Peace and Good

*Through the Year with
Francis of Assisi*

Pat McCloskey, O.F.M.

Franciscan
MEDIA
Cincinnati, Ohio

Excerpts from Omer Englebert, *St. Francis of Assisi: A Biography* and Marion A. Habig, ed., *St. Francis of Assisi: Writings and Early Biographies: English Omnibus for the Sources for the Life of St. Francis* (2 vols.) are used by permission. All rights reserved. Scripture passages have been taken from *New Revised Standard Version Bible*, copyright ©1989 by the Division of Christian Education of the National Council of the Churches of Christ in the U.S.A., and used by permission. All rights reserved.

Cover and book design by Mark Sullivan
Cover image © Fotolia | Giemmephoto

LIBRARY OF CONGRESS CATALOGING-IN-PUBLICATION DATA
McCloskey, Patrick.
Peace and good : through the year with Francis of Assisi / Pat McCloskey, O.F.M.
pages cm
Includes bibliographical references and index.
ISBN 978-1-61636-730-5 (alk. paper)
1. Francis, of Assisi, Saint, 1182-1226. 2. Devotional calendars—Catholic Church. I. Title.
BX2182.3.M38 2014
242'.2—dc23
2014030235

ISBN 978-1-61636-730-5
Copyright ©2014, Pat McCloskey, O.F.M. All rights reserved.

Published by Franciscan Media
28 W. Liberty St.
Cincinnati, OH 45202
www.FranciscanMedia.org

Printed in the United States of America.
Printed on acid-free paper.
15 16 17 18 5 4 3 2

CONTENTS

MAY 11

His Name Was Francis

His name was Francis, and he used to praise God the Artist in every one of God's works. Whatever joy he found in things made he referred to their maker. He rejoiced in all the works of God's hands. Everything cried out to him, "He who made us is infinitely good!"

He called animals "brother" or "sister," and he exhorted them to praise God. He would go through the streets and byways, inviting everyone to sing with him. And one time when he came upon an almond tree, he said, "Brother Almond, speak to me of God." And the almond tree blossomed.

That is what St. Francis of Assisi did, and that is what he does for us once we are caught up in his life and teachings. He makes us blossom, wherever and whoever we are. We blossom because we see in Francis what could happen to us if we were to embrace the overflowing goodness of God revealed in everything that exists, and let that embrace change us.

You may know this man Francis only as the sweet saint who adorns birdbaths and whose statues proliferate in gardens all over the world. But he was much more than that. He was a rich and spoiled young man who was born in 1182 in Assisi, Italy, and died in 1226 below and outside of Assisi next to the little church of St. Mary of the Angels where he and his followers, whom he called the Lesser Brothers, lived lives of Gospel poverty and ministered to the lepers who lived nearby.

He was the man who said in his Testament, "When I was in sin, it seemed to me repulsive to see lepers, and then the Lord Himself led me among them, and what was repulsive to me was turned into sweetness of soul and body for me."

He was a man who longed to become a knight, who went to war accoutered in knightly vesture, who suffered defeat in battle and lived a year as a prisoner of war in the neighboring town of Perugia, and he became in the end a pacifist, going to Egypt on the Fifth Crusade, not to make war against Islam but to try to reconcile the Crusaders and the Sultan, Malik al-Kamil.

He was a rich cloth merchant's son who gave all his possessions to the poor. And when the Bishop of Assisi said to him that the life of Francis and his Brothers was too hard because they had nothing in this world, Francis replied, "My Lord Bishop, if we had possessions, we would need weapons to defend them." He had learned the hard-earned lesson of the futility of war and power, to which he was so attracted as a young man.

He is the man, young, confused, and battle shocked, who heard the voice of Christ speak to him from the crucifix that hung in the run down, semi-abandoned church of San Damiano: "Francis, go and repair my house, which as you see is falling into ruin." And he responded immediately, not only by restoring the small chapel with his own hands, but with the help of his Brothers, he began to restore the Catholic Church itself. The Gospel of Jesus changed their hearts, and their transformed hearts overflowed into the way they lived and the way they preached to others by their words and their actions.

He is the saint whose love for the crucified Jesus Christ was so intense that, in a celebrated ecstatic experience, he received in his own body the wounds of Christ, the so-called sacred stigmata, and in his heart felt the great love that moved Jesus to live and die for us. It was as if his love for Jesus was so deep and so complete that it broke out in his own body as wounds imprinted on his own flesh.

Jesus. The very name moved him to tears; and when asked why he wept so, he would say, "I weep because Love is not loved." Love for him was the overflowing goodness of God made real for us in Jesus.

This Francis, this great saint, did so much more in response to that incredible Love, that all of it cannot be put into this brief introduction. But what follows in the daily meditations of this book will begin to open up for you the amazing life of Francis of Assisi and why he is considered the Mirror of Christ, one of the greatest saints whose life and spirituality are as relevant today as they were eight hundred years ago.

As St. Thomas More is "a man for all seasons," St. Francis of Assisi is a man for all ages, one who became so light and airy, so free of all possessiveness and selfishness that multitudes of men and women followed in his footsteps. Even animals listened to him. In the words of Coleman Banks, St. Francis "was so empty of nervous haste and fear and aggression that the birds would light on him." And when he died at twilight on October 4, 1226, the larks rose up to the roof of his cell and circled it with wing beat and song.

In *Peace and Good: Through the Year with Francis of Assisi*, you will come to better know this man of God, this holy father who changed the lives of so many people in his time, and through the ages up until this very day.

Through the practices and challenges that encourage you to apply Francis's teachings through your own life, you are invited to experience the simple way that Francis preached, a way deeply grounded in the word of God and in a love of all creation.

Francis is, indeed, a man for all ages, a man who brought peace and good to all God's creatures.

—Murray Bodo, O.F.M.

CHRONOLOGY OF THE LIFE OF FRANCIS

1181, summer or fall	Francis born in Assisi. Baptized Giovanni de Pietro di Bernardone, renamed Francesco by his father
1198, January 8	Innocent III elected pope
1198, spring	Duke Conrad of Urslingen's Rocca fortress besieged, taken, and razed by people of Assisi, as he yields Duchy of Spoleto to Innocent III
1199–1200	Civil war in Assisi; destruction of feudal nobles' castles; families of later St. Clare and Brother Leonardo move to Perugia
1202, November	War between Perugia and Assisi. Latter's army is defeated at Battle of Collestrada. Francis spends a year in prison in Perugia, until ransomed by his father as ill
1204	Long illness
1204, end, or spring 1205	Francis sets out for war in Apulia, but returns the next day, after a vision and message in Spoleto. Beginning of the gradual process of conversion
1205, June	Gautier de Brienne dies in southern Italy
1205, fall and winter	Message of the crucifix of San Damiano. Conflict with father

1206, January or February	Bishop's trial
1206, spring	Francis in Gubbio nursing victims of leprosy
1206, summer, probably July	Returns to Assisi, assumes hermit's habit and begins to repair San Damiano: end of conversion process; beginning of Thomas of Celano's "years of conversion" chronology
1206, summer, to January or early February 1208	Repairs San Damiano, San Pietro, and Portiuncula
1208, February 24	Francis hears Gospel of St. Matthias's Mass. Changes from hermit's habit to that of barefoot preacher; begins to preach
1208, April 16	Brothers Bernard and Peter Catanii join Francis. On April 23, Brother Giles is received at the Portiuncula
1208, spring	First mission: Francis and Giles to the Marches of Ancona
1208, summer	Three more, including Philip, join them
1208, fall and winter	Second mission: all seven go to the Poggio Bustone in the Valley of Rieti After being assured of the remission of his sins and the future growth of the Order, Francis sends the six, plus a new seventh follower, on the third mission, two by two. Bernard and Giles go to Florence
1209, early	The eight return to the Portiuncula. Four more join them

1209, spring	Francis writes brief Rule and goes to Rome with his eleven first companions. There he obtains the approval of Pope Innocent III. On the way back, they stay a while at Orte then settle at Rivo Torto
1209, September	German Emperor-elect Otto IV passes by Rivo Torto
1209 or 1210	The friars move to the Portiuncula
1209–1210	Possible beginning of the Third Order
1211, summer	Francis goes to Dalmatia and returns
1212, May	After a few days at San Paolo and a few weeks at Panzo Benedictine convents, Clare moves to San Damiano
1213, May 8	At San Leo, near San Marino, Count Orlando offers Mount La Verna to Francis as a hermitage
1213–1214 or 1214–1215	Francis travels to Spain and back
1215, November	Fourth Lateran Council. Francis in Rome
1216, July 16	Pope Innocent III dies in Perugia. July 18: Honorius III elected. French Archbishop Jacques de Vitry at Perugia
1216, summer	Francis obtains the Portiuncula Indulgence from Pope Honorius in Perugia
1217, May 5	Pentecost general chapter at the Portiuncula. First missions beyond the Alps and overseas. Giles leaves for Tunis, Elias for Syria, and Francis for France, but Cardinal Hugolin meets him in Florence and persuades him to stay in Italy

1224, August 15– September 29	(Assumption to St. Michael's Day)—Francis fasts at La Verna, receiving the stigmata about September 14
1224, October and early November	Francis returns to the Portiuncula via Borgo San Sepolcro, Monte Casale, and Citta di Castello
1224/1225, December–February	Riding on a donkey, he makes a preaching tour in Umbria and the Marches
1225, March	On a visit to St. Clare at San Damiano, his eye-sickness suddenly turns much worse. Almost blind, he has to stay there in a cell in or by the chaplain's house. At the insistence of Brother Elias, at last consents to receive medical care, but weather is too cold and treatment is postponed
1225, April–May	Still at San Damiano, undergoes treatment without improvement. Receives divine promise of eternal life and composes Canticle of Brother Sun
1225, June	Adding to the Canticle, reconciles feuding bishop and podesti of Assisi. Summoned by a letter from Cardinal Hugolin, leaves San Damiano for Rieti Valley
1225, early July	Welcomed in Rieti by Hugolin and papal court (there from June 23 to February 6). Goes to Fonte Colombo to undergo eye treatment urged by Hugolin, but has it postponed owing to absence of Brother Elias

1225, July–August	Doctor cauterizes the saint's temples at Fonte Colombo, without improvement
1225, September	Francis moves to San Fabiano near Rieti to be treated by other doctors, who pierce his ears. Restores the trampled vineyard of the poor priest
1225–1226, October–March	In either Rieti or Fonte Colombo
1226, April	Francis is in Siena for further treatment
1226, May or June	Returns to the Portiuncula via Cortona
1226, July–August	In summer heat, he is taken to Bagnara in the hills near Nocera
1226, late August or early September	His condition growing worse, he is taken via Nottiano to the palace of the bishop in Assisi. Bishop Guido is absent on a pilgrimage to Monte Gargano
1226, September	Knowing that his death is imminent, Francis insists on being carried to the Portiuncula
1226, October 3	Francis dies. Sunday, October 4, Francis buried in San Giorgio Church
1227, March 19	His friend Hugolin becomes Pope Gregory IX
1228, July 16	In Assisi, Gregory IX canonizes St. Francis
1230, May 25	Translation of the saint's remains to his new basilica, San Francesco

INTRODUCTION

"Why after you?" Brother Masseo once questioned St. Francis. "Why after you? You are not a very handsome man or possessed of great learning or wisdom. So why is all the world running after you?" (Little Flowers of St. Francis, chapter ten). Francis answered that God could not find a greater sinner through whom to display his infinite mercy.

The appeal of St. Francis remains undimmed almost eight centuries after his death. In looking at him, people have always been helped to see Christ.

Peace and Good presents writings by and about St. Francis, with each month having its own theme and each day featuring two sections, "Living as Francis Did" and "Growing with Francis," to help readers connect the teachings of St. Francis to their own lives. The title of the book comes from the phrase *pace e bene*—translated from the Italian as "peace and good"—which was the greeting Francis offered to all whom he encountered.

A major work about the life of Francis, *St. Francis of Assisi: Writings and Early Biographies: English Omnibus of the Sources for the Life of St. Francis,* edited by Marion Habig, O.F.M., was published in 1973 and it brought together the previously published work of six translators from both the United States and Great Britain. Franciscan Media now holds the copyright and has reissued this work in two paperback volumes. The 1973

Omnibus played a key role in launching a new era of Franciscan studies.

Each month's quotes reflect the order in which that material appears in the Omnibus: first the writings of St. Francis, then Thomas of Celano's First Life of St. Francis (1228), his Second Life of St. Francis (1247), and St. Bonaventure's Legenda Major (1263). A few of the quotations come from the Little Flowers of St. Francis, a book that was written after 1337.

This arrangement means that Celano may have two versions of the same incident, and Bonaventure may present a third one. Each writer, however, presents the information he had at the time and his own attempts to place the story of Francis within the larger story of God's providential self-revelation to the human family.

I am indebted to Murray Bodo, O.F.M., for writing the foreword to this book, to Lisa Biedenbach (who helped me write up the book proposal), to Mary Carol Kendzia (who saw its timeliness and shepherded this volume through the editing and publishing process, to Patti Normile (who edited the final text, in many cases standardizing spelling and punctuation that appeared in the *Omnibus* according to the usage in that section's original publication), to Mark Sullivan (for the stunning cover and book design), and to Robert Lucero, O.F.M. (for computer assistance). The *Omnibus* used the Vulgate numbering of the Psalms; this book uses the now more commonly accepted Hebrew numbering.

May *Peace and Good* point readers not indeed to Francis but rather to Jesus Christ after the example of the Poor Man of Assisi!

JANUARY

Peace

Perhaps no other virtue is more associated with St. Francis of Assisi than peace. He made peace with people, with animals, in the Church, and within civil society. This peace grew out of his honesty about his relationship to God, others, and himself. Before seeking peace with people and creation around him, Francis had to find peace within himself. That was a challenge faced with times of deep prayer.

In his time, the peace that Francis showed with birds, wolves, lambs, larks, and worms reminded his contemporaries that Adam and Eve lived in total harmony with all creatures before they were sent from the Garden of Eden. The serpent in the Garden of Eden promised Eve and Adam knowledge and power that would equal God's, but the serpent's promise was worthless.

Women and men suffering from leprosy were perhaps the most universally despised social group in Francis's day. The Lord led Francis to recognize them as his brothers and sisters. His respect for them as equals in God's creation brought peace to these afflicted ones.

Peace is both a wonderful and a much-abused word. Because we seek peace constantly, it has many counterfeits. For example, peace at any price always yields no peace at a very steep price.

Francis promoted peace among his friars, among the Poor Clares, among the Secular Franciscans, among all people. Thomas of Celano writes that the immensely popular Francis "seemed to be a man of another world" (*First Life*, 36). Francis called people back into the peace and harmony of a world into which God had created the human family and which was as fragile in Francis's day as it is in our own.

Peace is a gift from God. Human actions that cooperate with God's grace activate peace in the world. On October 27, 1986, St. John Paul II invited leaders of world religions to Assisi to pray and fast there for the sake of world peace. At the concluding prayer service, the pope called those present and everyone who would hear or read his words to be "artisans of peace." Francis of Assisi was certainly an artisan of peace.

Earlier the same pope had designated Francis as the patron of ecology. Francis learned to appreciate God's gift of natural resources, not to dominate them selfishly. All of creation pointed Francis toward God. He would have agreed with Dante Alighieri, who wrote in the *Divine Comedy* that over the gate of heaven is the affirmation, "In his will is our peace."

"Peace be with you" echoed from Jesus's life through the life of St. Francis of Assisi. We are called to allow it to reverberate through our lives as well.

JANUARY 1

Justice Seeks Peace

The friars should be delighted to follow the lowliness and poverty of our Lord Jesus Christ, remembering that of the whole world we must own nothing; but having food and sufficient clothing, with these let us be content (1 Timothy 6:8), as St. Paul says. They should be glad to live among social outcasts, among the poor and helpless, the sick and the lepers, and those who beg by the wayside. If they are in want, they should not be ashamed to beg alms, remembering that our Lord Jesus Christ, the Son of the living, all-powerful God set his face like a very hard rock (Isaiah 50:7) and was not ashamed. He was poor and he had no home of his own and he lived on alms, he and the Blessed Virgin and his disciples. (Rule of 1221, chapter 9)

LIVING AS FRANCIS DID

Today is a day of prayer for world peace. Peace is a work of justice; it does not come about by a display of superior strength or military might. In fact, it can be argued that those who "live among social outcasts, among the poor and helpless, the sick and the lepers, and those who beg by the wayside" most truly effect the cause of peace and justice by changing society at its very roots: its people.

GROWING WITH FRANCIS

Make a sign of peace today in some small way. Help to effect a change in the world with an act of justice and love.

JANUARY 2

Work Is Honorable

Those of us who were clerics said the Office like other clerics, while the lay brothers said the Our Father, and we were only too glad to find shelter in abandoned churches. We made no claim to learning and we were submissive to everyone. I worked with my own hands and I am still determined to work; and with all my heart I want all the other friars to be busy with some kind of work that can be carried on without scandal. Those who do not know how to work should learn, not because they want to get something for their efforts, but to give good example and to avoid idleness. When we receive no recompense for our work, we can turn to God's table and beg alms from door to door. God revealed a form of greeting to me, telling me that we should say, "God give you peace." (Testament)

Living as Francis Did

In the social circle into which Francis was born, manual labor was looked down on. Servants did household tasks under the supervision of someone like Francis's mother, Pica. His determination as an adult to engage in manual labor, therefore, was a radical conversion from his upbringing.

Growing with Francis

Some types of work may be beyond our skills, but do we feel any form of work is beneath our dignity? If so, how do we regard people who do that type of work? Does God see them the same way that we do?

JANUARY 3

Peaceful Thinking

Blessed are the peacemakers, for they shall be called the children of God (Matthew 5:9). They are truly peacemakers who are able to preserve their peace of mind and heart for love of our Lord Jesus Christ, despite all that they suffer in this world. (Admonition XV)

LIVING AS FRANCIS DID

It is very easy to engage in "if only" thinking: If only I had been born into a wealthier family, if only I had the advantage of a better education, if only I knew more influential people who could advance my career, and so on. "If only" thinking suggests that I am a spectator of my life, not an active participant in it.

Someone who constantly engages in "if only" thinking will never truly be at peace. She or he imagines that the key to happiness lies in someone else's hands, someone who is withholding that key. Jesus's words will often seem an obstacle because the "if only" thinkers tend to forget that Jesus suffered and died on a cross. If Jesus had followed their example, his time on the cross would have been filled with rumination over his bad luck. The Gospels, especially the Gospel of John, show Jesus as very deliberate in his choices. He rules—even from the cross.

GROWING WITH FRANCIS

How are you engaged in "if only" thinking? Does it contribute anything positive to your life? Resolve today to play the hand that has been dealt to you with optimism and joy, respecting everyone else in the process.

JANUARY 4

Goodness Triumphs

Where there is Love and Wisdom, there is neither Fear nor Ignorance.

Where there is Patience and Humility, there is neither Anger nor Annoyance.

Where there is Poverty and Joy, there is neither Cupidity nor Avarice.

Where there is Peace and Contemplation, there is neither Care nor Restlessness.

Where there is the Fear of God to guard the dwelling, there no enemy can enter.

Where there is Mercy and Prudence, there is neither Excess nor Harshness.

(*Admonition* XXVII)

LIVING AS FRANCIS DID

Francis's way of thinking constantly challenges us, as this quote shows. We are tempted to worry, for example, that the first pair of virtues in this series will not protect us from the second pair of situations that we would understandably like to avoid. Francis is correct. The first pair will prevent the unfavorable outcome mentioned at the end of each line above.

GROWING WITH FRANCIS

Do I see love, patience, humility, poverty, contemplation, fear of God, mercy, and prudence as desirable? Am I tempted to think they are ways that losers console themselves for losing? Be extra patient with one person today, beginning with yourself, not because doing so might change them but because that decision will point you in a better direction.

JANUARY 5

Lead Gently

We should not want to be in charge of others; we are to be servants, and should be subject to every human creature for God's sake (1 Peter 2:13). On all those who do this and endure to the last, the Spirit of God will rest (Isaiah 11:2); he will make his dwelling in them and there he will stay, and they will be children of your Father in heaven (Matthew 5:45) whose work they do. It is they who are the brides, the brothers and the mothers of our Lord Jesus Christ. A person is his bride when his faithful soul is united with Jesus Christ by the Holy Spirit; we are his brothers when we do the will of his Father who is in heaven (see Matthew 12:50), and we are mothers to him when we enthrone him in our hearts and souls by love with a pure and sincere conscience, and give him birth by doing good. This, too, should be an example to others. (Letter to All the Faithful)

LIVING AS FRANCIS DID

Francis moved beyond gender stereotypes. The same people can be brides, brothers, and mothers. It seems dizzying. Francis wrote this quote to help laypeople follow the Gospel more closely. Leaders must be servants who guide wisely and gently. "Control freaks," an unpleasant term society applies to those who use authority to bend others to their will, create unrest and dissension.

GROWING WITH FRANCIS

Exercise authority meekly today. Observe the positive results in both yourself and others.

The Next Step

Every creature in heaven and on earth and in the depths of the sea should give God praise and glory and honor and blessing (Revelation 5:13); he has borne so much for us and has done and will do so much good to us; he is our power and our strength, and he alone is good (see Luke 18:19), he alone most high, he alone all-powerful, wonderful, and glorious; he alone is holy and worthy of all praise and blessing for endless ages and ages. Amen. (Letter to All the Faithful)

LIVING AS FRANCIS DID

We praise God because that is the only way that we can live truthfully. We are not the sources of all goodness, every blessing. God is. Whatever strength we possess comes not from our efforts alone but from cooperating with God's grace and direction in our lives.

GROWING WITH FRANCIS

Francis wrote to his friars that once he embraced a leper, what had previously seemed bitter then seemed sweet. God's ways always challenge conventional wisdom. Are you on the cusp of deeper conversion but reluctant to take the next step because you fear that it will be too costly, that other people may consider you foolish? What step do you think God wants you to take next? Take it gratefully.

JANUARY 7

Reconciliation Heals

All praise be yours, my Lord, through those who grant pardon
   For love of you; through those who endure
   Sickness and trial.
Happy those who endure in peace,
   By you, Most High, they will be crowned.
All praise be yours, my Lord, through Sister Death,
   From whose embrace no mortal can escape.
Woe to those who die in mortal sin!
   Happy those She finds doing your will!
   The second death can do no harm to them.
Praise and bless my Lord, and give him thanks,
   And serve him with great humility.
(The Canticle of Brother Sun)

Living as Francis Did

Francis composed these verses to help the bishop of Assisi and its mayor end a bitter feud that disrupted the entire city.

Growing with Francis

Do you see forgiveness as a sign of weakness or a sign of strength? Forgive someone today, not necessarily because they deserve it but because you deserve to live without the anger you have directed at them that also festers in you.

JANUARY 8

Peaceable People

They are not to take up lethal weapons, or bear them about, against anybody.

As regards making peace among the brothers and sisters or non-members at odds, let what the ministers find proper be done; even, if it be expedient, upon consultation with the Lord Bishop.

If contrary to their right and privileges trouble is made for the brothers and sisters by the mayors and governors of the places where they live, the ministers of the place shall do what they shall find expedient on the advice of the Lord Bishop. (Rule of Third Order)

LIVING AS FRANCIS DID

Not everyone admired St. Francis. Some people feared that society would be weakened terribly if people followed the Gospel as he did. This quote urges members of the Third Order not to bear arms.

Francis urges laypeople following this Rule of Life to follow the advice of their local ministers and their bishop. In our language, Francis was urging them to be conscientious objectors on the subject of weapons. People argued then as today that this approach is simply not prudent, maybe working in some different world but not in this one. Peacemaking is difficult work because God's values can appear utopian, unrealistic. In fact, genuine peacemakers are the true realists.

GROWING WITH FRANCIS

Perhaps Francis's way of peace has never worked because it has never really been tried. How can you support his way in your life?

JANUARY 9

Choose Peace

In all his preaching, before he proposed the word of God to those gathered about, he first prayed for peace for them, saying: "The Lord give you peace." He always most devoutly announced peace to men and women, to all he met and overtook. For this reason many who had hated peace and had hated also salvation embraced peace, through the cooperation of the Lord, with all their heart and were made children of peace and seekers after eternal salvation. (Celano, First Life of St. Francis, 23)

LIVING AS FRANCIS DID

Francis of Assisi was one of the world's greatest peacemakers. He started by recognizing that peace is never simply a human achievement; it always depends on God as its source. God will not impose peace on us but will always encourage us to choose the ways of peace. That's a key part of our being made in the image and likeness of God.

Adam and Eve thought that they had a better plan. After all, wouldn't disobeying God's command turn them into God's equals? There is a reason why Satan has long been called "the father of lies." Genuine peace is never to his advantage. Peace always benefits us.

GROWING WITH FRANCIS

If someone called you a "peacemaker," would you feel complimented? What if someone else called you naïve or an idealist unprepared to live in the real world? Take one peacemaking action today—even if you know you may be criticized for doing so.

JANUARY 10

Go Two by Two

At this same time also, when another good man had entered their religion [religious community], their number rose to eight. Then the blessed Francis called them all together, and telling them many things concerning the kingdom of God, the contempt of the world, the renunciation of their own will, and the subduing of their own body, he separated them into four groups of two each and said to them: "Go, my dearest brothers, two by two into the various parts of the world, announcing to men peace and repentance unto the forgiveness of sins [Mark 1:4]; and be patient in tribulation [Romans 12:12], confident that the Lord will fulfill his purpose and his promise. To those who put questions to you, reply humbly; bless those who persecute you; give thanks to those who injure you and calumniate you; because for these things there is prepared for you an eternal kingdom" [Matthew 5:11]. (Celano, First Life of St. Francis, 29)

LIVING AS FRANCIS DID

Jesus sent out his apostles two by two to fellow Jews because Jewish law required the testimony of two witnesses in a court of law. Another reason for doing this is so that the apostles could witness this Good News by word and action. How they treated one another would either strengthen or undermine their words.

GROWING WITH FRANCIS

Find a partner and together take a step toward peace today.

JANUARY 11

Dig Deeper

Francis, therefore, the most valiant knight of Christ, went about the cities and villages [Matthew 9:35], announcing the kingdom of God, preaching peace, teaching salvation and penance unto the remission of sins, not in the persuasive words of human wisdom [1 Corinthians 2:4], but with the learning and power of the Spirit. He acted boldly in all things [Acts 9:28], because of the apostolic authority granted to him, using no words of flattery or seductive blandishments. He did not know how to make light of the faults of others, but he knew well how to cut them out; neither did he encourage the life of sinners, but he struck hard at them with sharp reproof, for he had first convinced himself by practicing himself what he wished to persuade others to do by his words; and fearing not the censurer, he spoke the truth boldly, so that even the most learned men, men enjoying renown and dignity, wondered at his words and were struck with wholesome fear by his presence. (Celano, First Life of St. Francis, 36)

LIVING AS FRANCIS DID

Like St. Paul before him, Francis did not rely on eloquent words to convince people; both of them relied on the integrity of lives shaped by God's grace. If faith rests on clever words, then it will always be in danger of being replaced by someone else wielding more eloquent words. In that case, the person becomes the message—not the message God wants preached.

GROWING WITH FRANCIS

Allow your conversion to go deeper and wider today and every day.

JANUARY 12

Sacrifice for the Kingdom

Men ran, and women too ran, clerics hurried, and religious hastened that they might see and hear the holy man of God who seemed to all to be a man of another world. Every age and every sex hurried to see the wonderful things that the Lord was newly working in the world through his servant. It seemed at that time, whether because of the presence of St. Francis or through his reputation, that a new light had been sent from heaven upon this earth, shattering the widespread darkness that had so filled almost the whole region that hardly anyone knew where to go. For so profound was the forgetfulness of God and the sleep of neglect of his commandments oppressing almost everyone that they could hardly be aroused even a little from their old and deeply rooted sins. (Celano, First Life of St. Francis, 36)

LIVING AS FRANCIS DID

Francis could have been reduced to a carnival attraction—interesting but hardly life-changing. What Celano describes here is a life-changing Francis—not by the force of Francis's personality but by God's grace. All levels of society recognized him as authentic. In a way, Francis was indeed a "man of another world" because he took the kingdom of God so seriously; it was a matter of life or death for him.

GROWING WITH FRANCIS

Sacrifice at least one thing—an idea, a behavior, a prejudice—for the kingdom to grow in you.

JANUARY 13

Cross a Boundary

They despised all worldly things so keenly that they hardly permitted themselves to receive even the necessities of life; and they were separated from bodily comforts for so long a time that they did not shrink from anything difficult. Amid all these things they strove for peace and gentleness with all men [Hebrews 12:14], and always conducting themselves modestly and peaceably, they avoided all scandals with the greatest zeal. They hardly spoke even when necessary; neither did anything scurrilous or idle proceed from their mouths, in order that nothing immodest or unbecoming might be found in their life and conversation. Their every action was disciplined, their every movement modest; all their senses were so mortified that they would hardly permit themselves to hear or see anything except what their purpose demanded. (Celano, First Life of St. Francis, 41)

LIVING AS FRANCIS DID

Celano is describing the actions of the earliest friars. People who were attracted to Francis saw that his values made a difference in the lives of people who might not otherwise readily associate with one another, and many came to realize that Francis was on to something that they lacked. In a very class-conscious society, Francis crossed many boundaries that he felt did not serve the kingdom of God well.

GROWING WITH FRANCIS

Cross a boundary today by making contact with someone whom you would normally ignore.

JANUARY 14

Tempter or Mentor?

With their eyes directed toward the ground, they clung to heaven with their minds. No envy, no malice, no rancor, no abusive speech, no suspicion, no bitterness found any place in them; but great concord, continual quiet, thanksgiving, and the voice of praise were in them. These were the teachings of their beloved father, by which he formed his new sons, not by words alone and tongue, but above all in deeds and in truth [1 John 3:18]. (Celano, First Life of St. Francis, 41)

LIVING AS FRANCIS DID

Francis was clearly centered on God and God's values. What Celano describes here is similar to the practice of mindfulness, an attitude of being centered in God. The other end of the spectrum is a great boredom that can have only momentary distractions but no abiding loyalties, a place where everything is fair game for praise or ridicule because nothing really matters in the long run.

In *The Screwtape Letters*, C.S. Lewis presents an experienced tempter who acts as a mentor for a young devil new to tempting. Regarding religion, the experienced tempter says that people are more easily convinced to be critics than to become disciples. Disciples are people who learn. That requires people to avoid the vices and embrace the virtues—an attitude of being centered in God—that Celano describes here.

GROWING WITH FRANCIS

Consider who is helping you to become a better disciple of Jesus; spend more time with that person.

JANUARY 15

Decision Making

That he might show himself in every way contemptible and give an example to the rest of true confession, Francis was not ashamed, when he had failed in something, to confess his failing in his preaching before all the people. Indeed, if it happened that he had had an evil thought about anyone, or if he had on occasion spoken an angry word, he would immediately confess his sins with all humility to the one about whom he had had the evil thought and beg his pardon. His conscience, which was a witness to his complete innocence, guarding itself with all solicitude, would not let him rest until it had gently healed the wound in his heart. Certainly he wanted to make progress in every kind of good deed, but he did not want to be looked up to on that account, but he fled admiration in every way, lest he ever become vain. (Celano, First Life of St. Francis, 54)

LIVING AS FRANCIS DID

Francis was keenly aware of his sins. Thus, he never tried to bluff his way through situations. If he was in the wrong, he was the first to admit it. Conscience was important to him as well, for here he knew that he was very close to God. Decisions of conscience are never trivial; they never look for a time when doing the right thing will come at a cheaper price.

GROWING WITH FRANCIS

Name the decisions in your life that are moving in the direction of conscientious decisions. Ask God to strengthen you to do the right thing no matter what the cost.

Be Gracious Whatever

O how beautiful, how splendid, how glorious did he appear in the inno-cence of his life, in the simplicity of his words, in the purity of his heart, in his love for God, in his fraternal charity, in his ardent obedience, in his peaceful submission, in his angelic countenance! [Esther 2:15] He was charming in his manners, serene by nature, affable in his conversation, most opportune in his exhortations, most faithful in what was entrusted to him, cautious in counsel, effective in business, gracious in all things. (Celano, First Life of St. Francis, 83)

LIVING AS FRANCIS DID

This description shows why Francis attracted followers, including laypeople who had already married or who would remain single outside a religious community. Francis led them to the Lord through his words but even more by his example. That did not make things easy for them, however.

Francis still had to make tough decisions, and so would they. Anyone who observed Francis realized that he did not lead a charmed life. Initial fervor for the Lord would mean nothing unless it redirected his entire life. Yes, embracing a leper in the early days of his conversion was a key moment, but it became decisive only in view of similar and perhaps even more costly future choices.

GROWING WITH FRANCIS

It's fairly easy to be gracious when everything seems to be going our way. Resolve today to be gracious—even with people whom you might prefer to avoid and with situations that you find difficult.

JANUARY 17

Prepare for the Day

He was serene of mind, sweet of disposition, sober in spirit, raised up in contemplation, zealous in prayer, and in all things fervent. He was constant in purpose, stable in virtue, persevering in grace, and unchanging in all things. He was quick to pardon, slow to become angry, ready of wit, tenacious of memory, subtle in discussion, circumspect in choosing, and in all things simple. He was unbending with himself, understanding toward others, and discreet in all things. (Celano, First Life of St. Francis, 83)

LIVING AS FRANCIS DID

Contemplation and prayer prepared Francis for each day's challenges—or gave him an opportunity to see more clearly God's ways in experiences that Francis may not have handled with his usual graciousness.

Our constant temptation is to admire saints from such a distance that we forget they were still human beings who cooperated with God's grace as best they could each day. Francis wasn't born serene. He could become as angry and upset as anyone else. The Lord led him to discover a great treasure (the kingdom of God) and to make the sacrifices necessary to live by its values.

GROWING WITH FRANCIS

Which of the virtues noted in the quote from Celano today might help you to better cope with the experiences of your day? Practice that virtue, with dedication and grace.

Aim High

For, though he was a man subject to the same infirmities as we ourselves [James 5:17], he was not content with observing the common precepts, but overflowing with the most ardent charity, he set out upon the way of total perfection; he aimed at the heights of perfect sanctity, and he saw the end of all perfection [Psalm 119:96]. Therefore, every order, every sex, every age has in him a visible pattern of the way of salvation and has outstanding examples of holy works. (Celano, First Life of St. Francis, 90)

LIVING AS FRANCIS DID

People were attracted to Francis because of the integrity of his life. Because he was radically honest with himself, he was ready to respond in word and deeds to the needs of others.

Sometimes we worry that God may ask too much of us, that God has too much confidence in us! We may offer to do great things as long as God doesn't ask us to do other things that we prefer to avoid. We can love people on the other side of the world, people whom we have never met, more easily than people in the next room at home, people who work close to us, people whom we know only too well.

GROWING WITH FRANCIS

Strive to imitate Francis's integrity in all your words and actions today. That's a challenge!

JANUARY 19

Love Is a Decision

If any propose to set their hand to difficult things and to strive after the greater gifts [1 Corinthians 12:31] of the more excellent way, let them look into the mirror of his life and learn every perfection. If any take to the lower and easier way, fearing to walk the difficult way and fearing the ascent to the top of the mountain, on this plain too they will find in him suitable guidance. If any, finally, seek signs and wonders, let them petition his sanctity and they will get what they seek. (Celano, First Life of St. Francis, 90)

LIVING AS FRANCIS DID

The kind of love that St. Paul famously praises in 1 Corinthians 13 may sound like an easy, dreamy love: always patient, kind, and self-sacrificing. Genuine love is always far more gritty, far less dependent on favorable circumstances or someone else's welcome choices.

Marriage counselors sometimes speak of love as a cycle of romance, disillusionment, and a decision to love. That is certainly true for married couples who have remained fresh in their love. But it is also true for every other type of love (including the celibate love that Francis showed).

GROWING WITH FRANCIS

Love never requires that we lie to ourselves about our actions or someone else's. Remember that love is much more a decision than an unchanging feeling.

Begin Again

But, though the glorious father had been brought to the fulness of grace before God and shone among men of this world by his good works, he nevertheless thought always to begin more perfect works and, like the most skilled soldier in the camps of God [Genesis 32:2], the enemy having been challenged, to stir up new wars. He proposed, under Christ the prince [Daniel 9:25], to do great things, and, with his limbs failing and his body dying, he hoped for a victory over the enemy in a new struggle. (Celano, First Life of St. Francis, 103)

LIVING AS FRANCIS DID

It's easy to read this passage and think that "the enemy" cited was someone or something other than Francis himself. In fact, we are constantly tempted by the siren song that other people who should be cooperating with us are refusing, that life isn't fair in many ways, that if Francis had lived in some earlier time or some other circumstance, holiness would have been much easier.

St. Bonaventure says that Francis's service to God began with a victory over himself. Centuries later, Napoleon Bonaparte is reported to have said that the only victories that are truly permanent are the ones over oneself. Even if that saying is only attributed to Napoleon, it is still profoundly true.

GROWING WITH FRANCIS

What would you like to ask God to help you conquer within yourself?

JANUARY 21

Silencing the Clamor

For true virtue knows not a limit of time, since the expectation of a reward is eternal. Therefore, he was afire with a very great desire to return to the first beginnings of humility and, by reason of the immensity of his love, rejoicing in hope [Romans 12:12], he thought to recall his body to its former subjection, even though it had already come to such an extremity. He removed from himself completely the obstacles of all cares, and he fully silenced the clamorings of all anxieties. (Celano, First Life of St. Francis, 103)

LIVING AS FRANCIS DID

Francis was "centered" long before that term became popular among spiritual writers. His values became more and more aligned with God's, but Francis did not use that as a reason to become self-righteous. That is a temptation many of his contemporaries did not resist. It was extremely easy to see any resistance to their ideas about God's ways as a personal snub.

Francis could eventually have become a candidate for a nervous breakdown: the rapid expansion of his brotherhood, the growing diversity of opinion about its priorities, the many demands on his time and energy, to name only a few reasons. Francis's centering in prayer enabled him to "silence the clamorings of all anxieties."

GROWING WITH FRANCIS

Allow Francis to help you "silence the clamorings of all anxieties."

JANUARY 22

Free Living

Truly Francis had a free and noble heart. Those who have experienced his magnanimity know how free, how liberal he was in all things; how confident and fearless he was in all things; with what great virtue, with what great fervor he trampled underfoot all worldly things. What indeed shall I say of the other parts of the world, where, by means of his clothing, diseases depart, illnesses leave, and crowds of both sexes are delivered from their troubles by merely invoking his name? (Celano, First Life of St. Francis, 120)

LIVING AS FRANCIS DID

Francis was a paradox in his own day. In many ways, he might not have seemed a very free person. His health was never terribly strong. The friars could take up a great deal of his time, and not all of them were saints!

And yet Francis was one of the freest people who ever lived. He had no fronts to put up, no masks behind which to hide, no image to maintain except that of a sinner open to the grace of God. Celano and other early biographers emphasize that Francis appealed to men and women of all economic and social classes. Most people felt extremely at ease in his presence. The only ones who did not were men and women who wanted him to endorse their self-deceptions about where they stood before God and in relation to others.

GROWING WITH FRANCIS

Are you enjoying the freedom that God wants you to have? If not, what needs to change?

JANUARY 23

Relinquish Envy

But there was a sudden change in things and new dangers arose meanwhile in the world. Suddenly the joy of peace was disturbed and the torch of envy was lighted and the Church was torn by domestic and civil war. The Romans, a rebellious and ferocious race of men, raged against their neighbors, as was their custom, and, being rash, they stretched forth their hands against the holy places [1 Maccabees 14:31]. The distinguished Pope Gregory tried to curb their growing wickedness, to repress their savagery, to temper their violence; and, like a tower of great strength, he protected the Church of Christ. Many dangers assailed her, destruction became more frequent, and in the rest of the world the necks of sinners [Psalm 129:4] were raised against God. (Celano, First Life of St. Francis, 122)

LIVING AS FRANCIS DID

This "Pope Gregory" was Pope Gregory IX, a great friend and advisor of Francis before becoming pope and the one who would eventually canonize him. Pope Gregory saw the Friars Minor and the Friars Preacher as men who could render great service to the Church by their Gospel way of life.

Some sins wear out the person committing them. No one can engage in gluttony, for example, 24/7. Envy, however, never wears out a sinner because it feeds upon itself. There is always someone, it claims, who has received far more than he or she truly deserved.

GROWING WITH FRANCIS

Is there someone or something you envy? Create kind thoughts about them to surpass the envy.

Stand for the Underdog

[During the war between] Perugia and Assisi, Francis was made captive with several others and endured the squalors of a prison. His fellow captives were consumed with sorrow, bemoaning miserably their imprisonment; Francis rejoiced in the Lord and laughed at his chains. His grieving companions resented his happiness and considered him insane. Francis replied: "Why do you think I rejoice? There is another consideration, for I will yet be venerated as a saint throughout the whole world." And so it has truly come about; everything he said has been fulfilled.

There was at that time among his fellow prisoners a certain proud and completely unbearable knight whom the rest were determined to shun, but Francis's patience was not disturbed. He put up with the unbearable knight and brought the others to peace with him. Capable of every grace, a chosen vessel of virtues, he poured out his gifts on all sides. (Celano, Second Life of St. Francis, 4)

Living as Francis Did

Francis befriended a prisoner of war who was shunned by other prisoners. By word and example, Francis recognized this man's dignity, encouraging his fellow prisoners to do the same. Francis could not impose peace on this man or on anyone else, but he could draw God's peace out of many people.

Growing with Francis

It takes no effort to pile up on someone who is already down. Speak positively today about some individual whose God-given dignity is not being recognized.

JANUARY 25

Rich in Poverty

Francis liked to stay at the brothers' place at Greccio, both because he saw that it was rich by reason of its poverty and because he could give himself more freely to heavenly things in a more secluded cell hewn from a projecting rock. Here is that place where he brought back to memory the birthday of the Child of Bethlehem, becoming a child with that Child. It happened, however, that the inhabitants were being annoyed by many evils, for a pack of ravening wolves was devouring not only animals but even men, and every year hailstorms were devastating the fields and vineyards. (Celano, Second Life of St. Francis, 35)

LIVING AS FRANCIS DID

"Rich by reason of its poverty." That phrase was as difficult to understand in Francis's day as it is in ours. Celano was not pulling this expression out of thin air. St. Paul had written that Christ became poor for our sake so that he might enrich us by his poverty. Francis could truly be himself among the friars in Greccio. Therefore, the "evils" that disrupted their life also threatened his.

GROWING WITH FRANCIS

Are you tempted to think that every poor person is poor because of bad choices he or she has made? In fact, the deck is stacked against some people. Jesus did not present the poverty of Lazarus at the rich man's gate as the result of bad choices or sinfulness on the part of Lazarus. Reflect on how you view the poor, and whether that perspective needs to change.

JANUARY 26

Speak Truth

One day, while he was preaching to them, Francis said: "To the honor and glory of Almighty God, hear the truth I announce to you. If every one of you confesses his sins and brings forth fruits befitting repentance [Luke 3:8], I give you my word that every pestilence will depart and the Lord, looking kindly upon you, will grant you an increase of temporal goods. But hear this also: again I announce to you that if you are ungrateful for his gifts and return to your vomit, the plague will be renewed, your punishment will be doubled, and even greater wrath will be let loose against you." (Celano, Second Life of St. Francis, 35)

LIVING AS FRANCIS DID

Francis encouraged the residents of Greccio to convert, to confess their sins, and to allow that conversion to keep going deeper in their lives. The sacrament of confession was rejected by the Albigensians, a Christian sect active in Francis's time, who saw the Church's sacramental system as too fleshy, too closely tied in with the material world.

The Albigensians lived in an overly simple world, thinking everything material was evil and everything spiritual was good. Baptism, Eucharist, anointings, marriage—all were too fleshy for the Albigensians, who could wax eloquent about the spiritual Church without wrinkle in heaven but who looked down on an obviously wrinkled Church here on earth.

GROWING WITH FRANCIS

Is there anything for which you would like to ask God's pardon? Bring this to God in prayer.

JANUARY 27

Ask and Receive

While the saint was living on Mount Alverna alone in a cell, one of his companions [Leo] longed with a great desire to have something encouraging from the words of the Lord noted down briefly in the hand of St. Francis. For he believed he would escape by this means a serious temptation that troubled him, not indeed of the flesh but of the spirit, or at least that he would be able to resist it more easily. Languishing with such a desire, he nevertheless was afraid to make known the matter to the most holy father. But what man did not tell Francis, the Spirit revealed to him. (Celano, Second Life of St. Francis, 49)

LIVING AS FRANCIS DID

Leo was one of Francis's first companions and one of a small group who accompanied Francis in his final years. It seems in this passage that Leo was troubled by something. We don't know the specifics, but perhaps he was worried that he might not persevere in the Gospel life that he had embraced. Possibly he felt oppressed by some previous sin that he had already confessed. Whatever the source of his worry, Leo felt that if only he had some message in Francis's handwriting, he would be able to face that temptation more effectively.

GROWING WITH FRANCIS

God's grace never abandoned Leo, and it will always be within calling distance for us if we open ourselves to it and cooperate with it. Where do you need God's grace to touch your life today?

JANUARY 28

Write Your Blessings

One day Blessed Francis called this brother and said: "Bring me some paper and ink, for I want to write down the words of the Lord and his praises which I have meditated upon in my heart." After these things he had asked for were quickly brought to him, he wrote down with his own hand the Praises of God and the words he wanted, and lastly a blessing for that brother, saying: "Take this paper and guard it carefully till the day of your death." Immediately every temptation was put to flight, and the writing was kept and afterwards it worked wonderful things [Genesis 30:25]. (Celano, Second Life of St. Francis, 49)

LIVING AS FRANCIS DID

The letter to Brother Leo (yesterday's entry) is on one side of a piece of parchment; the Praises of God are on the other side. Gratitude so filled Francis of Assisi that he praised God frequently, always blessing God for the natural world, for the people whom God created, and for God's constant love for them. Reading the Scriptures, receiving Holy Communion regularly, praying privately and with his brothers—all of these shaped Francis's life to such an extent that everything that we admire about him became second nature to him.

GROWING WITH FRANCIS

What positive traits are becoming second nature in your life? Each day we can reinforce the good things we have done and lessen the effects of the shortcomings in our lives.

JANUARY 29

Good for All

Not only were Francis' words effective when he was present in person, but at times when they were transmitted through others they did not return to him void [Isaiah 55:11]. It happened once that he came to the city of Arezzo, when behold, the whole city was shaken by civil war to the extent that destruction seemed very close. The man of God therefore lodged in a town outside the city, and he saw devils rejoicing over that place and stirring up the citizens to each other's destruction. But calling a brother, Sylvester by name, a man of God of worthy simplicity, he commanded him saying: "Go before the gate of the city, and on the part of Almighty God command the devils to leave the city as quickly as they can." (Celano, Second Life of St. Francis, 108)

LIVING AS FRANCIS DID

There are some people who are constantly upset about one thing or another, for example, what someone else should have said or done but failed to do. They live in a very large "if only" world where their happiness is totally dependent on someone else's decisions. They are so wrapped up in themselves that they neither speak nor think of "the common good" of society but only of themselves.

GROWING WITH FRANCIS

What destructive intentions can you take action against? For example, email messages that seem to be hate mail against political figures or others, or criticism without constructive suggestions for improvement for helping the common good.

JANUARY 30

Speak Truth to Power

Pious simplicity hastened to carry out the command and speaking psalms of praise before the face of the Lord, he cried out loudly before the gate: "On the part of Almighty God and at the command of our father Francis, depart from here, all you devils." Soon thereafter the city returned to peace and the people preserved their civic rights in great tranquility. Wherefore afterwards blessed Francis, when preaching to them, said at the beginning of his sermon: "I speak to you as men who were once subjected to the devil and in the bonds of the devils, but I know that you have been set free by the prayers of a certain poor man." (Celano, Second Life of St. Francis, 108)

LIVING AS FRANCIS DID

Brother Sylvester (yesterday's reading) was able to cast the demons out of Arezzo, and civil harmony returned to the city. People were able to move beyond selfish interests, seeing themselves always on the side of the angels and their opponents as the devil's agents.

Two centuries after Francis, St. Bernardine of Siena (another Franciscan) became famous for preaching devotion to the Holy Name of Jesus as a way of moving people beyond selfish political or economic interests.

GROWING WITH FRANCIS

Are you tempted to stereotype any group of people in society at large? Is God calling you to live more truthfully about their good deeds and about your own sins?

JANUARY 31

Confess Temptation

As the merits of St. Francis increased, so too did his struggle with the ancient serpent. For the greater the gifts bestowed upon him, the more subtle were the temptations and the more serious the assaults hurled against him.... At one time there was sent to the holy father a most serious temptation of the spirit, of course for the increase of his crown. He was in anguish as a result; and filled with sorrows, he tormented and tortured his body, he prayed and he wept bitterly. After being thus assailed for several years, he was praying one day at St. Mary of the Portiuncula when he heard a voice within his spirit saying: "Francis, if you have faith like a mustard seed, you will say to this mountain, 'Remove from here and it will remove'" [Matthew 17:19]. The saint replied: "Lord, what mountain do you want me to remove?" And again he heard: "The mountain is your temptation." And weeping, Francis said: "Let it be unto me, Lord, as you have said." Immediately all the temptation was driven out, and he was made free and put completely at peace within himself. (Celano, Second Life of St. Francis, 115)

LIVING AS FRANCIS DID

God freed Francis of his temptation once Francis did his part.

GROWING WITH FRANCIS

What temptation will you ask God to enable you to overcome?

Jesus

Francis of Assisi based everything he said and did on following Jesus Christ within the faith community that had preserved and revered the Scriptures. He loved the Old Testament and the New Testament for what they tell us of God's wondrous love uniquely manifested in the person of Jesus Christ. Many of Francis's contemporaries saw the Incarnation of Jesus as almost secondary to the Scriptures, a step that had to happen to make redemption possible. Yet Blessed John Duns Scotus and other Franciscans have made a strong case that the Incarnation would have happened even if Adam and Eve had never sinned. Jesus's life would have had a very different trajectory, but we would, in fact, never dare to acknowledge God as Father, Son, and Holy Spirit if it weren't for the Incarnation, our strongest sign of God's abiding love and presence in the world.

In Francis's day, many Christians were tempted to love Jesus whom they could not see while looking askance on a Church that was all too full of sinners. Francis recognized that it is the community of faith, comprised of forgiven sinners, who proclaims the word of God, celebrates the sacraments, recognizes saints, calls people into generously cooperating with God's grace, and accompanies believers on their journey of faith.

In fact, some Christians at the time of Francis were terribly scandalized by the concept of the Incarnation of Jesus; it was entirely too fleshy for them. Bread, wine, oil, Jesus in a human body and speaking human words! These were all too material for people who thought of themselves as very spiritual and far above such mundane realities.

Throughout his life Francis grew in his understanding of and love for Jesus. Individual and communal prayer contributed to that—but so did the corporal and spiritual works of mercy that Francis and his followers bestowed on very flawed people whom God loves extravagantly.

Following Jesus made complacency impossible for Francis. There were always more ways that Francis discovered to follow the self-emptying Jesus. Within one hundred years after the death of Francis, Meister Eckhart, a Dominican theologian and mystic, wrote that we need not have a spirituality of addition in terms of adding more pious practices, but a spirituality of subtraction in terms of emptying ourselves of false images of God, self, and others. Eckert did not point to Francis as a prime example of a spirituality of subtraction, but he certainly could have.

This month's quotes take us into St. Bonaventure's Major Life of St. Francis, or Legenda Major. As an excellent theologian, Bonaventure saw Francis as a humble and increasingly generous follower of Jesus. Bonaventure saw the gift of the stigmata, the five wounds of Jesus, as a unique confirmation of Francis's conformity to Christ.

Francis's life makes no sense apart from Jesus Christ. Would our lives make sense apart from Jesus Christ? Francis will lead us to follow Christ's self-emptying way if we so choose.

FEBRUARY 1

Follow Faithfully

This is the life Brother Francis asked to be permitted him and approved by the lord Pope Innocent. The Pope granted his request and approved the Rule for him and for his friars, present and to come....

The Rule and life of the friars is to live in obedience, in chastity and without property, following the teaching and the footsteps of our Lord Jesus Christ who says, If you wish to be perfect, go, sell your possessions, and give the money to the poor, and you will have treasure in heaven; then come, follow me (Matthew 19:21); and, If anyone wishes to come after me, let him deny himself, and take up his cross, and follow me (Matthew 16:24). Elsewhere he says, If anyone comes to me and does not hate his father and mother, and wife and children, and brothers and sisters, yes, and even his own life, he cannot be my disciple (Luke 14:26). (Rule of 1221, preface and chapter 1)

LIVING AS FRANCIS DID

Francis took Jesus's words as something to be lived, and wrote his Rule around this belief. He asked nothing more of his brothers than he himself was willing to give, especially if it concerned becoming a more true disciple of Jesus.

GROWING WITH FRANCIS

Saints are realists. To do likewise and make your life genuine, follow Francis by following Jesus.

Be a Real Deal

The Rule and life of the Friars Minor is this, namely, to observe the Holy Gospel of our Lord Jesus Christ by living in obedience, without property, and in chastity. Brother Francis promises obedience and reverence to his holiness Pope Honorius and his lawfully elected successors and to the Church of Rome. The other friars are bound to obey Brother Francis and his successors. (Rule of 1223, chapter 1)

LIVING AS FRANCIS DID

The three vows that Francis took—poverty, chastity, and obedience—were the same as those that monks had taken for centuries. However, he lived without the safety net that most monks had in their monasteries. If working with his hands did not earn enough to live on, Francis begged. But first the friars had to work hard and live simply. They did not wait for people to come to them. The friars went to the people and preached the word of God that too often was not preached effectively. Today, we "preach" by the way we live out the Gospel in our own lives.

GROWING WITH FRANCIS

Francis was "the real deal," and his integrity attracted followers to the Lord. People who came in contact with Francis found personal strengths they had not sufficiently appreciated. How can we become humble, "real deals"?

FEBRUARY 3

Exam Time

[Francis] outdid all his contemporaries in vanities and he came to be a promoter of evil [2 Maccabees 4:1–2] and was more abundantly zealous for all kinds of foolishness [Galatians 1:14]. He won the admiration of all and strove to outdo the rest in the pomp of vainglory, in jokes, in strange doings, in idle and useless talk, in songs, in soft and flowing garments, for he was very rich, not however avaricious but prodigal, not a hoarder of money but a squanderer of his possessions, a cautious business man but a very unreliable steward. On the other hand, he was a very kindly person, easy and affable, even making himself foolish because of it; for because of these qualities many ran after him, doers of evil and promoters of crime. And thus overwhelmed by a host of evil companions, proud and high-minded, he walked about the streets of Babylon until "the Lord looked down from heaven" [Psalm 33:13a]. (Celano, First Life of St. Francis, 2)

LIVING AS FRANCIS DID

Francis wasn't born a saint. His early companions may not have been truly evil, just crazy kids, but they did not live in God's way. Eventually, Francis chose God's values.

GROWING WITH FRANCIS

Reexamine your basic assumptions about life. Conversion may follow.

FEBRUARY 4

Conversion Continues

When this new soldier of Christ came up to this church [San Damiano], moved with pity over such great need, he entered it with fear and reverence. And when he found there a certain poor priest, he kissed his sacred hands with great faith, and offered him the money he had with him, telling him in order what he proposed to do. The priest was astonished and, wondering over a conversion so incredibly sudden, he refused to believe what he heard…. For he had seen him just the day before, so to say, living in a riotous way among his relatives and acquaintances [Luke 2:44] and showing greater foolishness than the rest. But Francis persisted obstinately and tried to gain credence for what he said, asking earnestly and begging the priest to suffer him to remain with him for the sake of the Lord. In the end the priest acquiesced to his remaining there, but out of fear of the young man's parents, he did not accept the money; whereupon this true condemner of money threw it upon a window sill, for he cared no more for it than for the dust. He wanted to possess that wisdom that is better than gold and to acquire that prudence that is more precious than silver [Proverbs 16:16]. (Celano, First Life of St. Francis, 9)

LIVING AS FRANCIS DID

Francis's conversion was far from complete when he began to live at San Damiano.

GROWING WITH FRANCIS

Your conversion has a next step. Trust that God will help you take it.

He Dares Us

Changed now perfectly in heart and soon to be changed in body too, he was walking one day near the church of St. Damian, which had nearly fallen to ruin and was abandoned by everyone. Led by the Spirit, he went in and fell down before the crucifix in devout and humble supplication; and smitten by unusual visitations, he found himself other than he had been when he entered. While he was thus affected, something unheard of before happened to him: the painted image of Christ crucified moved its lips and spoke. Calling him by name it said: "Francis, go, repair my house, which, as you see, is falling completely to ruin." Trembling, Francis was not a little amazed and became almost deranged by these words. He prepared himself to obey and gave himself completely to the fulfillment of this command…. From then on, compassion for the crucified was rooted in his holy soul, and, as it can be piously supposed, the stigmata of the venerable passion were deeply imprinted in his heart, though not as yet upon his flesh. (Celano, Second Life of St. Francis, 10)

LIVING AS FRANCIS DID

Thomas of Celano jumps ahead in Francis's story, seeing a profound link between his experience at San Damiano and his later reception of Christ's wounds, the stigmata. Francis's conversion progressively opened him to cooperate more generously with God's grace.

GROWING WITH FRANCIS

Do you sometimes fear that God will ask too much of you? God won't!

A Gradual Process

Indeed, he never forgot to be concerned about that holy image, and he never passed over its command with negligence. Right away he gave a certain priest some money that he might buy a lamp and oil, lest the sacred image should be deprived of the due honor of a light even for a moment. Then he diligently hastened to do the rest and devoted his untiring efforts toward repairing that church. For, though the divine command concerned itself with the church that Christ had purchased with his own blood [Acts 20:28], Francis would not suddenly become perfect, but he was to pass gradually from the flesh to the spirit. (Celano, Second Life of St. Francis, 11)

LIVING AS FRANCIS DID

Francis "did not suddenly become perfect, but he was to pass gradually from the flesh to the spirit." Celano said a great deal in those few words. We tend to like our conversion stories quick and dramatic; a gradual reorienting of a person's values tends not to hold our attention as strongly. But more often than not, conversion is a gradual process.

Francis rebuilt the Church of San Damiano and entrusted it to Lady Clare and to her cloistered sisters. Soon after Clare died in 1253, the city of Assisi persuaded the nuns to relocate to a new monastery; the city walls were extended so that it would enclose that monastery and church.

GROWING WITH FRANCIS

Be willing to allow your conversion to move deeper and wider. Stay the course.

FEBRUARY 7

Toward Reconciliation

It happened, however, when Francis' father had left home for a while on business and the man of God remained bound in the basement of the house, his mother, who was alone with him and who did not approve of what her husband had done, spoke kindly to her son. But when she saw that he could not be persuaded away from his purpose, she was moved by motherly compassion for him, and loosening his chains, she let him go free. He, however, giving thanks to Almighty God, returned quickly to the place where he had been before…. Meanwhile his father returned, and not finding Francis, he turned to upbraid his wife, heaping sins upon sins. Then, raging and blustering, he ran to that place hoping that if he could not recall him from his ways, he might at least drive him from the province. (Celano, First Life of St. Francis, 13)

LIVING AS FRANCIS DID

Francis and his father came to have very different values in life. This is not an uncommon situation in families: however, it is one that all too often sets family members against each other for life. In this case, there is no record that Francis and his father were ever reconciled.

GROWING WITH FRANCIS

Seek out someone with whom you would like to be reconciled. If you do not succeed, at least put down the resentment that you have carried far too long.

FEBRUARY 8

Humility Conquers Pride

And behold, he [a companion of Francis] went into ecstasy and saw among the many thrones in heaven one that was more honorable than the rest, ornamented with precious stones, and radiant with all glory. He wondered within himself at this noble throne and considered silently whose it might be. And while he was considering these things, he heard a voice saying to him: "This throne belonged to one of the fallen angels, but now it is reserved for the humble Francis." At length, coming back to himself, the brother saw the blessed Francis coming from his prayers, and quickly prostrating himself at Francis' feet in the form of a cross, he said to him, not as to one living in this world, but as to one already reigning in heaven: "Pray for me to the Son of God, Father, that he will not impute to me my sins." The man of God stretched forth his hand [Matthew 14:31] and raised him up [Acts 3:7], realizing that something had been shown to him in his prayers. (Celano, Second Life of St. Francis, 123)

LIVING AS FRANCIS DID

In the vision of the follower of Francis, we see the pride of Lucifer, a fallen angel, answered by the humility of Francis.

GROWING WITH FRANCIS

Acknowledge one of your personal gifts and one of your blind spots.

FEBRUARY 9

Truth Matters

Humility is the guardian and the ornament of all virtues. If the spiritual building does not rest upon it, it will fall to ruin, though it seems to be growing. This virtue filled Francis in a more copious abundance, so that nothing should be wanting to a man adorned with so many gifts. In his own opinion, he was nothing but a sinner, despite the fact that he was the ornament and splendor of all sanctity. He tried to build himself up upon this virtue, so that he would lay the foundation he had learned from Christ [Matthew 11:29]. Forgetting the things he had gained, he set before his eyes only his failings in the conviction that he lacked more than he had gained. There was no covetousness in him except the desire to become better, and not content with what he had, he sought to add new virtues. (Celano, Second Life of St. Francis, 140)

LIVING AS FRANCIS DID

Shakespeare once wrote, "The more fair and crystal is the sky, the uglier seem the clouds that in it fly" (*Richard II*). The closer Francis came to God, the more aware he was of his sins, and the more he sought to turn away from them. There was nothing fake about his humility.

GROWING WITH FRANCIS

The more truthfully we live with everyone, the more natural humility will become. It takes a great deal of energy to maintain a false image. Use your energy wisely today.

FEBRUARY 10

Are We Listening?

Worn down by his serious illness that was being brought to an end with every suffering, he had himself placed naked upon the naked ground, so that in that final hour when the enemy could still rage against him, he might wrestle naked with a naked enemy. He waited without fear for his triumph, and with his hands clasped he was grasping a crown of justice [2 Timothy 4:8]. Placed thus upon the ground, with his garment of sackcloth laid aside, he raised his face to heaven as was his custom, and giving his whole attention to that glory, he covered the wound in his right side with his left hand lest it be seen. And he said to his brothers: "I have done what was mine to do; may Christ teach you what you are to do." (Celano, Second Life of St. Francis, 214)

LIVING AS FRANCIS DID

This passage explains a great deal about Francis's life. He served God with the best of his ability, and he was not going to worry about how his friars imitated him once he had died. Placed in God's hands, the friars could be open to God's grace and learn whatever God still needed to teach them.

GROWING WITH FRANCIS

God is trying to teach all of us what we should do. Are we listening? Or are we holding back out of fear?

FEBRUARY 11

Risk Rebuilding

Christ himself was Francis' only guide during all this time and now in his goodness he intervened once more with the sweet influence of his grace. Francis left the town one day to meditate out-of-doors and as he was passing by the church of San Damiano which was threatening to collapse with age, he felt urged to go in and pray. There as he knelt in prayer before a painted image of the Crucified, he felt greatly comforted in spirit and his eyes were full of tears as he gazed at the cross. Then, all of a sudden, he heard a voice coming from the cross and telling him three times, "Francis, go and repair my house. You see it is all falling down."… [Francis] was quite willing to devote himself entirely to repairing the ruined church of San Damiano, although the message really referred to the universal Church which Christ "won for himself at the price of [h]is own blood" (Acts 20:28), as the Holy Spirit afterwards made him realize and he himself explained to the friars. (Bonaventure, Major Life of St. Francis, II, 1)

Living as Francis Did

San Damiano was about a twenty minute walk outside of Assisi, and it was the first of three churches that Francis rebuilt. As St. Bonaventure indicates, Francis eventually realized that his rebuilding mission was to reach beyond structures to the heart of the Church.

Growing with Francis

How might you help rebuild Christ's Church?

Gospel Guidance

Francis was filled with the encouragement of the Holy Spirit, when he realized he was being joined by his first follower, and he said, "We shall have
to ask God's advice about this." In the morning they went to the church of
St. Nicholas where they spent some time in prayer. Then Francis opened
the Gospel book three times in honor of the Blessed Trinity, asking God to
approve Bernard's plan with a three-fold testimony. The book opened the
first time at the words, "If you wish to be perfect, go, sell your possessions,
and give the money to the poor" (Matthew 19:21a). The second time they
found the phrase, "Take nothing with you to use on your journey" (Luke
9:3), and the third time the words of our Lord caught their eyes, "If any
want to become my followers, let them deny themselves, and take up their
cross, and follow me" (Matthew 16:24). "This is our life and our rule," said
Francis, "and everyone who comes to join our company must be prepared
to do this. And so, if you have a mind to be perfect, go home and do as you
have heard." (Bonaventure, Major Life of St. Francis, III, 3)

Living as Francis Did

Life changed for Francis when Bernard of Quintavalle became his follower,
and he faced the challenges of living in a brotherhood. Francis and his
followers kept their eyes on the Lord for directions.

Growing with Francis

Is God leading you in a new direction, giving you a new vision?

FEBRUARY 13

God's Healing Power

At this time, too, a religious of the Order of the Crucigeri who was called Moricus was lying ill in a hospital near Assisi. It was a long drawn-out illness and his condition was so bad that the doctors had given up all hope, but then he appealed to St. Francis and sent a message to him, entreating him of his goodness to pray to God for him. Francis agreed immediately and said a prayer for him; then he took some bread-crumbs and dipped them in oil taken from the lamp which burned before our Lady's altar, making a sort of pill out of them. This he sent with one of the friars to the sick man saying: "Take this medicine to our brother Moricus. By means of it Christ's power will restore him to perfect health and when he is strong and ready for the fray once more, he will bring him into our company for the rest of his life." The moment the sick man took the medicine which had been prepared under the inspiration of the Holy Spirit, he immediately recovered and was able to get up. (Bonaventure, Major Life of St. Francis, IV, 8)

LIVING AS FRANCIS DID

Francis would be the first person to affirm that this cure was done under God's power and for God's glory. Moricus praised God for many years by his words and good example.

GROWING WITH FRANCIS

Praise God's goodness today.

Low Maintenance or High?

On his missionary journeys, in preaching the Gospel, he [Francis] always took whatever food was put before him by those who gave him hospitality. But when he returned home, he kept strictly to the rule of fasting. He was hard on himself but accommodating towards his neighbor. In this way he obeyed Christ's Gospel in everything and did people as much good by eating as by fasting. More often than not, his weary body had only the bare earth for a bed and he usually slept in an upright position with a piece of wood or a stone at his head. He was content with one worn habit, as he served God in cold and nakedness. (Bonaventure, Major Life of St. Francis, V, 1)

LIVING AS FRANCIS DID

Francis's needs were few, but he accepted hospitality when it was offered; as such, both he and his hosts benefitted by this. In all circumstances, Francis witnessed to the Good News of Jesus Christ. Because Francis knew that this Good News was addressed to all people, he did not spare himself in its service. Francis's richest benefactors witnessed the Lord's love as much as the poorest women and men whom Francis served. In many ways, Francis was a low-maintenance person, in physical needs and in interior desires. Everyone felt comfortable around him—except people for whom his life seemed a silent reproach.

GROWING WITH FRANCIS

Are you a low-maintenance person? Could you become one?

FEBRUARY 15

Be Available

Francis had humility in abundance, the guardian and the crowning glory of all virtue. He was a mirror and a shining example of Christian perfection but in his own eyes he was only a sinner, and it was on this that he based his spiritual progress, laying the foundation he had learned from Christ, as a careful architect should (1 Corinthians 3:10). The Son of God, he used to say, descended from the sublimity of the Father's bosom to share our misery and become our Lord and Teacher, in order to teach us humility by word and example. Therefore, as Christ's true disciple, he was careful to preserve a low opinion of himself and appear worthless in the eyes of others, keeping in mind the words of the supreme Teacher, "What is prized by human beings is an abomination in the sight of God" (Luke 16:15b). (Bonaventure, Major Life of St. Francis, VI, 1)

LIVING AS FRANCIS DID

Francis had deep appreciation for the fact that Jesus, rich as he was, emptied himself for us so that we might become rich in God's eyes, rich in what truly matters. He did not seek out a good image of himself or avoid what might cause other people to think less of him. Only God's opinion mattered. Francis's time and energy were always available to preach and live the Gospel.

GROWING WITH FRANCIS

People often hold back from doing good because they fear that others will consider their time and energy wasted. Look past this, and humbly live the Gospel.

Discard "Stuff"

The realization that everything comes from the same source filled Francis with greater affection than ever and he called even the most insignificant creatures his brothers and sisters, because he knew they had the same origin as himself. However, he reserved his most tender compassion for those creatures which are a natural reflection of Christ's gentleness and are used in Sacred Scripture as figures of him. He often rescued lambs, which were being led off to be slaughtered, in memory of the Lamb of God who willed to be put to death to save sinners. (Bonaventure, Major Life of St. Francis, VIII, 6)

LIVING AS FRANCIS DID

Jesus Christ meant everything to Francis because, as St. Paul says, everything was created for the Word-made-flesh. Francis had a sacramental worldview; he believed that everything comes from God and can lead us back to God. When people have a false sense of ownership ("appropriation" Francis called it), this rhythm is disrupted.

Living honestly before God and in relation to all creation, we are less tempted to yield to claims about what we "deserve." Gratitude becomes second nature. People are not seen as competitors for scarce resources but as men and women loved by God as much as we are loved by God.

GROWING WITH FRANCIS

How much "stuff" do you really need? This can be more than physical possessions; attitudes can also become stuff that interferes with living as persons created and loved by God.

FEBRUARY 17

Pray, Then Act

The memory of Christ Jesus crucified was ever present in the depths of his heart like a bundle of myrrh, and he longed to be wholly transformed into him by the fire of love. In his extraordinary devotion to Christ, he fasted every year for forty days, beginning at the Epiphany, the time when Christ himself lived in the desert. Then he would go to some lonely place and remain there shut up in his cell, taking as little food and drink as possible, as he spent all his time praying and praising God. He loved Christ so fervently and Christ returned his love so intimately that he seemed to have his Savior before his eyes continually, as he once privately admitted to his companions. He burned with love for the Sacrament of our Lord's Body with all his heart, and was lost in wonder at the thought of such condescending love, such loving condescension. He received Holy Communion often and so devoutly that he roused others to devotion too. (Bonaventure, Major Life of St. Francis, IX, 2)

LIVING AS FRANCIS DID

Christ's love transformed Francis. He surrendered whatever was not needed in order to live the Gospel. Francis followed an extra Lent (from Epiphany to Ash Wednesday) not out of vanity or for the sake of publicity, but because he drew near to Jesus in prayer and fasting. This supported his preaching and his deeds of compassion.

GROWING WITH FRANCIS

Pray by yourself for fifteen minutes today. Act on your prayer.

Pray and Act…Again

Christ, the power of God, Christ the wisdom of God (1 Corinthians 1:24), whom the Spirit of God had anointed, was with his servant Francis in everything he did, lending him eloquence in preaching sound doctrine and glorifying him by the extraordinary power of his miracles. Francis' words were like a blazing fire which penetrated the depths of the heart and filled the minds of his hearers with wonder. They had no claim to any literary style, but gave every sign of being the result of divine inspiration. (Bonaventure, Major Life of St. Francis, XII, 7)

LIVING AS FRANCIS DID

Seeing things from God's perspective takes time and readiness to question conventional wisdom. By prayer, fasting, preaching, and works of mercy, Francis of Assisi learned to look at life from God's viewpoint. Francis's words were a blazing fire because of the integrity of his life. He was the same whether in the public eye or praying by himself in some cave. Francis did not have to worry about being overheard when he thought no one was listening; his life was centered on Jesus.

GROWING WITH FRANCIS

Have you accepted Jesus as the power and wisdom of God? What blocks that effort? Pray for fifteen minutes today and then go out and do something generous that you had not planned on doing when you got up this morning.

FEBRUARY 19

Put God in the Driver's Seat

Because of the extraordinary miracles which highlighted his preaching, the people listened to St. Francis' words as if an angel from God were speaking. The extraordinary degree of virtue he had attained and his spirit of prophecy; the power of his miracles, together with his divine appointment to preach, and the obedience irrational creatures paid him; the profound change of heart in those who heard him, and the fact that he had been taught by the Holy Spirit without the aid of man, and commissioned to preach by the Supreme Pontiff as a result of a revelation, in addition to the rule in which the approach to preaching is laid down, and what was approved by Christ's Vicar; together with the mark of the Great King which was impressed on his body like a seal [the stigmata]—these were all so many testimonies which proclaimed before the whole world that Christ's Francis deserved to be respected because of his office, to be believed because of his teaching, and to be admired for his sanctity, and that therefore he preached Christ's Gospel as a spokesman from God himself. (Bonaventure, Major Life of St. Francis, XII, 12)

LIVING AS FRANCIS DID

There is no substitute for a life of integrity. Francis had it, but so can we. His conversion is complete; ours is still in process. The more we turn to the Lord's ways, the more natural they will become.

GROWING WITH FRANCIS

God's grace will naturally lead us to lives of integrity; stay open to it.

Scripture Alive

By divine inspiration he learned that if he opened the Gospels, Christ would reveal to him what was God's will for him and what God wished to see realized in him. And so Francis prayed fervently and took the Gospel book from the altar, telling his companion, a devout and holy friar, to open it in the name of the Blessed Trinity. He opened the Gospel three times, and each time it opened at the passion, and so Francis understood that he must come like Christ in the distress and the agony of his passion before he left the world, just as he had been like him in all that he did during his life. His body had already been weakened by the austerity of his past life and the fact that he had carried our Lord's Cross without interruption, but he was not afraid and he felt more eager than ever to endure any martyrdom. The unquenchable fire of love for Jesus in his goodness had become a blazing light of flame, so that his charity could not succumb even before the flood-waters of affliction [Song of Solomon 8:6–7]. (Bonaventure, Major Life of St. Francis, XIII, 2)

LIVING AS FRANCIS DID

Bonaventure probably knew more Bible texts than Francis knew, but he must have admired how much Francis's life made those texts come alive because, after all, they are God's self-revelation.

GROWING WITH FRANCIS

Take a few minutes to read a favorite Scripture passage; then try to live it out today.

FEBRUARY 21

Soul Piercing

One morning about the feast of the Exaltation of the Holy Cross, while he was praying on the mountainside, Francis saw a Seraph with six fiery wings coming down from the highest point in the heavens. The vision descended swiftly and came to rest in the air near him. Then he saw the image of a Man crucified in the midst of the wings, with his hands and feet stretched out and nailed to a cross. Two of the wings were raised above his head and two were stretched out in flight, while the remaining two shielded his body. Francis was dumbfounded at the sight and his heart was flooded with a mixture of joy and sorrow. He was overjoyed at the way Christ regarded him so graciously under the appearance of a Seraph, but the fact that he was nailed to a cross pierced his soul with a sword of compassionate sorrow. (Bonaventure, Major Life of St. Francis, XIII, 3)

LIVING AS FRANCIS DID

For St. Bonaventure, Francis's reception of the stigmata, the five wounds of the crucified Christ, was the ultimate proof of the conformity of Francis to Christ. In that same spirit, Francis was very careful not to let many people know about his stigmata because he rightly feared that many people would focus on him instead of on Christ.

GROWING WITH FRANCIS

Allow your soul to be pierced with "compassionate sorrow" today.

FEBRUARY 22

Signed by the Spirit

Eventually [Francis] realized by divine inspiration that God had shown him this vision in his providence, in order to let him see that, as Christ's lover, he would resemble Christ crucified perfectly not by physical martyrdom, but by the fervor of his spirit. As the vision disappeared, it left his heart ablaze with eagerness and impressed upon his body a miraculous likeness. There and then the marks of nails began to appear in his hands and feet, just as he had seen them in his vision of the Man nailed to the Cross. His hands and feet appeared pierced through the center with nails, the heads of which were in the palms of his hands and on the instep of each foot, while the points stuck out on the opposite side. The heads were black and round, but the points were long and bent back, as if they had been struck with a hammer; they rose above the surrounding flesh and stood out from it. His right side seemed as if it had been pierced with a lance and was marked with a livid scar which often bled, so that his habit and trousers were stained. (Bonaventure, Major Life of St. Francis, XIII, 3)

LIVING AS FRANCIS DID

After receiving the stigmata, Francis grew in fervor of spirit, always witnessing to God's kingdom.

GROWING WITH FRANCIS

Is there a particular way that you have been signed by the Spirit? Take a few moments to reflect on this.

FEBRUARY 23

Love Transforms

True love of Christ had now transformed his lover into his image, and when the forty days which he had intended spending in solitude were over and the feast of St. Michael had come, St. Francis came down from the mountain. With him he bore a representation of Christ crucified which was not the work of an artist in wood or stone, but had been reproduced in the members of his body by the hand of the living God. "Kings have their counsel that must be kept secret" (Tobit 12:7), and so Francis who realized that he shared a royal secret did his best to conceal the sacred stigmata. However, it is for God to reveal his wonders for his own glory; he had impressed the stigmata on St. Francis in secret, but he publicly worked a number of miracles by them, so that their miraculous, though hidden, power might become clearly known. (Bonaventure, Major Life of St. Francis, XIII, 5)

LIVING AS FRANCIS DID

As affirmed in this passage, love transforms lovers. They retain their identities yet become different people—the ones they were always intended to be, people who point others to God. No matter who our beloveds may be, or what station in life we choose, love will transform us if we but surrender to it.

GROWING WITH FRANCIS

Every spiritual journey has a next step. Be ready for the next step on your pilgrimage toward God.

FEBRUARY 24

Respond with Grace

The very first vision you [Francis] saw has now been fulfilled; it was
revealed to you then that you were to be a captain in Christ's army and
that you should bear arms which were emblazoned with the sign of the
cross. At the beginning of your religious life the sight of the Crucified
pierced your soul with a sword of compassionate sorrow. There can be
no doubt that you heard Christ's voice from the cross, which seemed to
come from his throne in his sanctuary on high, because we have your own
word for it. Later on, Brother Sylvester saw two swords piercing you in the
form of a cross. When St. Anthony was preaching on the proclamation
fixed to the Cross, Monaldus saw you raised up in the air with your arms
outstretched in the form of a cross, and we know now beyond all shadow of
doubt that these were not imaginary visions, but revelations from heaven.
(Bonaventure, Major Life of St. Francis, XIII, 10)

Living as Francis Did

Bonaventure here is connecting the dots in Francis's life, showing readers
how things that have already been described have now come to fruition—
in God's time and in God's way. The reason for this description is not to
heap honors on Francis (he doesn't really need them) but to give readers
the courage to respond to God's grace as generously as Francis did.

Growing with Francis

Consider how events in your life that were seemingly unrelated have come
together in a very positive way.

Let's Begin Again

Francis now hung, body and soul, upon the Cross with Christ; he burned with love for God worthy of a seraph and, like Christ, he thirsted for the salvation of the greatest possible number of human beings. He could no longer walk because of the nails protruding from his feet, and so he had himself carried, half-dead as he was, through the towns and villages, to encourage others to bear Christ's Cross. To the friars he used to say, "My brothers, we must begin to serve our Lord and God. Until now we have done very little." He longed with all his heart to return to the humble beginning he had made at first and to nurse the lepers once more, as he had done before, making his body which was already worn out with toil serve him once again as it had served him before. With Christ for his leader, he proposed to achieve great victories and, even as his limbs bordered on collapse, he hoped to triumph over his enemy the Devil once again, because he was fervent and courageous in spirit. (Bonaventure, Major Life of St. Francis, XIV, 1)

LIVING AS FRANCIS DID

Although the earlier service on behalf of lepers was no longer physically possible for Francis, in every season of his life, he served God faithfully—in large part because he was always ready to begin again.

GROWING WITH FRANCIS

God may be inviting you to begin again. Pray for the clarity of vision and the readiness to sacrifice that this may require.

What Is Yours to Do?

[Francis] asked to be brought to St. Mary of the Portiuncula, so that he might yield up his spirit where he had first received the spirit of grace. When he arrived there, he was anxious to show that he had no longer anything in common with the world, after the example of Eternal Truth. In his last serious illness, which was destined to put an end to all his suffering, he had himself laid naked on the bare earth, so that with all the fervor of his spirit he might struggle naked with his naked enemy in that last hour which is given him to vent his wrath. As he lay there on the ground, stripped of his poor habit, he raised his eyes to heaven, as his custom was, and was lost in the contemplation of its glory. He covered the wound in his right side with his left hand, to prevent it being seen, and he said to the friars, "I have done what was mine to do. May Christ teach you what is yours." (Bonaventure, Major Life of St. Francis, XIV, 3)

LIVING AS FRANCIS DID

We read Thomas Celano's account of Francis's death earlier in this chapter. Francis's life had come full circle. He had rebuilt St. Mary of the Angels, and there he would die. Consider the good you have done in life.

GROWING WITH FRANCIS

How might you prepare to be ready to come full circle graciously in your life?

The Ultimate Poverty

His [Francis's] companions were overcome with sorrow and wept bitterly; one of them whom the saint called his guardian was inspired by God and took a habit with a cord and trousers, and offered them to Christ's beggar, as he realized this was what he wanted. "I am giving you the loan of these," he said, "as a beggar, and you are to take them in virtue of obedience." The saint was delighted and his heart overflowed with happiness; this proved that he had kept his faith with Lady Poverty to the end. Raising his hands to heaven, he gave praise to Christ for freeing him from all his burdens and allowing him to go freely to meet him. He had acted as he did in his anxiety for poverty, and he was unwilling even to keep a habit unless it was on loan. Christ hung upon his Cross, poor and naked and in great pain, and Francis wanted to be like him in everything. (Bonaventure, Major Life of St. Francis, XIV, 4)

LIVING AS FRANCIS DID

Different accounts of Francis's death suggest that his desire to die naked may have finally yielded to wearing his habit again—but only after it was clear that this habit was "on loan" to him.

GROWING WITH FRANCIS

How much does any of us truly own? A stroke, an accident, or an ultimately death put our ownership in a new light. Death is the ultimate poverty because no one can be assured how she or he will be remembered by future generations.

FEBRUARY 28

Live as Christ

That was why at the beginning of his religious life he [Francis] stood naked before the bishop, and at the end he wished to leave the world naked. In obedience and love he begged the friars who were standing by him to let him lie naked on the ground, when they saw he was dead, for as long as it takes to walk a mile unhurriedly.

Surely he was the most Christ-like of men! His only desire was to be like Christ and imitate him perfectly, and he was found worthy to be adorned with the marks of his likeness; in his life he imitated the life of Christ and in his death he imitated his death, and he wished to be like him still when he was dead. (Bonaventure, Major Life of St. Francis, XIV, 4)

LIVING AS FRANCIS DID

Francis lived for another twenty years after he heard the call to rebuild the Church while in prayer before the San Damiano crucifix. His service to that Church took many twists and turns, but it was always guided by the example of Christ's love for the human family. For us, too, what is most important are the countless decisions we make that draw us closer to Christ, closer to sharing the life of the Blessed Trinity.

GROWING WITH FRANCIS

Francis's life spoke for itself. Live in such a way that your life clearly witnesses to your deepest values and your life might lie exposed to the world.

Holy Reading

Our holy father left this world on Saturday evening, October 3, in the year of our Lord 1226, and he was buried the following day. He immediately became famous for the numerous and extraordinary miracles which were worked through his intercession, because God looked with favor upon him. In his lifetime his sublime holiness was made known to the world in order to show people how they should live by the example of his perfect uprightness. Now that he was reigning with Christ, his sanctity was to be proclaimed from heaven through the miracles worked by God's power, to strengthen the faith of the whole world. All over the world the glorious miracles and the wonderful favors which were obtained through his intercession inspired countless numbers to serve Christ faithfully and venerate his saint. (Bonaventure, Major Life of St. Francis, XV, 6)

Living as Francis Did

Almost forty years would pass before St. Bonaventure completed the Major Life of St. Francis, or Legenda Major. The proof of Francis's life was there for everyone to see. Today, reading can take us to places in Francis's life to which we could not venture otherwise. Reading the Legenda Major in the same devout spirit in which it was written by St. Bonaventure will lead you more deeply into the life and spirit of St. Francis.

Growing with Francis

Consider reading the entire Legenda Major, noticing how Francis's following of Jesus became progressively more generous. Allow it to influence your own following of Jesus Christ.

Conversion

We tend to like dramatic conversions—for example, the story of St. Paul on the road to Damascus (Acts 9:3–8). If someone introduces the word *process* or *journey*, our eyes may glaze over because those expressions indicate that we are in for a long haul.

For this reason, we may prefer reducing Francis's conversion to a single event: embracing a leper alongside the road, hearing the crucifix of San Damiano tell him to rebuild God's house that was falling into ruin, or stripping himself before his father and the local bishop while proclaiming that he now recognized only God as his father.

The life of Francis of Assisi certainly had its dramatic moments. But these were not isolated events; they were an integral part of a faith journey that lasted forty-four years! The early conversions prepared Francis for later and more costly ones.

Francis tended to see all sin as some form of appropriation, as an attempt to claim for oneself what belongs to God alone. Once Francis had simplified his life physically (food, clothing, and shelter, for example), he still had to simplify his life internally (letting go of anger, resentment, or grudges). As his outward life became more humble, his inner life could have become a treasure house of attitudes that Francis refused to surrender to God's grace and love. Francis could have died a bitter man; the reason that he did not is simply that his conversion to the Lord's ways was constantly going deeper and wider.

Francis's contemporaries either knew that he was on the right track, or they had to discredit him; there was no middle course. In every century, saints have stirred up similar reactions. Our temptation is to admire bits and pieces of a saint's life but to affirm that, considered as a whole, this person's life is simply too extreme and God simply could not expect that much conversion and dedication from anyone.

The first twenty days in this chapter contain quotes from Francis himself. All of us are tempted to protect our comfort zone at any price. We easily believe that God must be satisfied with our conversion thus far and is not pointing to any new paths. We can easily believe that we have a good-enough God, and that we are certainly good-enough disciples of that God.

Francis of Assisi constantly shows us otherwise. If, as he believed, all sin is a form of appropriation, of claiming for oneself what belongs to God alone, then conversion can never be complete this side of heaven. The moment that it becomes complete here on earth, a person tends to self-righteousness because no further conversion is needed—or indeed imaginable.

Francis cautioned his friars against thinking that praising the holy lives of saints was enough. We must imitate their generous cooperation with God's grace, regardless of where those conversions may lead and how much they cost.

MARCH 1

Servant Leadership

It is the duty of the friars who are elected ministers, and therefore servants of the other friars, to assign their subjects to the various houses of their provinces. Afterwards they must visit them often, giving them encouragement and spiritual advice. My other beloved brothers must all obey them in all that concerns the salvation of their souls, and is not contrary to our way of life.

The friars should behave towards one another the way the Lord tells us: "In everything, do to others as you would have them do to you" (Matthew 7:12a); and, "What you hate, do not do to anyone" (Tobit 4:16). The ministers who are servants should remember the words of our Lord, "The Son of Man came not to be served but to serve" (Matthew 20:28a). They should remember, too, that they have been entrusted with the care of the souls of the friars. If any one of them is lost through their fault or bad example, they must account for it before our Lord Jesus Christ on the Day of Judgment. (Rule of 1221, chapter 4)

LIVING AS FRANCIS DID

Francis of Assisi deliberately chose the term "minister" to describe leaders among Franciscans. Ministers are leaders who are to serve others, remembering that ministers must give an accounting to God for what they have done or not done.

GROWING WITH FRANCIS

Are there any services you are asked to provide that seem beneath your dignity? If so, examine your pride and offer that service gracefully.

MARCH 2

Be a Model of Francis

All the friars, both the ministers, who are servants, and their subjects, should be careful not to be upset or angry when anyone falls into sin or gives bad example; the devil would be only too glad to ensnare many others through one man's sin. They are bound, on the contrary, to give the sinner spiritual aid, as best they can. "Those who are well have no need of a physician, but those who are sick" (Matthew 9:12)....

Far from doing or speaking evil to one another, the friars should be glad to serve and obey one another in a spirit of charity. This is the true, holy obedience of our Lord Jesus Christ. (Rule of 1221, chapter 5)

LIVING AS FRANCIS DID

Without the advice that Francis gives above, we could be perpetually upset with those around us who are quite obviously still sinners. Although we should not act as enablers when others make poor choices, we must remember that we, too, are sinners. Whereas people in institutions such as the Church tend to see their leader as a father figure, Francis preferred the image of elder brother, sister, or mother to describe leaders among Franciscans and those who wish to follow Francis.

GROWING WITH FRANCIS

Complete this sentence, "I could be a better leader if…" If you identified someone else's actions as your biggest obstacle, go back and reword that sentence to describe how your behavior needs to change. Model the change that you would like to see in them.

MARCH 3

A Great Irony

We must be firmly convinced that we have nothing of our own, except our vices and sins....We must all be on our guard against pride and empty boasting and beware of worldly or natural wisdom. A worldly spirit loves to talk a lot but do nothing, striving for the exterior signs of holiness that people can see, with no desire for true piety and interior holiness of spirit. It was about people like this that our Lord said, "Truly I tell you, they have received their reward" (Matthew 6:2b). The spirit of God, on the other hand, inspires us to mortify and despise our lower nature and regard it as a source of shame, worthless and of no value. Humility, patience, perfect simplicity, and true peace of heart are all its aim, but above everything else it desires the fear of God, the divine wisdom and the divine love of the Father, Son, and Holy Spirit. (Rule of 1221, chapter 17)

LIVING AS FRANCIS DID

The great irony of our lives is that we tend to claim—Francis would say "appropriate"—things that truly belong to God alone while rejecting the only things that are, in fact, ours: our sins and our vices. "Humility, patience, perfect simplicity, and true peace of heart" should be what we seek to acquire.

GROWING WITH FRANCIS

Is the irony described above present in your life? If so, what steps can you take to live more honestly before God?

MARCH 4

All Good from God

We must refer every good to the most high supreme God, acknowledging that all good belongs to him; and we must thank him for it all, because all good comes from him. May the most supreme and high and only true God receive and have and be paid all honor and reverence, all praise and blessing, all thanks and all glory, for to him belongs all good and "no one is good but God alone" (Luke 18:19b). And when we see or hear people speaking or doing evil or blaspheming God, we must say and do good, praising God, who is blessed for ever. (Rule of 1221, chapter 17)

LIVING AS FRANCIS DID

We do not really own anything as though we possessed it apart from God. That was the original sin of Adam and Eve. In a sense, the serpent sealed the deal by promising Eve (and by extension, Adam) that disobeying God's command would make them as powerful as God is. That was obviously not the case.

Every blessing we experience comes from God. Every sin we commit is a failed attempt to separate some blessing from its source. Our best response to someone else's sin is the good example that we give. Ultimately, God will straighten things out.

GROWING WITH FRANCIS

Identify three blessings from God that you experienced yesterday. Be alert today for any temptations you may encounter not to connect this day's blessings to God.

MARCH 5

Living Honestly

Almighty, most high and supreme God, Father, holy and just, Lord, King of heaven and earth, we give you thanks for yourself. Of your own holy will you created all things spiritual and physical, made us in your own image and likeness, and gave us a place in paradise, through your only Son, in the Holy Spirit. And it was through our own fault that we fell. We give you thanks because, having created us through your Son, by that holy love with which you loved us, you decreed that he should be born, true God and true man, of the glorious and ever blessed Virgin Mary and redeem us from our captivity by the blood of his passion and death. (Rule of 1221, chapter 23)

LIVING AS FRANCIS DID

Although we may not warm up to the expression "doing penance," Francis could just as easily have described a life of penance as "living honestly." Conversion always moves us away from personal illusions and closer to God's reality, away from our blind spots and into God's grace. The humility of Jesus evident in his Incarnation should rub off on us.

GROWING WITH FRANCIS

How honest are you? Not simply honest in your financial dealings with other people or your golf score but also honest about your gifts and your blind spots. Francis was being brutally honest when, toward the end of his life, he described himself as a sinner. Are we ready to follow his example?

MARCH 6

Grace Enables Good

We Friars Minor, servants and worthless as we are, humbly beg and implore everyone to persevere in the true faith and in a life of penance; there is no other way to be saved. We beseech the whole world to do this, all those who serve our Lord and God within the holy, catholic, and apostolic Church, together with the whole hierarchy, priests, deacons, subdeacons, acolytes, exorcists, lectors, porters, and all clerics and religious, male or female; we beg all children, big and small, the poor and the needy, kings and princes, laborers and farmers, servants and masters; we beg all virgins and all other women, married or unmarried; we beg all lay folk, men and women, infants and adolescents, young and old, the healthy and the sick, the little and the great, all peoples, tribes, families and languages, all nations and all men everywhere, present and to come; we Friars Minor beg them all to persevere in the true faith and in a life of penance. (Rule of 1221, chapter 23)

LIVING AS FRANCIS DID

Every group of people in Francis's society was included in the quote above, invited to trade any inflated sense of self for the truth that God's grace enables whatever good we accomplish.

GROWING WITH FRANCIS

In what ways do you "persevere in the true faith and in a life of penance"?

MARCH 7

Living Your Values

We should wish for nothing else and have no other desire; we should find no pleasure or delight in anything except in our Creator, Redeemer, and Saviour; he alone is true God, who is perfect good, all good, every good, the true and supreme good, and he alone is good, loving and gentle, kind and understanding; he alone is holy, just, true, and right; he alone is kind, innocent, pure, and from him, through him, and in him is all pardon, all grace, and all glory for the penitent, the just, and the blessed who rejoice in heaven. (Rule of 1221, chapter 23)

LIVING AS FRANCIS DID

Francis knew that idolatry was the key sin in the Old Testament. Sometimes it expressed itself through the worship of statues made of wood, stone or metal. More often, however, it involved the worship of something less than God as though it *were* God: money, economic resources, political power, an out-of-control nationalism, or anything else to which we can become addicted. These temptations are still with us.

GROWING WITH FRANCIS

If you listed the three most important values in your life and then shared them with the people closest to you, would any of them be surprised when they compared your list to their experience of you? Identify one positive action you can take today to express your deepest values.

MARCH 8

Don't Fool Yourself

Nothing, then, must keep us back, nothing separate us from him, nothing come between us and him. At all times and seasons, in every country and place, every day and all day, we must have a true and humble faith, and keep him in our hearts, where we must love, honor, adore, serve, praise and bless, glorify and acclaim, magnify and thank, the most high supreme and eternal God, Three and One, Father, Son, and Holy Spirit, Creator of all and Saviour of those who believe in him, who hope in him, and who love him; without beginning and without end, he is unchangeable, invisible, indescribable and ineffable, incomprehensible, unfathomable, blessed and worthy of all praise, glorious, exalted, sublime, most high, kind, lovable, delightful and utterly desirable beyond all else, for ever and ever. (Rule of 1221, chapter 23)

LIVING AS FRANCIS DID

Every sin—what separates us from God—presents itself as a shortcut to something good. In fact, every sin is some form of a lie; it's a dead end dressed up as a shortcut. Once we've been down the same path a few times, we should start to recognize the scenery.

GROWING WITH FRANCIS

People tend to praise the humility and generosity of St. Francis of Assisi— and rightly so. But these virtues mean nothing apart from the deep-down honesty with which he lived. An honest person is not simply someone who avoids telling lies; it's someone, above all, who doesn't lie to herself or himself. Live a radical honesty today.

MARCH 9

Mending Fences

And this is my advice, my counsel, and my earnest plea to my friars in our Lord Jesus Christ that, when they travel about the world, they should not be quarrelsome or take part in disputes with words (2 Timothy 2:14) or criticize others; but they should be gentle, peaceful, and unassuming, courteous and humble, speaking respectfully to everyone, as is expected of them. (Rule of 1223, chapter 3)

LIVING AS FRANCIS DID

The apostles shared the Good News that Jesus gave them; they always knew that they were not the Good News, but its servants. It's easy to turn even a minor disagreement into a personal attack. It's also quite easy to become very self-righteous. "How dare they not appreciate my good idea." we may say. "I was only trying to help. What ingrates! After all I've done for them!"

Conversion always leads us deeper into the truth about our relationship to God and other people. That deeper truth influences the way we see ourselves and enables us to laugh at ourselves if need be.

GROWING WITH FRANCIS

With whom did I most recently have a serious disagreement? Were my motives and my defenses really as pure as I presented them? Mend a personal fence today—perhaps not the biggest one you need to mend, but one fence at least. That will make mending the next one that much easier.

MARCH 10

Banish "If Only"

With all my heart, I beg the friars in our Lord Jesus Christ to be on their guard against pride, boasting, envy, and greed, against the cares and anxieties of this world, against detraction and complaining. Those who are illiterate should not be anxious to study. They should realize instead that the only thing they should desire is to have the spirit of God at work within them, while they pray to him unceasingly with a heart free from self-interest. They must be humble, too, and patient in persecution or illness, loving those who persecute us by blaming us or bringing charges against us, as our Lord tells us, "Love your enemies and pray for those who persecute you" (Matthew 5:44). (Rule of 1223, chapter 10)

LIVING AS FRANCIS DID

The "if only" litany never ends. "If only my parents had understood me better. If only my coworkers were more receptive to my suggestions. If only my children appreciated how much I sacrifice myself for them. If only my friends realized how much I do for them!" Yes, that litany can be never-ending. Francis admonishes his friars here to accept what they are and desire only that the spirit of God be at work in them.

GROWING WITH FRANCIS

Is your heart as free of self-interest as it should be? Are you frequently resentful of someone else's good fortune? You will be happier if you come to terms with your gifts and shadows.

MARCH 11

Change Me, Lord

This is how God inspired me, Brother Francis, to embark upon a life of penance. When I was in sin, the sight of lepers nauseated me beyond measure; but then God himself led me into their company, and I had pity on them. When I had once become acquainted with them, what had previously nauseated me became a source of spiritual and physical consolation for me. After that I did not wait long before leaving the world. (Testament)

LIVING AS FRANCIS DID

The story of Francis's first positive experience with a leper is well known. He encountered a leprous man while out riding and was tempted to ride away. Instead, Francis chose to dismount, kiss the man, and give him some coins.

When Francis recognized a leper as someone made in God's image and likeness, that didn't change the leper's appearance or smell, but it profoundly changed how Francis saw himself. He finally recognized what he had in common with lepers: being created and loved by God. The Lord did not lead Francis among lepers in order to punish him but to force him to confront what he accepted as self-evident: that he was blessed by God and they were obviously not. No, God was leading Francis to make connections he had previously resisted.

GROWING WITH FRANCIS

Today, pray for the person or group of people you have the hardest time recognizing as being loved by God. Tomorrow, do something to put today's prayer into action.

MARCH 12

Watering Faith

God told Adam: "You may freely eat of every tree of the garden; but of the tree of the knowledge of good and evil you shall not eat" (Genesis 2:16–17). Adam, then, could eat his fill of all the trees in the garden, and as long as he did not act against obedience, he did not sin. A man eats of the tree that brings knowledge of good when he claims that his good will comes from himself alone and prides himself on the good that God says and does in him. And so, at the devil's prompting and by transgressing God's command, the fruit becomes for him the fruit that brings knowledge of evil, and it is only right that he should pay the penalty. (Admonition II)

LIVING AS FRANCIS DID

For Francis of Assisi, the most basic sin is some form of appropriation, claiming for oneself what belongs to God alone. We may try to make our appropriations look more respectable by saying that we are simply being honest or prudent. But are we? Do we protest vigorously if someone suggests that our motives for a certain action may not be as selfless as we claim?

GROWING WITH FRANCIS

When the Christians in Corinth started bickering among themselves about their importance within that community, St. Paul wrote to them that he planted, Apollos (another evangelist) watered, "but God gives the growth." Do we really believe that? How do we act on it?

MARCH 13

Surrender to Mercy

What have you to be proud of? If you were so clever and learned that you knew everything and could speak every language, so that the things of heaven were an open book to you, still you could not boast of that. Any of the devils knew more about the things of heaven, and knows more about the things of earth, than any human being, even one who might have received from God a special revelation of the highest wisdom. If you were the most handsome and the richest man in the world, and could work wonders and drive out devils, all that would be something extrinsic to you; it would not belong to you and you could not boast of it. But there is one thing of which we can all boast; we can boast of our humiliations (2 Corinthians 12:15) and in taking up daily the holy cross of our Lord Jesus Christ. (Admonition V)

LIVING AS FRANCIS DID

Francis knew that knowledge can be appropriated, that it can be used as a weapon against other people. In the end, the only thing we truly own are our sins. Jesus invites us to surrender them to God's mercy.

GROWING WITH FRANCIS

The cross of Jesus Christ did not scare Francis because he knew that God's help was never lacking. What is most important in my life is not in someone else's hands; it's in mine and God's. If my grasp weakens, God's will not.

MARCH 14

A Hidden Reserve of Patience

We can never tell how patient or humble a person is when everything is going well with him. But when those who should co-operate with him do the exact opposite, then we can tell. A man has as much patience and humility as he has then, and no more. (Admonition XIII)

LIVING AS FRANCIS DID

People can learn to cover their tracks very well, to smile and appear one way while interiorly they are judging things by a very different set of values. Over the years, Francis had to deal with some friars whose conversion was real but very stunted. Their conversion would not go deeper and wider—as it naturally will—because they were not willing to surrender any more of their life to God. Thus, they could seem very patient until someone was so foolish as to cross them. Then they showed their true colors!

The most patient person you have ever known was not patient because that person had an easy life or because everyone else did things on the patient person's timetable. No, patient people know two things intensely: (1) There are always options, and (2) Some options are better than others. A truly patient person deals with conflict maturely, not turning every disagreement into a life-or-death challenge or referendum on their worth as a person.

GROWING WITH FRANCIS

Be patient with at least one difficult person today.

MARCH 15

Only Before God

Blessed the religious who has no more regard for himself when people praise him and make much of him than when they despise and revile him and say that he is ignorant. What a man is before God, that he is and no more. Woe to that religious who, after he has been put in a position of authority by others, is not anxious to leave it of his own free will. On the other hand, blessed is that religious who is elected to office against his will but always wants to be subject to others. (Admonition XX)

LIVING AS FRANCIS DID

In his Major Legend (6:1), St. Bonaventure says that Francis frequently repeated, "What a man is before God, that he is and no more." Perhaps no statement is more typical of Francis than this one. We could rightly end this statement by adding "and no less"

Conversion led Francis deeper into the truth about God, himself, and other people. The more truthful Francis was, the more he saw leadership among the brothers as a service, not an honor to be flaunted—and certainly it was not a key part of a friar's identity. A person can be as greedy for power as for gold.

GROWING WITH FRANCIS

Conversion led Francis into greater freedom. It will do the same for us. Allow your dignity as someone made in God's image and likeness to lead you into more generous service today.

MARCH 16

Balanced in God

Blessed that religious who takes blame, accusation, or punishment from another as patiently as if it were coming from himself. Blessed the religious who obeys quietly when he is corrected, confesses his fault humbly and makes atonement cheerfully. Blessed the religious who is in no hurry to make excuses, but accepts the embarrassment and blame for some fault he did not commit. (Admonition XXIII)

LIVING AS FRANCIS DID

Picture in your mind a pyramid. Because it has a wide base, it cannot be tipped over easily because its center of gravity is well within the pyramid's base. If, however, you could evenly cut the top off the pyramid, you could flip it upside down and balance it on its very narrow base. The least little pressure from the side, however, would cause it to tip over immediately because its center of gravity would soon fall outside that narrow base.

In various ways, we can make our lives into inverted pyramids, constantly in danger of being tipped over. The humility praised by Francis keeps us solidly grounded in God's grace and, therefore, much less likely to tip over.

GROWING WITH FRANCIS

Is it enough for you that God knows you perfectly even if others do not? If we rest in God's love and providence, we are less likely to feel the need to correct everyone else's mistaken notions. The truth will come out in God's good time. Stay firmly balanced today.

MARCH 17

Conversion Hones Conscience

We are bound to order our lives according to the precepts and counsels of our Lord Jesus Christ, and so we must renounce self and bring our lower nature into subjection under the yoke of obedience; this is what we have all promised God. However, no one can be bound to obey another in anything that is sinful or criminal. (Letter to All the Faithful)

LIVING AS FRANCIS DID

Obedience is a great virtue, but "just following orders" has its limits. In fact, it could be positively sinful. The Nuremberg trials of Nazi officials after World War II showed that obeying a law could, in fact, be a crime against humanity.

Francis wrote the words cited above to laypeople who were trying to live the Gospel as radically as he was doing. A deepening conversion will always sharpen our sense of conscience. If a certain issue becomes a matter of conscience for us, we cannot act against our considered and prayerful judgment without hurting ourselves to some degree, without succumbing to some well-disguised form of idolatry. Christ was obedient even unto death on the cross, but that did not violate his conscience.

GROWING WITH FRANCIS

Is civil disobedience ever justified? A conscientious person cannot rule out that possibility. Am I allowing my conscience all the room that it needs to grow? Am I willing to follow it even if doing so may cause others to judge me negatively?

MARCH 18

Step By Step

Almighty, eternal, just and merciful God, grant us in our misery that we may do for your sake alone what we know you want us to do, and always want what pleases you; so that, cleansed and enlightened interiorly and fired with the ardour of the Holy Spirit, we may be able to follow in the footsteps of your Son, our Lord Jesus Christ, and so make our way to you, Most High, by your grace alone, you who live and reign in perfect Trinity and simple Unity, and are glorified, God all-powerful, for ever and ever. Amen. (Letter to a General Chapter)

LIVING AS FRANCIS DID

We tend to like our conversions short-term and not very messy. But in fact, all change starts as a seed deep within us, and while sometimes it may burst out suddenly in a blaze of glory, more often it progresses slowly and steadily toward transformation.

Being cleansed and interiorly enlightened, allowing oneself to be filled with the ardor of the Holy Spirit—these things take time. The ante keeps going up, so to speak. We are tempted to tell God that we've done enough, that God should count on someone else for whatever may leave our consciences unsettled.

GROWING WITH FRANCIS

"In His will is our peace," sing the saints in Dante's *Divine Comedy*. We cannot, however, truly be at peace unless we allow our conversion to God's ways to be open-ended. Every faith journey has a next step. What is yours today?

MARCH 19

Who Today?

I should like you to prove that you love God and me, his servant and yours, in the following way. There should be no friar in the whole world who has fallen into sin, no matter how far he has fallen, who will ever fail to find your forgiveness for the asking, if he will only look into your eyes. And if he does not ask forgiveness, you should ask him if he wants it. And should he appear before you again a thousand times, you should love him more than you love me, so that you may draw him to God; you should always have pity on such friars. Tell the guardians, too, that this is your policy. (Letter to a Minister)

LIVING AS FRANCIS DID

This minister wrote to Francis and apparently wanted to resign his office so that he did not have to deal with so many imperfect friars. Francis does not encourage him in that direction. Instead, he tells the minister to draw any errant friar back to the Lord's ways through the minister's prayer and good example. Forgiveness does not mean that the minister should lie about the damage done by this friar, but forgiveness also prevents him from acting as though he can pass God's judgment on that friar.

GROWING WITH FRANCIS

Forgiveness happens when I want for the person who wronged me what God wants for that person: to live as someone created in God's image and likeness. Who's next on my list of people to forgive?

Be a Living Sign

Brother Leo, send greetings and peace to your Brother Francis.

As a mother to her child, I speak to you, my son. In this one word, this one piece of advice, I want to sum up all that we said on our journey, and, in case hereafter you still find it necessary to come to me for advice, I want to say this to you: In whatever way you think you will best please our Lord God and follow in his footsteps and in poverty, take that way with the Lord God's blessing and my obedience. And if you find it necessary for your peace of soul or your own consolation and you want to come to me, Leo, then come. (Letter to Brother Leo)

Living as Francis Did

Brother Leo was one of the first followers of Francis and remained a very close friend until Francis died. Leo may also have been a bit scrupulous, afraid to trust his own judgment. This letter was obviously meant to bring Leo greater peace of mind and a stronger sense of the freedom that God wants all of us to have. Brother Leo probably felt encouraged by Francis's request that Leo bless *him*.

Growing with Francis

Is there someone in your life who very much needs to hear an encouraging word from you? Call, email, or write that person today; be a living sign of God's love and the freedom that God wants this person to have.

MARCH 21

Whose Will?

It is indeed very hard to give up things one is accustomed to, and things that once enter into the mind are not easily eradicated; the mind, even though it has been kept away from them for a long time, returns to the things it once learned; and by constant repetition vice generally becomes second nature. So Francis still tried to flee the hand of God, and, forgetting for a while his paternal correction, he thought, amid the smiles of prosperity, of the things of the world [1 Corinthians 7:34]; and, ignorant of the counsel of God [Wisdom 9:13], he still looked forward to accomplishing great deeds of worldly glory and vanity. For a certain nobleman of the city of Assisi was preparing himself in no mean way with military arms, and, puffed up by a gust of vainglory, vowed that he would go to Apulia to increase his wealth and fame. Upon hearing this, Francis, who was flighty and not a little rash, arranged to go with him. (Celano, First Life of St. Francis, 4)

LIVING AS FRANCIS DID

Francis's conversion was a lifelong process that enabled him to take the next steps the Lord placed before him. He dreamed of becoming a knight and doing great things for God, others—and for himself. But this was not to happen in the way he thought it would.

GROWING WITH FRANCIS

Consider today that God may already be fulfilling your deepest desires, but not in the way that you initially expected.

MARCH 22

Going Where?

On a certain night, therefore, after he had given himself with all delibera-
tion to the accomplishment of these things, and while, burning with desire,
he longed greatly to set about the journey, he who had struck him with the
rod of justice visited him in the sweetness of grace by means of a nocturnal
vision; and because Francis was eager for glory, he enticed him and raised
his spirits with a vision of the heights of glory. For it seemed to Francis
that his whole home was filled with the trappings of war, namely, saddles,
shields, lances, and other things; rejoicing greatly, he wondered silently
within himself what this should mean.... The answer was given him that
all these arms would belong to him and to his soldiers. When he awoke,
he arose in the morning with a glad heart, and considering the vision an
omen of great success, he felt sure that his journey to Apulia would come
out well. (Celano, First Life of St. Francis, 5)

LIVING AS FRANCIS DID

Francis had a sense of what furthered his goals and what obstructed them.
The dream described above suggests that God was working in ways that
Francis had not originally foreseen. Francis indeed won glory, but with
very different weapons than he expected.

GROWING WITH FRANCIS

GPS devices are known for "recalculating." Prayer and continuous conversion are part of how we recalculate and thus follow the Lord's lead.

MARCH 23

Change Required

He [Francis] said that he did not want to go to Apulia, but he promised that he would do noble and great things in his native place. People thought he wished to take to himself a wife, and they asked him, saying: "Francis, do you wish to get married?" But he answered them, saying: "I shall take a more noble and more beautiful spouse than you have ever seen; she will surpass all others in beauty and will excel all others in wisdom." Indeed, the immaculate spouse of God is the true religion which he embraced; and the hidden treasure is the kingdom of heaven, which he sought with such great desire; for it was extremely necessary that the Gospel calling be fulfilled in him who was to be the minister of the Gospel in faith and in truth. (Celano, First Life of St. Francis, 7)

LIVING AS FRANCIS DID

Francis's sense of what constituted loss and gain changed as a result of his conversion. In time, he was ready to sacrifice everything else for the Gospel treasure he had found. Before that reached a critical stage, however, he had to deal with the fact that many of his friends did not understand what was happening to him interiorly. He learned to live with that, trusting God would lead him in the right direction.

GROWING WITH FRANCIS

Is your sense of loss and gain the same as it was twenty years ago? If not, what has changed?

MARCH 24

Patient or Proud?

He [Francis] arose, therefore, immediately, active, eager, and lively; and, bearing the shield of faith to fight for the Lord, armed with a great confidence, he took the way toward the city; aglow with a divine fire, he began to accuse himself severely of laziness and cowardice. When those who knew him saw this, they compared what he was now with what he had been; and they began to revile him miserably. Shouting out that he was mad and demented, they threw the mud of the streets and stones at him. They saw that he was changed from his former ways and greatly worn down by mortification of the flesh, and they therefore set down everything he did to exhaustion and madness. But since a patient man is better than a proud man, the servant of God showed himself deaf to all these things and, neither broken nor changed by any of these injuries, he gave thanks to God for all of them. (Celano, First Life of St. Francis, 11)

LIVING AS FRANCIS DID

Francis said that a patient man is better than a proud man. That takes some effort to understand. A sinfully proud person is never far from being tipped over: The proud person is misunderstood, not sufficiently appreciated, never given the help needed to complete a project, on and on and on. Where do you fall on the line of patience or pride?

GROWING WITH FRANCIS

Give someone a well-deserved compliment today. That person might even be yourself if the compliment is shared with God.

MARCH 25

Act for Justice

He [Francis's father, Pietro Bernardone] rushed upon him [Francis] like a wolf upon a sheep, and looking upon him with a fierce and savage countenance, he laid hands upon him and dragged him shamelessly and disgracefully to his home. Thus, without mercy, he shut him up in a dark place for several days, and thinking to bend his spirit to his own will, he first used words and then blows and chains. But Francis became only the more ready and more strong to carry out his purpose; but he did not abandon his patience either because he was insulted by words or worn out by chains. For he who is commanded to rejoice in tribulation [Matthew 4:10–12] cannot swerve from the right intention and position of his mind or be led away from Christ's flock, not even by scourgings and chains; neither does he waver in a flood of many waters [Psalm 31:6], whose refuge from oppression is the Son of God, who, lest our troubles seem hard to us, showed always that those he bore were greater. (Celano, First Life of St. Francis, 12)

LIVING AS FRANCIS DID

Weather vanes are very useful because they tell us which direction the wind is blowing. Human beings, however, can turn themselves into weather vanes by having no firm convictions about anything. Is there something in your life to which you are committed enough that you would endure the kind of oppression Francis sometimes faced?

GROWING WITH FRANCIS

Speak up for justice today, even if that is risky.

MARCH 26

Stripping Down

When he [Francis] was brought before the bishop, he would suffer no delay or hesitation in anything; indeed, he did not wait for any words nor did he speak any, but immediately putting off his clothes and casting them aside, he gave them back to his father. Moreover, not even retaining his trousers, he stripped himself completely naked before all. The bishop, however, sensing his disposition and admiring greatly his fervor and constancy, arose and drew him within his arms and covered him with the mantle he was wearing. He understood clearly that the counsel was of God, and he understood that the actions of the man of God that he had personally witnessed contained a mystery. He immediately, therefore, became his helper and cherishing him and encouraging him, he embraced him in the bowels of charity. (Celano, First Life of St. Francis, 15)

LIVING AS FRANCIS DID

Francis's conversion kept going deeper and deeper. The confrontation with his father, who expected the bishop of Assisi to side with him, was an important but painful part of Francis's conversion. For what treasure was he willing to risk everything? Life would help him sort that out. Sometimes we are tempted to say, "O God, ask me to give up anything except…" That may well be the next step on our faith journey.

GROWING WITH FRANCIS

Believe that God always provides the strength to live by God's values, and consider where you need God's strength.

MARCH 27

Building on the Old

The first work that blessed Francis undertook after he had gained his freedom from the hand of his carnally minded father was to build a house of God.

He did not try to build one anew, but he repaired an old one, restored an ancient one. He did not tear out the foundation, but he built upon it, ever reserving to Christ his prerogative, though he was not aware of it, "For no one can lay any foundation other than the one that has been laid; that foundation is Christ Jesus" (1 Corinthians 3:11). When he had returned to the place where, as has been said, the church of St. Damian had been built in ancient times, he repaired it zealously within a short time with the help of the grace of the Most High. This is the blessed and holy place, where the glorious religion and most excellent order of Poor Ladies and holy virgins had its blessed origin about six years after the conversion of St. Francis and through that same blessed man. (Celano, First Life of St. Francis, 18)

LIVING AS FRANCIS DID

In Francis's day, some people admired him very much for thinking in new ways. The danger there was that Francis was simply calling attention to himself. Francis's first biographer wanted to show that the saint's newness was actually the rediscovery of something very old: that the Gospel could be lived here and now, not simply admired from afar.

GROWING WITH FRANCIS

What new way of thinking might help in your own conversion?

MARCH 28

Who Counts?

He [Bernard of Quintavalle] hastened therefore to sell all his goods and gave the money to the poor, though not to his parents; and laying hold of the title to the way of perfection, he carried out the counsel of the holy Gospel: "If you wish to be perfect, go, sell your possessions, and give the money to the poor, and you will have treasure in heaven; then come, follow me" (Matthew 19:21). When he had done this, he was associated with St. Francis by his life and by his habit, and he was always with him until, after the number of the brothers had increased, he was sent to other regions by obedience to his kind father. His conversion to God was a model to others in the manner of selling one's possessions and giving them to the poor. St. Francis rejoiced with very great joy over the coming and conversion of so great a man, in that the Lord was seen to have a care for him by giving him a needed companion and a faithful friend. (Celano, First Life of St. Francis, 24)

LIVING AS FRANCIS DID

People often think that all of Assisi was abuzz when Francis began to live in a new way. Yet in fact, the conversion of Bernard of Quintavalle may have caused more of a sensation in Assisi because he was a nobleman. Status was as important then as it is today—perhaps even more so.

GROWING WITH FRANCIS

Who counts in your world and why? Is that group becoming larger or smaller?

MARCH 29

I'm the Sinner!

Therefore the blessed father Francis was being daily filled with the consolation and the grace of the Holy Spirit; and with all vigilance and solicitude he was forming his new sons with new learning, teaching them to walk with undeviating steps the way of holy poverty and blessed simplicity. One day, when he was wondering over the mercy of the Lord with regard to the gifts bestowed upon him, he wished that the course of his own life and that of his brothers might be shown him by the Lord; he sought out a place of prayer, as he had done so often, and he persevered there for a long time "with fear and trembling" [Tobit 13:6]. Standing before the Lord of the whole earth [Zechariah 4:14], he thought "because of the bitterness of my soul" [Isaiah 38:15] of the years he had spent wretchedly, frequently repeating this word: "God, be merciful to me, the sinner!" (Luke 18:13). (Celano, First Life of St. Francis, 26)

Living as Francis Did

The tax collector whom Celano quotes here prayed as he did precisely because he was an honest man. He knew that he was a sinner in need of God's mercy. The more honest Francis became, the fewer things that he needed to defend. Poverty, simplicity, honesty, and repentance all go together.

Growing with Francis

Repeat the tax collector's prayer—"God, be merciful to me, the sinner!"— at least once today and then act on it.

MARCH 30

Do It!

Little by little a certain unspeakable joy and very great sweetness began to flood his innermost heart. He began also to stand aloof from himself, and, as his feelings were checked and the darkness that had gathered in his heart because of his fear of sin dispelled, there was poured into him a certainty that all his sins had been forgiven and a confidence of his restoration to grace was given him. He was then caught up above himself, and absorbed in a certain light; the capacity of his mind was enlarged and he could see clearly what was to come to pass. When this sweetness finally passed, along with the light, renewed in spirit, he seemed changed into another man. (Celano, First Life of St. Francis, 26)

LIVING AS FRANCIS DID

Sometimes we resist conversion to the Lord's way because we fear giving it full freedom will shrink our world, will make us more closed in. Like every other saint, Francis of Assisi reminds us that conversion to the Lord's ways will always enlarge our world, stretching us in a good way.

Francis "seemed changed into another man" because conversion indeed made him a new man. He retained his original DNA and fingerprints, but his heart became ever new and young.

GROWING WITH FRANCIS

Have you ever mulled over what deeper conversion might take away from your life or bring to it? How might you give God a bit more room to work in your life? Do it! You won't regret it.

MARCH 31

Jesus Everywhere

These things the most blessed father Francis fulfilled most perfectly; he bore the image and form of a seraph and, persevering upon the cross, merited to rise to the ranks of the heavenly spirits. For he was always on the cross, fleeing no labor or suffering, if only he could fulfill the will of the Lord in himself and concerning himself.

The brothers, moreover, who lived with him knew how his daily and continuous talk was of Jesus and how sweet and tender his conversation was, how kind and filled with love his talk with them. His mouth spoke out of the abundance of his heart [Isaiah 51:3], and the fountain of enlightened love that filled his whole being bubbled forth outwardly. Indeed, he was always occupied with Jesus; Jesus he bore in his heart, Jesus in his mouth, Jesus in his ears, Jesus in his eyes, Jesus in his hands, Jesus in the rest of his members. (Celano, First Life of St. Francis, 115)

Living as Francis Did

Conversion did not scare Francis because he knew that it would lead him into the deeper and wider truth about who he was before God, in relation to other people, and in his own eyes.

Growing with Francis

Francis once reminded his friars that they needed to live the very virtues for which they praised the saints. How can you live the virtue you most admire in the most saintly person you have ever met?

Prayer

Our lives are so easily fragmented between responsibilities to friends, family, employers, neighbors, and the larger human family that we may think we don't have the time or energy for prayer. That was the experience of Francis of Assisi up until his mid-twenties. Then he discovered that prayer was more real than many of the things he had been considering more important.

Only in prayer were his knightly ambitions turned in a new direction; only in prayer did he find the strength to lead the people who wanted to follow him—but on their own terms. Prayer enabled him to discover the link between the Church that Jesus established and the Church that needed much more conversion to Jesus's ways.

We often think of prayer as an activity that is guaranteed to leave us more serene than when we began it. It does ultimately lead to serenity, but only after it has led us into deeper honesty about God, other people, and ourselves. As long as certain parts of a person's life are "off limits" as the subject of prayer, that person's possibilities for conversion will be stunted.

Prayer is not for sissies, and Francis of Assisi knew that. Prayer is not simply rearranging a person's mental furniture; it leads to discarding some furniture (attitudes) that is no longer compatible with God's ways and acquiring other furniture (different attitudes) as necessary in order to live honestly before God, with other people, and with ourselves.

Perhaps no part of the Bible provides a bigger help to prayer than the Psalms. They spring from every part of our emotional spectrum and lead us to the same point: gratitude for God's generosity and a desire to imitate it as much as we can here and now. Francis knew the Psalms by heart, and those who followed him quickly did so too. They learned the Bible's other most famous prayers and could pray them as they walked from place to place, reflecting on what God had accomplished through them in their previous location and preparing for what God might be asking from them in the next place.

Francis was as much subject to self-doubt as any of us. His motives were purified in prayer; his ego became right-sized there. His prayer was both private and public; one without the other tends to lead the person praying into some type of illusion. Instead, prayer leads us into deeper and more radical honesty while enabling us to deal with the consequences of any newfound honesty.

John Dewey, an educational theorist, once wrote that all education is about making connections. Prayer enabled Francis of Assisi to see the connections in what otherwise could have been a very fragmented life: preacher, healer, leader of friars, spiritual guide for many lay people, and advisor to popes and bishops.

Rather than ask how he could find time and energy to pray, Francis asked himself, "How could I not pray?"

APRIL 1

Only Through Prayer

Our Lord tells us in the Gospel, "This kind of evil spirit can come only by through prayer" (Mark 9:28), and in another place, "And whenever you fast, do not look dismal like the hypocrites" (Matthew 6:16). And so all the friars, both clerics and lay brothers, must say the Divine Office with the praises and prayers, as they are obliged to.

The clerics should celebrate the liturgy, praying for the living and the dead, like the clerics of the Roman Curia. Each day they should say the "Have mercy on me, O God" (Psalm 51) and one Our Father for the faults and failings of the friars, together with the "Out of the depths, I cry to you, O Lord" (Psalm 130) and an Our Father for the dead friars....

The lay brothers who can read the psalter may have a copy of it, but those who cannot read are not allowed to have one. (Rule of 1221, chapter 3)

LIVING AS FRANCIS DID

People who share prayer regularly may be able to handle tensions that arise in common life better than people who do not pray together—assuming that common prayer deepens their conversion to the Lord's ways. Prayer allows us time to distance ourselves from everyday concerns and see the bigger picture of life. This in itself can create a more calm and balanced spirit.

GROWING WITH FRANCIS

Pray alone or with a friend today for the peace only God can give.

Pray the Day

The lay brothers are to say the Creed and twenty-four Our Fathers with the Glory Be to the Father for Matins [the first of eight "hours" in the Liturgy of the Hours]. For Lauds they are to say five; for Prime the Creed and seven Our Fathers together with the Glory Be to the Father. For Terce, Sext, and None they are to say seven; for Vespers, twelve; and for Compline, the Creed followed by seven Our Fathers with the Glory be to the Father. For the dead they must say seven Our Fathers with the prayer Eternal rest, and each day they are to say three Our Fathers for the faults and failings of the friars. (Rule of 1221, chapter 3)

Living as Francis Did

The Liturgy of the Hours, also known as the Divine Office, is the daily prayer of the Church. It structured the ebb and flow of monasteries, and continues to do so even today. As such, the Divine Office formed a backbone of Francis's community. The Hours also have been said by laypeople since medieval times, particularly the two most important Hours: Lauds (Morning Prayer) and Vespers (Evening Prayer).

Praying the Our Fathers was an advantage for traveling friars who did not have the easily portable breviaries that exist today.

Growing with Francis

Say three Our Fathers today for your needs and those of your loved ones.

APRIL 3

Remember the Dead

The clerics are to recite the Divine Office according to the rite of the Roman Curia, except the psalter; and so they may have breviaries. The lay brothers are to say twenty-four Our Fathers for Matins and five for Lauds; for Prime, Terce, Sext, and None, for each of these, they are to say seven; for Vespers twelve and for Compline seven. They should also say some prayers for the dead. (Rule of 1223, chapter 3)

Living as Francis Did

The Rule of 1223's section on praying is shorter than the corresponding section in the Rule of 1221. The "hour" of Prime was suppressed at Vatican II. Matins (now called the Office of Readings) includes several psalms, responses, a longer reading from the Old Testament, and a reading from one of the Church Fathers (Sts. Augustine, Jerome, or other writers). Those readings may be coordinated with that day's feast if there is one.

The prayers for the dead are not specified. In fact, the Franciscan family has an annual feast to commemorate all its faithful departed. Smaller portions of the Franciscan family may have their own prescribed prayers for the dead, who are also remembered in the intercessions at Morning and Evening Prayer.

Growing with Francis

Pray today for your deceased relatives—parents, grandparents, aunts, siblings—and friends, reflecting on how their faith has influenced yours.

APRIL 4

Where Lies Your Worth?

The friars to whom God has given the grace of working should work in a spirit of faith and devotion and avoid idleness, which is the enemy of the soul, without however extinguishing the spirit of prayer and devotion, to which every temporal consideration must be subordinate. As wages for their labor they may accept anything necessary for their temporal needs, for themselves or their brethren, except money in any form. And they should accept it humbly as is expected of those who serve God and strive after the highest poverty. (Rule of 1223, chapter 5)

LIVING AS FRANCIS DID.

Francis wanted friars to work as hard as each could, but never to the detriment of their life of prayer and penance. If friars worked together in someone's fields, they might pray the psalms from memory, or use the Our Father to pray the Liturgy of the Hours. He preferred payment in goods rather than money. In his day, cash was becoming more than a convenience; it was used by some (for example, moneylenders) as a means of oppression, by others as a way of accumulating wealth.

According to their Rule, Franciscans should work with faith and devotion, earning their daily bread. If they cannot, they could "have recourse to the table of the Lord" (beg), seeking help through their fraternities, friends, and families. Their lives should always point to God through regular prayer.

GROWING WITH FRANCIS

Is your sense of personal worth overly connected to your ability to work?

APRIL 5

Faithful Following

All the other friars, too, are bound to obey their guardians in the same way, and say the Office according to the Rule. If any of them refuse to say the Office according to the Rule and want to change it, or if they are not true to the Catholic faith, the other friars are bound in virtue of obedience to bring them before the custos [superior] nearest the place where they find them....

The friars should not say, this is another Rule. For this is a reminder, admonition, exhortation, and my testament which I, Brother Francis, worthless as I am, leave to you, my brothers, that we may observe in a more Catholic way the Rule we have promised to God. The Minister General and all the other ministers and custodes are bound in virtue of obedience not to add anything to these words or subtract from them. They should always have this writing with them as well as the Rule and at the chapters they hold, when the Rule is read, they should read these words also. (Testament)

LIVING AS FRANCIS DID

For Francis, it was essential that the friars thoroughly reflect their Catholic faith. How the friars prayed the Divine Office was one indication of their Catholic identity.

GROWING WITH FRANCIS

It's easy to find fault with the Church here on earth. While we need to be honest about the Church's faults it is important to see it as an instrument for sharing the Good News of Jesus.

APRIL 6

Marthas and Marys

Not more than three or at most four friars should go in together to a hermitage to lead a religious life there. Two of these should act as mothers, with the other two, or the other one, as their children. The mothers are to lead the life of Martha; the other two, the life of Mary Magdalene.

Those who live the life of Mary are to have a separate enclosure and each should have a place to himself, so that they are not forced to live or sleep together. At sunset they should say Compline of the day. They must be careful to keep silence and say their Office, rising for Matins. Their first care should be to seek the kingdom of God and his justice (Luke 12:31). Prime and Terce should be said at the proper time, and after Terce the silence ends and they can speak and go to their mothers. (Religious Life in Hermitages)

LIVING AS FRANCIS DID

This passage refers to the story found in Luke 10:38–42, which speaks of Martha, who "was distracted by her many tasks" and Mary, who sat the feet of Jesus and listened to him teach. Francis wrote that the "Marthas" should tend to the needs of friars, while the "Marys" remain deeply involved in prayer. The friars would then switch roles.

GROWING WITH FRANCIS

If you are more Martha than Mary, try to take on some of Mary's characteristics today. Reverse this if you are more Mary than Martha.

APRIL 7

Flexible or Rigid

The friars who are mothers must be careful to stay away from outsiders and in obedience to their custos keep their sons away from them, so that no one can speak to them. The friars who are sons are not to speak to anyone except their mother or their custos, when he chooses to visit them, with God's blessing. Now and then, the sons should exchange places with the mothers, according to whatever arrangement seems best suited for the moment. But they should all be careful to observe what has been laid down for them, eagerly and zealously. (Religious Life in Hermitages)

LIVING AS FRANCIS DID

Most friars who used hermitages did so temporarily. Their prayer nurtured the ministry when they were no longer living in a hermitage. It was expected that this life would lead them more deeply into the truth about God, themselves, and one another. For this reason, it should never become a springboard for self-righteousness.

Francis was in many ways a very flexible person. He could write a rule for Religious Life in Hermitages, but he made sure that it would never foster a caste system. The friars who prayed more intensely would have to take their turn of waiting on other friars who would engage in prayer more full-time.

GROWING WITH FRANCIS

How flexible are you? Does your prayer foster flexibility or rigidity? Are you tempted to think that more mundane work such as cooking and cleaning is beneath your dignity?

APRIL 8

Spirit and Life

In that love which is God (1 John 4:16), I, Brother Francis, the least of our servants and worthy only to kiss your feet, beg and implore all those to whom this letter comes to hear these words of our Lord Jesus Christ in a spirit of humility and love, putting them into practice with all gentleness and observing them perfectly. Those who cannot read should have them read to them often and keep them ever before their eyes, by persevering in doing good to the last, because they are "spirit and life" (John 6:64). Those who fail to do this shall be held to account for it before the judgment-seat of Christ at the last day. And may God, Father, Son, and Holy Spirit, bless those who welcome them and grasp them and send copies to others, if they persevere in them to the last (Matthew 10:22). (Letter to All the Faithful)

LIVING AS FRANCIS DID

The Letter to the All the Faithful may have been written in early 1220, before Francis wrote his Rule in 1221. The audience is laywomen and laymen interested in living the Gospel life after the example of Francis. He represented not only a new path to holiness for priests and brothers, but also a new path for married spouses and single persons. This passage occurs toward the end of a letter that is filled with Scripture references.

GROWING WITH FRANCIS

Be "spirit and life" to someone today, even if it is through prayer alone.

APRIL 9

Head to Heart

I beseech the Minister General, my superior, to see that the Rule is observed inviolably by all, and that the clerics say the Office devoutly, not concentrating on the melody of the chant, but being careful that their hearts are in harmony so that their words may be in harmony with their hearts and their hearts with God. Their aim should be to please God by purity of heart, not to soothe the ears of the congregation by their sweet singing. I myself promise to observe this strictly, as God gives me the grace, and I will hand it on to the friars who are with me so that they too may put it into practice in the Office and in other prescriptions of the Rule. If a friar refuses to do this, I will not regard him as a Catholic or as one of my friars and I even refuse to see or speak with him until he repents. I say the same of all those others who go wandering about with no thought for regular discipline. (Letter to a General Chapter)

LIVING AS FRANCIS DID

Francis wrote this letter because he wanted to avoid disagreements among his clerical followers over how to chant the Divine Office. Prayerful words penetrate the hearts of Francis's followers, moving them to deeper conversion to the Lord's ways.

GROWING WITH FRANCIS

How can your prayer move from your head to your heart?

APRIL 10

Delve into Scripture

"Holy, holy, holy, the Lord God almighty,
  Who was, and who is, and who is coming." (Revelation 4:8)
R. Let us praise and glorify him for ever.
  Worthy is the Lamb who was slain
  to receive power and divinity
  and wisdom and strength
  and honor and glory and blessing." (Revelation 5:12)
R. Let us praise and glorify him for ever.
  Let us bless the Father and the Son and the Holy Spirit.
R. Let us praise and glorify him for ever.
  "Bless the Lord, all you works of the Lord." (Daniel 3:57a)
R. Let us praise and glorify him for ever.
(The Praises Before the Office)

LIVING AS FRANCIS DID

Francis composed a number of these "Praises," which reflect his deep, biblically based spirituality.

GROWING WITH FRANCIS

How might you develop a deeper appreciation of Scripture? Take a first step this week.

APRIL 11

Joining in Prayer

Changed, therefore, but in mind, not in body, he refused to go to Apulia and he strove to bend his own will to the will of God. Accordingly, he withdrew for a while from the bustle and the business of the world and tried to establish Jesus Christ dwelling within himself [Ephesians 3:16]. Like a prudent business man, he hid the treasure he had found from the eyes of the deluded, and, having sold all his possessions, he tried to buy it secretly [Matthew 13:44]. Now since there was a certain man in the city of Assisi whom he loved more than any other because he was of the same age as the other, and since the great familiarity of their mutual affection led him to share his secrets with him; he often took him to remote places, places well-suited for counsel, telling him that he had found a certain precious and great treasure. This one rejoiced and, concerned about what he heard, he willingly accompanied Francis whenever he was asked. (Celano, First Life of St. Francis, 6).

LIVING AS FRANCIS DID

We don't know the name of Francis's friend mentioned above. It seems that he never became a friar, but he joined Francis in prayer and was important in Francis's conversion—as was Francis in his.

GROWING WITH FRANCIS

Take some extra time today to pray in a special way for a family member, friend, or someone in your community who is in need.

APRIL 12

Prayer Changes Us

There was a certain grotto near the city where they frequently went and talked about this treasure. The man of God...would enter the grotto, while his companion would wait for him outside; and filled with a new and singular spirit, he would pray to his Father in secret. He wanted no one to know what he did within, and taking the occasion of the good to wisely conceal the better, he took counsel with God alone concerning his holy proposal. He prayed devoutly that the eternal and true God would direct his way and teach him to do his will. He bore the greatest sufferings in mind and was not able to rest until he should have completed in deed what he had conceived in his heart; various thoughts succeeded one another and their importunity disturbed him greatly. He was afire within himself with a divine fire and he was not able to hide outwardly the ardor of his mind; he repented that he had sinned so grievously and had offended the eyes of God's majesty [Isaiah 3:8], and neither the past evils nor those present gave him any delight.... When he came out again to his companion, he was so exhausted with the strain, that one person seemed to have entered, and another to have come out. (Celano, First Life of St. Francis, 6)

Living as Francis Did

Francis could be easily consumed by prayer. Its intensity often manifested itself as a physical experience.

Growing with Francis

Allow prayer to change you as God desires.

APRIL 13

Prayer of Discernment

They all conferred together, as true followers of justice, whether they should dwell among men or go to solitary places. But St. Francis, who did not trust in his own skill, but had recourse to holy prayer before all transactions, chose not to live for himself alone, but for him who "died for all" [2 Corinthians 5:15], knowing that he was sent for this that he might win for God the souls the devil was trying to snatch away. (Celano, First Life of St. Francis, 35)

LIVING AS FRANCIS DID

This discussion took place early in the life of Francis's brotherhood. Most of Francis's followers chose a life of active ministry, but some of them lived in hermitages (as Francis himself did) from time to time. The friars esteemed those who made a choice opposite theirs. What mattered was that God was praised in all things and that God's people be supported in their faith journey—either by preaching, other work, or the prayers of the friars.

Francis prayed at Mount La Verna in Tuscany and in other secluded places. He sometimes withdrew from preaching during the Church's Lent (Ash Wednesday through Easter) or during other "Lents" that he observed (Epiphany to Ash Wednesday or Assumption of Mary to the feast of St. Michael the Archangel).

GROWING WITH FRANCIS

Is prayer part of your important decisions? Prayer is often a moment of greater truth and insight for people. Avail yourself of its graces.

APRIL 14

Prayer for Churches

At that time, walking in simplicity of spirit [Proverbs 20:7], they did not know as yet the ecclesiastical office [Divine Office]. He [Francis] said to them: "When you pray, say Our Father [Luke 11:2], and We adore thee, Christ, here and in all thy churches which are in the whole world, and we bless thee, because by thy holy cross thou hast redeemed the world." [This prayer is also found in the Testament of St. Francis.] But this the brothers strove to observe with the greatest diligence as disciples of their beloved master, for they strove to carry out most efficaciously not only those things which the blessed father Francis said to them in fraternal advice or fatherly command, but also the things that were in his mind or on which he was meditating, if in some way they would come to know them. (Celano, First Life of St. Francis, 45)

LIVING AS FRANCIS DID

Francis never lost sight of the connection of Jesus, prayer, and the Church of his day. Every church reminded Francis of God's love and mercy; thus, he asked the friars to recite the prayer given above. Franciscans around the world still use this prayer regularly, often when they finish praying Morning Prayer, Evening Prayer, or one of the hours of the Divine Office.

GROWING WITH FRANCIS

Say the prayer cited above, keeping in mind the good of the Church throughout the world. Pray too for a spirit of unity with all people of faith, no matter what religion they profess.

APRIL 15

Beginning with Me

Moreover, if a church were standing in any place whatsoever, even though the brothers were not present there but could only see it from some distance, they were to prostrate themselves upon the ground in its direction and, having bowed low with body and soul, they were to adore Almighty God, saying:

"We adore thee, Christ, here and in all thy churches," as the holy father [Francis, Testament] had taught them. And, what is no less to be admired, wherever they saw a crucifix or the mark of a cross, whether upon the ground, or upon a wall, or on trees, or in the hedges along the way, they were to do the same thing. (Celano, First Life of St. Francis, 45)

LIVING AS FRANCIS DID

The Church was far from perfect in Francis's day, as is also the case today. It has always given a less than perfect witness to the Good News it is called to proclaim. Even so, Francis's sense of Jesus's Incarnation was so strong that he never surrendered to the temptation to look down on the Church that was present around him while praising the heavenly Church that he did not yet see.

Francis asked the friars to recite this prayer whether they actually were in a church building or could only see it from afar. A cross or crucifix should lead them to recite this prayer.

GROWING WITH FRANCIS

Pray that the whole Church may better witness Jesus's Good News—beginning with you.

APRIL 16

Time for God

The man of God Francis had been taught not to seek his own [1 Corinthians 13:5], but to seek especially what in his eyes would be helpful toward the salvation of others; but above everything else he desired to depart and to be with Christ [Philippians 1:23]. Therefore, his greatest concern was to be free from everything of this world, lest the serenity of his mind be disturbed even for an hour by the taint of anything that was mere dust. He made himself insensible to all external noise, and, bridling his external senses with all his strength and repressing the movements of his nature, he occupied himself with God alone. In the clefts of the rock he would build his nest and in the hollow places of the wall his dwelling [Song of Songs 2:14].... He therefore frequently chose solitary places so that he could direct his mind completely to God; yet he was not slothful about entering into the affairs of his neighbors, when he saw the time was opportune, and he willingly took care of things pertaining to their salvation. (Celano, First Life of St. Francis, 71)

LIVING AS FRANCIS DID

One of the great ironies in the life of Francis is that the more he sought solitude and concentrated on God's ways, the more Francis's contemporaries sought him out. His calling was to be found among people, rather than alone in caves.

GROWING WITH FRANCIS

Make additional time for God today.

APRIL 17

Depth not Length

For his safest haven was prayer; not prayer of a single moment, or idle or presumptuous prayer, but prayer of long duration, full of devotion, serene in humility. If he began late, he would scarcely finish before morning. Walking, sitting, eating, or drinking, he was always intent upon prayer. He would go alone to pray at night in churches abandoned and located in deserted places, where, under the protection of divine grace, he overcame many fears and many disturbances of mind. (Celano, First Life of St. Francis, 71)

Living as Francis Did

It's easy to become discouraged that we do not pray as often or with the intensity that Francis had. Yet prayer is the last place where we should compare ourselves to others. We don't know if another person's prayer reflects a life already turned over to God's grace or a life with much to be relinquished to God's grace.

Long prayers are not necessarily better—as Jesus's story about a Pharisee and a tax collector praying in the Temple shows (Luke 18:10–14). What matters is the integrity of prayer, the openness the person praying shows to conversion to the Lord's ways. Someone timing the prayer of that Pharisee and that tax collector would have wrongly concluded that the Pharisee had offered the better prayer. Jesus didn't see it that way.

Growing with Francis

Use your prayer to trim away whatever obscures the fact that you are created in the image and likeness of God.

APRIL 18

Greater Conversion

At a certain time the blessed and venerable father Francis left behind the crowds of the world that were coming together daily with the greatest devotion to hear and see him, and he sought out a quiet and secret place of solitude, desiring to spend his time there with God and to cleanse himself of any dust that may have clung to him from his association with men [Luke 10:11a]. It was his custom to divide up the time given him to merit grace, and, as seemed necessary to him, to give part of it to working for the good of his neighbors and the rest to the blessed retirement of contemplation. He therefore took with him just the very few companions to whom his holy life was better known than it was to the rest, so that they might protect him from the invasion and disturbance of men and respect and preserve his quiet in all things. (Celano, First Life of St. Francis, 91)

LIVING AS FRANCIS DID:

People knew that Francis was the real deal. They were so attracted to Francis that their presence sometimes threatened the very thing they admired most about Francis: that he pointed them to God. Some people were attracted to Francis more out of curiosity than from a desire to follow his example of conversion and adopt a deeper practice of prayer and good works.

GROWING WITH FRANCIS

Consider whether you might be afraid that a deeper prayer life could lead to greater conversion, and of the change that would bring.

APRIL 19

Be Open

After he had remained there for a while and had acquired in an inexpressible way familiarity with God by his constant prayer and frequent contemplation, he longed to know what might be more acceptable to the eternal King concerning himself or in himself or what might happen. Most carefully he sought out and most piously longed to know in what manner, by what way, and by what desire he might cling perfectly to the Lord God according to his counsel and according to the good pleasure of his will. This was always his highest philosophy; this very great desire always flamed in him while he lived, namely, to seek out from the simple, from the wise, from the perfect and imperfect, how he might attain the way of truth and come to his highest good. (Celano, First Life of St. Francis, 91)

LIVING AS FRANCIS DID

Francis believed that others could help him discern God's will about his life and ministry. He was drawn to a life of more intense prayer, but he also felt the need to share what he learned in prayer—not to call attention to himself but to help others on their spiritual journey. Francis accepted advice from a wide range of people and then evaluated it. Yet whatever he decided was truly his decision.

GROWING WITH FRANCIS

I'm listening, God! What are you trying to tell me?

Ready, Set, Go

Filled with the Spirit of God [1 Corinthians 7:40b], he was ready to suffer every distress of mind and to bear every bodily torment, if only his wish might be granted, that the will of the Father in heaven might be mercifully fulfilled in him. One day therefore he went before the holy altar which was erected in the hermitage where he was staying, and taking the book in which the holy Gospel was written, he reverently placed it upon the altar. Then he prostrated himself in prayer to God, not less in heart than in body, and he asked in humble prayer that the good God, "the Father of mercies and the God of all consolation" [2 Corinthians 1:3b], would deign to make known his will to him, and that he might be able to carry out what he had earlier begun simply and devoutly; and he prayed that it might be shown to him at the first opening of the book what was more fitting for him to do. (Celano, First Life of St. Francis, 92)

LIVING AS FRANCIS DID

It would have been fairly easy for Francis to assume that God wanted the same thing throughout his life. In fact, Francis was led through times of intense preaching, concentrated praying, and even speaking with the sultan of Egypt. He was always prepared to go where God led him.

GROWING WITH FRANCIS

Be as attuned to God's will as Francis was, ready to go where the Lord leads.

APRIL 21

Drawing Closer

Two years before Francis gave his soul back to heaven, while he was living in the hermitage which was called Alverna, after the place on which it stood, he saw in the vision of God [Isaiah 6:2] a man standing above him, like a seraph with six wings, his hands extended and his feet joined together and fixed to a cross. Two of the wings were extended above his head, two were extended as if for flight, and two were wrapped around the whole body [Isaiah 6:2]. When the blessed servant of the Most High saw these things, he was filled with the greatest wonder, but he could not understand what this vision should mean. Still, he was filled with happiness and he rejoiced very greatly because of the kind and gracious look with which he saw himself regarded by the seraph, whose beauty was beyond estimation; but the fact that the seraph was fixed to a cross and the sharpness of his suffering filled Francis with fear. And so he arose, if I may so speak, sorrowful and joyful, and joy and grief were in him alternately. Solicitously he thought what this vision could mean, and his soul was in great anxiety to find its meaning. (Celano, First Life of St. Francis, 94)

LIVING AS FRANCIS DID

Divine visions marked key turning points in Francis's life, such as this event, which was followed by him receiving the stigmata.

GROWING WITH FRANCIS

Seek out a way to draw closer to God today.

APRIL 22

A Rare Gift

His hands and feet seemed to be pierced through the middle by nails, with the heads of the nails appearing in the inner side of the hands and on the upper sides of the feet and their pointed ends on the opposite sides. The marks in the hands were round on the inner side, but on the outer side they were elongated; and some small pieces of flesh took on the appearance of the ends of the nails, bent and driven back and rising above the rest of the flesh. In the same way the marks of the nails were impressed upon the feet and raised in a similar way above the rest of the flesh. Furthermore, his right side was as though it had been pierced by a lance and had a wound in it that frequently bled so that his tunic and trousers were very often covered with his sacred blood. Alas, how few indeed merited to see the wound in his side while this crucified servant of the crucified Lord lived! But happy was [Brother] Elias who, while the saint lived, merited to see this wound; and no less happy was [Brother] Rufino who touched the wound with his own hands. (Celano, First Life of St. Francis, 95)

LIVING AS FRANCIS DID

Celano goes into detail because the stigmata was such a rare event. Francis's first biographer stressed how fitting this gift was, even though it cost the saint dearly.

GROWING WITH FRANCIS

Be ready for whatever gift God offers you today.

APRIL 23

Resist Temptation

But while he frequented hidden places as more suitable to prayer, the devil tried to drive him away from such places by an evil suggestion. He put into his mind a certain woman who was monstrously hunchbacked, an inhabitant of his city, and who was a hideous sight to all. He threatened to make him like her if he did not leave off what he had begun. But strengthened in the Lord [Ephesians 6:10], he rejoiced to hear a reply of salvation and grace: "Francis," God said to him in spirit, "what you have loved carnally and vainly you should now exchange for spiritual things, and taking the bitter for sweet [Proverbs 27:7], despise yourself, if you wish to acknowledge me; for you will have a taste for what I speak of even if the order is reversed." Immediately he was compelled to obey the divine command and was led to actual experience. (Celano, Second Life of St. Francis, 9)

LIVING AS FRANCIS DID

Even saints have temptations. Francis had them. Jesus had them. Satan, the father of lies, seeks to undermine anyone's movement toward God's grace and the freedom that God has always wanted us to enjoy. The father of lies constantly tries to discourage us, to convince us that God's ways are too difficult, too slow, and ultimately don't bring us where we want to go. Not so!

GROWING WITH FRANCIS

Pray for yourself and for everyone who is tempted to give in to discouragement. God has rich gifts to offer us!

APRIL 24

Willing and Ready

When Francis returned from his private prayers, through which he was changed almost into another man, he tried with all his strength to conform himself to others, lest, if the inner fire were apparent to others, he should lose what he had gained under the glow of human favor. Often too he spoke things like these to his familiar friends: "When a servant of God is praying and is visited by a new consolation from the Lord, he should, before he comes away from his prayer, raise his eyes to heaven and with hands joined say to the Lord: 'This consolation and sweetness you have sent from heaven, Lord, to me, an unworthy sinner, and I return it to you so you may keep it for me, for I am a robber of your treasure.' And again: 'Lord, take your good things away from me in this world and keep them for me in the life to come.' Thus," he said, "he ought to speak. And when he comes away from prayer, he should show himself to others as poor and as a sinner, as though he had attained no new grace." (Celano, Second Life of St. Francis, 99)

LIVING AS FRANCIS DID

Francis's prayer, as described here, is a model of humility and honesty.

GROWING WITH FRANCIS

Pray humbly and honestly that you may be willing to receive everything the Lord wants to give you.

APRIL 25

Trust in God

When one brother who was undergoing temptations was sitting alone with the saint, he said to Francis: "Pray for me, kind Father, for I am sure that I will be immediately freed from my temptations if you will be kind enough to pray for me. For I am afflicted above my strength and I know that this is no secret to you." St. Francis said to him: "Believe me, son, for I think you are for that reason more truly a servant of God; and know that the more you are tempted, the more will you be loved by me." And he added: "I tell you in all truth, no one must consider himself a servant of God until he has undergone temptations and tribulations…. There are many who flatter themselves over their long-standing merits and are happy because they have had to undergo no temptations. But because fright itself would crush them even before the struggle, they should know that their weakness has been taken into consideration by the Lord. For difficult struggles are hardly ever put in the way of anyone, except where virtue has been perfected." (Celano, Second Life of St. Francis, 118)

LIVING AS FRANCIS DID

Temptation can crush a person who forgets God's ever-present help. What matters is not the size of our temptations but how readily we see ourselves as God sees us—and act accordingly.

GROWING WITH FRANCIS

Trust in God's assistance today.

End in Praise

A few years after his conversion, Francis, to preserve the virtue of holy humility, resigned the office of superior of the order in a certain chapter before all the brothers, saying: "From now on I am dead to you. But see, here is Brother Peter of Catania, whom I and all of you shall obey." And bowing down before him, he promised him obedience and reverence. The brothers, therefore, wept, and their sorrow brought forth deep sighs, when they saw themselves, in a certain way, to be orphaned from such a father. But Francis, rising and with his hands joined and his eyes raised to heaven, said: "Lord, I commend to you the family that you heretofore have entrusted to me. But now, because of my infirmities, as you know, most sweet Lord, I am unable to care for it and so I entrust it to the ministers. Let them be obliged to render an account before you, Lord, on judgment day, if any brother of them perishes because of their negligence, or example, or harsh correction." He remained thereafter until his death a subject, conducting himself more humbly than anyone else. (Celano, Second Life of St. Francis, 143)

LIVING AS FRANCIS DID

Regular and intense prayer gave Francis freedom to recognize that his brotherhood needed a type of leadership that he could no longer provide. Prayer led him into heartfelt praise.

GROWING WITH FRANCIS

Even if you are in a difficult situation, take time today to praise God in prayer.

APRIL 27

Doubt Happens

Francis was greatly consoled by the visitations of God, by which he was made to feel sure that the foundations of his order would always remain unshaken. It was also promised to him that without a doubt the number of those who would fall away would be replaced by the substitution of elect. For once when he was disturbed over bad examples and, thus distressed, gave himself over to prayer, he brought back this rebuke from the Lord: "Why are you disturbed, little man? Did I not place you over my order as its shepherd, and now you do not know that I am its chief protector? I chose you, a simple man, for this task, that what I would do in you to be imitated by the rest they might follow who wished to follow. I have called, I will preserve and feed, and I will choose others to repair the falling away of others, so that if a substitute is not born, I will make him to be born. Do not be disturbed, therefore, but work out your salvation [Philippians 2:12b], for though the order were reduced to the number of three, it will by my grace remain unshaken." (Celano, Second Life of St. Francis, 158)

LIVING AS FRANCIS DID

Despite his great faith, Francis occasionally doubted what the next step in following God might be. We do the same thing.

GROWING WITH FRANCIS

Don't be surprised if God brings you closer to reality before this day ends.

APRIL 28

Enriching Lives

Since the strength of Francis' love made him a brother to all other creatures, it is not surprising that the charity of Christ made him more than a
brother to those who are stamped with the image of their Creator. For he
used to say that nothing is more important than the salvation of souls, and
he often offered as proof the fact that the Only-begotten of God deigned
to hang on the cross for souls. This accounts for his struggles at prayer, his
tirelessness at preaching, his excess in giving examples. He did not consider
himself a friend of Christ unless he loved the souls that Christ loved. And
this was the main reason why he reverenced doctors so much, namely,
because, as Christ's helpers, they exercised one office with him. He loved
his brothers beyond measure with an affection that rose from his innermost being, because they were of the same ["family of faith" (Galatians
6:10)] and united by participation in "the promised eternal inheritance"
(Hebrews 9:15b). (Celano, Second Life of St. Francis, 172)

LIVING AS FRANCIS DID

Prayer led Francis inward at first, but ultimately it made him a more
compassionate preacher, a more generous brother to his friars, a more
transparent example of God's love for everyone. For this reason, women
and men of every social group saw the love of God working through the
life of Francis.

GROWING WITH FRANCIS

Is your prayer enriching the lives of other people? Is it moving you to
greater compassion and transparency?

APRIL 29

Rebuild!

Francis left the town one day to meditate out-of-doors and as he was passing by the church of San Damiano which was threatening to collapse with age, he felt urged to go in and pray. There as he knelt in prayer before a painted image of the Crucified, he felt greatly comforted in spirit and his eyes were full of tears as he gazed at the cross. Then, all of a sudden, he heard a voice coming from the cross and telling him three times, "Francis, go and repair my house. You see it is all falling down." Francis was alone in the church and he was terrified at the sound of the voice, but the power of its message penetrated his heart and he went into an ecstasy. Eventually, he came back to himself and prepared to obey the command he had received. He was quite willing to devote himself entirely to repairing the ruined church of San Damiano, although the message really referred to the universal Church which Christ "won for himself at the price of his own blood" (Acts 20:28), as the Holy Spirit afterwards made him realize and he himself explained to the friars. (Bonaventure, Major Life of St. Francis, II, 1)

LIVING AS FRANCIS DID

Through prayer Francis realized how much rebuilding was needed—and whose Spirit must animate that rebuilding.

GROWING WITH FRANCIS

Is there something you are being called to rebuild? How can prayer help?

APRIL 30

Boundless Love

A cicada used to perch on a fig-tree beside St. Francis' cell at the Portiuncula and sing there, inspiring the saint to praise God for its song, because he could admire the glory of the Creator in the most insignificant creature. Then one day he called it and when it hopped on to his hand as if it had been taught by God, he told it, "Sing, my sister cicada. Sing a song of praise to God your Creator." Immediately the cicada started to chirp and never stopped until the saint told it to go back to its usual perch. There it remained for a whole week and it came and went every day, singing at his command. Finally the saint remarked to his companions, "We must give our sister cicada permission to go away. She has given us enough pleasure by her singing and inspired us to praise God for a whole week." Immediately he gave it leave, the cicada disappeared and was never seen there again, as if it did not dare transgress his command in the slightest way. (Bonaventure, Major Life of St. Francis, VIII, 9)

LIVING AS FRANCIS DID

Francis might have considered the cicada's chirping a distraction to prayer; instead, he used it, as he used all of creation, as a ladder leading him back to God, the giver of every good gift.

GROWING WITH FRANCIS

Turn a potential distraction to your prayer into a reminder of God's boundless love for you and all of creation.

Mother Mary

Throughout his life, Francis was devoted to Mary, particularly because of her role in Jesus's birth. He easily made the connection between the Jesus born of Mary in Bethlehem and the Jesus uniquely present in the Eucharist. Francis imitated Mary's practice of pondering the events of her life in the light of God's providence and followed her in using the Scriptures as a springboard for his prayer. He wrote a "Salutation of the Blessed Virgin Mary," praising her virtues and her generous cooperation with God's grace. Mary's custom of meditating on Old Testament passages encouraged Francis to write his "Office of the Passion," which is quoted several times in the reflections for the last days of this month.

That she shared in her son's poverty cast Mary in a very different light for Francis. Artists chose to portray Mary in art as a queen, garbed in costly garments and fine jewelry. Francis saw her as the Gospel writers did and, undoubtedly as early Christians did, as a faithful disciple of Jesus during his lifetime and a tremendous inspiration to his followers after his ascension into heaven. Mary needed no finery; her simplicity of lifestyle spoke of her true wealth as the Mother of God.

Within a century after Francis's death, Blessed John Duns Scotus, a Franciscan theologian in Oxford, Paris, and eventually Cologne, strongly defended the teaching of Mary's Immaculate Conception—that is, the teaching that Mary was conceived without original sin. The first Franciscans in the New World promoted that devotion as well, never being ashamed of the material poverty that Mary shared with her son, Jesus. She became a model for their style of evangelization.

Francis chose to make his headquarters at St. Mary of the Angels, a very small church that he rebuilt on the plain below Assisi. Here the friars would gather for Pentecost and feast of the Archangel Michael (September 29). As the number of friars grew and they became more geographically expanded, the friars would meet regionally in September; the Pentecost chapter (meeting) was eventually restricted to the provincial ministers.

The Friars Minor continue to hold most of their general chapters at St. Mary of the Angels—as well as international meetings of directors of postulants, novices, friars in temporary profession, vocation directors, and directors of ongoing formation. The feast of the "Pardon of Assisi" draws thousands of people each year to St. Mary of the Angels on August 2, the anniversary of that chapel's dedication. The sons of St. Francis care for the Basilica of the Annunciation in Nazareth and have staffed the Basilica of the Nativity in Bethlehem since 1333. They also staff the Latin-rite parish in Cana, where Jesus worked his first miracle—at Mary's request.

Mary's *fiat* at Nazareth was repeated throughout her faith-filled life as she said, "Yes," to God (Luke 1:38). Her humble servitude helped Francis remain a servant leader and inspires his followers today to do the same.

MAY 1

Use Freedom Wisely

We are all poor sinners and unworthy even to mention your name, and so we beg our Lord Jesus Christ, your beloved Son, in whom you are well pleased (Matthew 17:5), and the Holy Spirit, to give you thanks for everything, as it pleases you and them.

And we beg his glorious mother, blessed Mary, ever Virgin, Saints Michael, Gabriel, Raphael, and all the choirs of blessed spirits, Seraphim, Cherubim, Thrones and Dominations, Principalities and Powers; we beg all the choirs of Angels and Archangels, St. John the Baptist, John the Evangelist, Saints Peter and Paul, all the holy Patriarchs, Prophets, Innocents, Apostles, Evangelists, Disciples, Martyrs, Confessors, Virgins, blessed Elias and Enoch and the other saints, living and dead or still to come, we beg them all most humbly, for love of you, to give thanks to you, the most high, eternal God, living and true, with your Son, our beloved Lord Jesus Christ, and the Holy Spirit, the Comforter, for ever and ever. Amen. (Rule of 1221, chapter 23)

LIVING AS FRANCIS DID

Francis saw Mary as having a unique place within the communion of saints. All the saints overflow with gratitude for God's gracious gifts, for the unique revelation that God has given us in Jesus Christ. Yet grace and freewill intersect in Mary in a unique way, because God the Father chose her as the human mother for Jesus.

GROWING WITH FRANCIS

Use freedom wisely today.

MAY 2

Respect Poverty

Our Lord Jesus Christ is the glorious Word of the Father, so holy and exalted, whose coming the Father made known by St. Gabriel the Archangel to the glorious and blessed Virgin Mary, in whose womb he took on our weak human nature. He was rich beyond measure and yet he and his holy Mother chose poverty. (Letter to All the Faithful)

LIVING AS FRANCIS DID

Francis's Letter to All the Faithful is directed to adults who wanted to live a Gospel life after the example of Francis but within their chosen vocation of marriage, single life, or diocesan priesthood.

The poverty of Mary was not emphasized by most people in Francis's day; they probably thought that indicated a lack of respect for the mother of Jesus. She was commonly represented in statues and paintings as a queen or as a member of the nobility. Likewise, Christ always appeared in royal garb. The self-emptying of Jesus that St. Paul praised so highly in the Letter to the Philippians was an embarrassment to many of Francis's contemporaries.

Because of the somewhat negative understanding of poverty in Francis's time, he took a risk that in remembering the poverty of Jesus, Mary, and Joseph, he would be ignored by Catholics and emphasized by others who did not accept the Catholic Church's teachings.

GROWING WITH FRANCIS

How do you view poverty? Can you see it as Francis did? Or is it something that is unappealing to you?

MAY 3

Open to God

Listen to this, my brothers: If it is right to honor the Blessed Virgin Mary because she bore him in her most holy womb; if St. John the Baptist trembled and was afraid even to touch Christ's sacred head; if the tomb where he lay for only a short time is so venerated; how holy, and virtuous, and worthy should not a priest be; he touches Christ with his own hands, Christ, who is to die no more but enjoy eternal life and glory, upon whom the angels desire to look (1 Peter 1:12). A priest receives him into his heart and mouth and offers him to others to be received. (Letter to a General Chapter)

LIVING AS FRANCIS DID

Mary had a unique role in giving us the Jesus who was born in Bethlehem, preached the kingdom of God, was crucified on Calvary, was raised from the dead on Easter, and later ascended into heaven. Mary witnessed these events and helped the early Church remain faithful to the Good News. What St. Luke writes of her twice in chapter two of his Gospel (that she pondered in her heart all that God was doing) became the Church's path as well. Its members could wish for a clearer roadmap than they had regarding how to announce the Good News of Jesus; through prayer they discovered what God wanted them to do.

GROWING WITH FRANCIS

Be as open to God's ways as Mary was.

MAY 4

Real Presence

Put away all worry and anxiety and receive the holy Body and Blood of our Lord Jesus Christ fervently in memory of him. See to it that God is held in great reverence among your subjects; every evening, at a signal given by a herald or in some other way, praise and thanks should be given to the Lord God almighty by all the people. If you refused to see to this, you can be sure that you will be held to account for it at the day of judgment before Jesus Christ, your Lord and God. (Letter to the Rulers of the People)

LIVING AS FRANCIS DID

This letter from Francis was part of his "Eucharistic crusade" to promote greater devotion to the Eucharist after Lateran Council IV. Francis was not a professional theologian, but he knew that the Eucharist was much more than a vague reminder of the Last Supper; Christ is truly present there.

The Acts of the Apostles makes no reference to Mary as partaking of the Eucharist after the ascension of Jesus into heaven, but we cannot doubt that she did. She who gave birth to Jesus also received him back in the Eucharist.

GROWING WITH FRANCIS

If possible, attend Mass today. Thank God for the gift of the Eucharist, a continuous reminder of Christ alive in the world.

MAY 5

Supreme Good

You are holy, Lord, the only God,
　and your deeds are wonderful.
You are strong.
　You are great.
　You are the Most High,
　You are almighty.
　You, holy Father, are
　King of heaven and earth.
You are Three and One,
　Lord God, all good.
　You are Good, all Good, supreme Good,
　Lord God, living and true.
(Praises of God)

LIVING AS FRANCIS DID

Francis could utter these praises because he appreciated Mary's unique role in God's plan for the world. Jesus is our best revelation of God.

GROWING WITH FRANCIS

Spend time today reflecting on God as the supreme good in your life.

MAY 6

God Is...

You [God] are love,
You are wisdom,
You are humility,
You are endurance.
You are rest,
You are peace.
You are joy and gladness.
You are justice and moderation.
You are all our riches,
And you suffice for us.
(Praises of God)

LIVING AS FRANCIS DID

Francis could never have praised God in this fashion without gratitude for Jesus's Incarnation. Even though God is supreme and almighty, God could never be distant once Jesus came as part of the human family.

GROWING WITH FRANCIS

Choose one line from this quote that stands out for you and pray over it today.

MAY 7

God Is All

You [God] are beauty.

 You are gentleness.

 You are our protector,

 You are our guardian and defender.

 You are courage.

 You are our haven and our hope.

You are our faith,

 Our great consolation.

 You are our eternal life,

 Great and wonderful Lord,

 God almighty,

 Merciful Savior.

(Praises of God)

LIVING AS FRANCIS DID

The Albigensians, a Catholic sect that believed all matter to be evil, claimed to be better Christians than the Catholics, but the Albigensians were embarrassed by Jesus's Incarnation because it was so fleshy.

GROWING WITH FRANCIS

God is my protector, defender, my hope, and my consolation. Thank you, God, for being all things to your people.

MAY 8

Hail Mary

Hail, holy Lady,
>   Most holy Queen,
>   Mary, Mother of God,
>   Ever Virgin;
Chosen by the most holy Father in heaven,
>   Consecrated by him,
>   With his most holy beloved Son
>   And the Holy Spirit, the Comforter.
On you descended and in you still remains
>   All the fullness of grace
>   And every good.
(Salutation of the Blessed Virgin)

LIVING AS FRANCIS DID

Someone who had only this description of Mary might claim that she was not genuinely free when she told the angel Gabriel, "Let it be done to me according to your word." Francis never made that mistake. He prized her freedom and the generous way she used it.

GROWING WITH FRANCIS

Follow Mary's example, and use your freedom generously today.

MAY 9

Seek Virtues

Hail, his Palace.

Hail, his Tabernacle.

Hail, his Robe.

Hail, his Handmaid.

Hail, his Mother.

And Hail, all holy Virtues,

   Who, by the grace

   And inspiration of the Holy Spirit,

   Are poured into the hearts of the faithful

   So that, faithless no longer,

   They may be made faithful servants of God

   Through you.

(Salutation of the Blessed Virgin)

LIVING AS FRANCIS DID

We are tempted to think and speak about virtues as though they grow separately in a person's life. Mary is the clearest example that virtues grow together. Each virtue reinforces every other virtue; each leads us to see God's ways as more life-giving and respectful of our freedom than the sins that promise shortcuts but yield only dead ends.

GROWING WITH FRANCIS

Be open to God's grace in helping you to develop the virtues you need most right now.

MAY 10

Discipleship

Holy Virgin Mary, among all the women of the world there is none like you; you are the daughter and handmaid of the most high King and Father of heaven; you are the mother of our most holy Lord Jesus Christ; you are the spouse of the Holy Spirit. Pray for us, with St. Michael the archangel and all the powers of heaven and all the saints, to your most holy and beloved Son, our Lord and Master. (Office of the Passion)

LIVING AS FRANCIS DID

Mary is unique and yet a model disciple of Jesus—in fact, his first and most perfect disciple. For this reason, Francis was not going to overlook her in his Office of the Passion, a "quilt" of Scripture passages referring to Jesus and his plan of salvation. St. Augustine reminded the Christians in his Diocese of Hippo Rhegius in North Africa that Mary was both mother and disciple. Jesus could have only one mother, but he can have many disciples. Mary shows us the way.

Mary did not lead a charmed life; she knew more sorrow than most if not all of her Son's disciples. She, however, was always able to believe that God was still present amid the confusing and heartbreaking events of her life. And she was correct!

GROWING WITH FRANCIS

Ask Mary's help in becoming the most generous disciple of Jesus that you can be.

MAY 11

Interior Growth

Worn down by a long illness, as man's stubbornness deserves when it can hardly be corrected except by punishments, he [Francis] began to think of things other than he was used to thinking upon. When he had recovered somewhat and had begun to walk about the house with the support of a cane to speed the recovery of his health, he went outside one day and began to look about at the surrounding landscape with great interest. But the beauty of the fields, the pleasantness of the vineyards, and whatever else was beautiful to look upon, could stir in him no delight. He wondered therefore at the sudden change that had come over him, and those who took delight in such things he considered very foolish. (Celano, First Life of St. Francis, 3)

LIVING AS FRANCIS DID

As a young man, Francis lived from one form of entertainment to another, probably soon bored by most of it. A life based exclusively on self-interest ultimately proves unsatisfying and, in fact, guarantees boredom.

The contrast with Mary, the mother of Jesus, is great. Boredom is a luxury that materially poor people can hardly afford. In pondering the events of her life and trying to connect them with God's providence, Mary developed a very rich interior life, one that was constantly nourished by prayer.

GROWING WITH FRANCIS

Are your horizons expanding or shrinking? Allow your inner life to grow.

MAY 12

Follow Mary

Meanwhile the holy man of God, having put on a new kind of habit and having repaired the aforesaid church, went to another place near the city of Assisi, where he began to rebuild a certain dilapidated and well-nigh destroyed church, and he did not leave off from his good purpose until he had brought it to completion. Then he went to another place, which is called the Portiuncula, where there stood a church of the Blessed Virgin Mother of God that had been built in ancient times, but was now deserted and cared for by no one. When the holy man of God saw how it was thus in ruins, he was moved to pity, because he burned with devotion toward the mother of all good; and he began to live there in great zeal. It was the third year of his conversion when he began to repair this church. (Celano, First Life of St. Francis, 21)

LIVING AS FRANCIS DID

Zeal to build a church to honor Mary does not guarantee that later generations will have the same zeal to keep it in good shape. Francis decided to rebuild the Portiuncula (Little Portion) of Mary, a church that was perhaps fifteen by forty feet. It is also known as Santa Maria degli Angeli (St. Mary of the Angels).

GROWING WITH FRANCIS

Let Mary's prayerful example lead you today.

MAY 13

My Treasure

He [Bernard of Quintavalle] had often given the blessed father [Francis] hospitality, and, having had experience of his life and conduct and having been refreshed by the fragrance of his holiness, he conceived a fear and brought forth the spirit of salvation [Job 51:35; Isaiah 59:4]. He noticed that Francis would pray all night, sleeping but rarely, praising God and the glorious Virgin Mother of God, and he wondered and said: "In all truth, this man is from God." (Celano, First Life of St. Francis, 24)

LIVING AS FRANCIS DID

Bernard of Quintavalle was a nobleman; his embrace of the Gospel life that Francis followed may have attracted more attention in Assisi than Francis's decision to follow such a life. The genuineness of Francis's praises of God and the Virgin Mary (when Francis thought no one was listening) convinced Bernard that Francis practiced what he preached. Like Francis and the man in the Gospels, Bernard found a great treasure and would never part with it for money or prestige.

Mary, the disciple, inspired Francis, the disciple, just as Francis later came to inspire Bernard. Neither Mary nor Francis had a roadmap of life, but each had an unshakable conviction that God is still in charge of this world.

GROWING WITH FRANCIS

What do you treasure most in your life? If someone observed you for an entire month, would they say your decisions reflect what your treasure is? If not, what can you change?

Be Generous

Filled with the spirit of God [1 Corinthians 7:40], he was ready to suffer every distress of mind and to bear every bodily torment, if only his wish might be granted, that the will of the Father in heaven might be mercifully fulfilled in him. One day therefore he went before the holy altar which was erected in the hermitage where he was staying, and taking the book in which the holy Gospel was written, he reverently place it upon the altar. Then he prostrated himself in prayer to God, not less in heart than in body, and he asked in humble prayer that the good God, the Father of mercies and the God of all comfort [2 Corinthians 1:3] would deign to make known his will to him, and that he might be able to carry out what he had earlier begun simply and devoutly. (Celano, First Life of St. Francis, 92)

Living as Francis Did

What Celano describes here is almost certainly what Mary did much less dramatically day in and day out. Francis did not have to quote Mary's *fiat* (let it be done to be according to your word) daily for it to become his life's guiding star.

Focusing exclusively on *my* plans, *my* priorities, *my* list of who counts and who does not—sooner or later such a life becomes deadly. No one, for example, can develop deep and lasting friendships or a strong family life from such a starting point.

Growing with Francis

Do something generous for someone else today.

MAY 15

Infinite Love

For though he knew that the kingdom of heaven was set up in all the habitations of the land [Isaiah 38:15] and believed that the grace of God was given to the elect of God [Luke 18:13] in every place he had however experienced that the place of the church of St. Mary of the Portiuncula was endowed with more fruitful graces and visited by heavenly spirits [Ephesians 6:10; Philippians 3:1]. Therefore he often said to his brothers: "See to it, my sons, that you never abandon this place. If you are driven out from one side, go back in at the other. For this place is truly holy and is the dwelling place of God. Here, when we were but a few, the Most High gave us increase; here he enlightened the hearts of his poor ones by the light of his wisdom; here he set our wills afire with the fire of his love. Here he who prays with a devout heart will obtain what he prays for and he who offends will be punished more severely. Wherefore, my sons, consider this dwelling place of God to be worthy of all honor." (Celano, First Life of St. Francis, 106)

LIVING AS FRANCIS DID

Every year people come to St. Mary of the Angels on August 2 to celebrate the Pardon of Assisi, a reminder of God's infinite love for us.

GROWING WITH FRANCIS

Praise God's infinite love today.

A Holy Place

The servant of God Francis, a person small in stature, humble in mind, a minor by profession, while yet in the world chose out of the world for himself and his followers a little portion, in as much as he could not serve Christ without having something of the world. For it was not without the foreknowledge of a divine disposition that from ancient times that place was called the Portiuncula which was to fall to the lot of those who wished to have nothing whatsoever of the world. For there had also been built in that place a church of the virgin mother who merited by her singular humility to be, after her son, the head of all the saints. In this church the Order of Friars Minor had its beginning; there, as on a firm foundation, when their number had grown, the noble fabric of the order arose. The holy man loved this place above all others; this place he commanded his brothers to venerate with a special reverence; this place he willed to be preserved as a model of humility and highest poverty for their order. (Celano, Second Life of St. Francis, 18)

Living as Francis Did

Francis died not twenty-five yards from this chapel, and another small chapel was soon erected to mark the spot. The Basilica of Our Lady of the Angels encloses them both—and much more.

Growing with Francis

In what place have you strongly felt God's love?

MAY 17

God's Movement

This was as it should be. For, according to what the old inhabitants used to say, the place was also called St. Mary of the Angels. The happy father used to say that it had been revealed to him by God that the Blessed Mother loved this church, among all the other churches built in her honor throughout the world, with a special love; for this reason the holy man loved it above all others. (Celano, Second Life of St. Francis, 19)

LIVING AS FRANCIS DID

Until Francis's brotherhood became too large and geographically extended, all the friars returned to the Portiuncula each year at Pentecost for a few days of prayer, reflection, penance, sharing what God had done through them and accepting an "obedience" to return to their previous place of prayer and ministry or to set off on a new apostolic mission. The first mission to Germany began at the Portiuncula but did not succeed; the second one did.

The patronage of Mary helped to place these discussions and decisions in their proper context: What does God want of our brotherhood at this moment in time? What risks is God calling us to take?

To this day, the Friars Minor usually hold their meetings at the Portiuncula, pondering what God is asking of them now and selecting leaders to lead their common journey of faith for the next few years.

GROWING WITH FRANCIS

How do you experience God's movement in your life? Where is God leading you?

MAY 18

Visiting the Sick

Another day when Francis was preaching, a certain poor and infirm man came to the place. Pitying his double affliction, namely, his want and his feebleness, Francis began to speak with his companion about poverty. And when, suffering with the sufferer, Francis' heart had become deeply afflicted, the companion of the saint said to him: "Brother, it is true that this man is poor, but it may also be true that nowhere in the whole province is there a man who is richer in his desires." Immediately the saint rebuked him and said to him when he admitted his guilt: "Hurry quickly and take off your tunic and cast yourself down at the feet of this poor man and acknowledge your guilt. And do not only ask for forgiveness, but ask him also to pray for you." He obeyed and went to make satisfaction and he came back. The saint said to him: "When you see a poor man, Brother, an image is placed before you of the Lord and his poor mother. So too in the sick consider the infirmities which the Lord took upon himself for us." (Celano, Second Life of St. Francis, 85)

LIVING AS FRANCIS DID

Francis could not remember the poor Christ without remembering the poor Virgin Mary as well. Both of them helped Francis to be compassionate when it might have been easy to be selfish or to feel overwhelmed.

GROWING WITH FRANCIS

Visit a sick friend or neighbor today. If a visit isn't possible, call, email, or send a card.

MAY 19

The Image of God

Toward the Mother of Jesus he was filled with an inexpressible love, because it was she who made the Lord of Majesty our brother. He sang special Praises to her, poured out prayers to her, offered her his affections, so many and so great that the tongue of man cannot recount them. But what delights us most, he made her the advocate of the order and placed under her wings the sons he was about to leave that she might cherish them and protect them to the end.—Hail, advocate of the poor! Fulfill toward us your office of protectress until the time set by the Father [Galatians 4:2]. (Celano, Second Life of St. Francis, 198)

LIVING AS FRANCIS DID

Medieval artists sometimes portrayed Mary as wearing a large cloak opened to reveal alongside her people of every social class. No single group has a monopoly on Mary.

The purity of Mary's compassion helped Francis and his brothers find their own reserves of compassion that they never realized they had. Mary would help the friars to avoid degenerating into cliques trying to seek power over one another. She would help them focus on God's agenda—with all the sacrifices that it might require. Their sacrifices could never exceed hers. Is it a coincidence that Mary typically appears to people at the margins of their society?

GROWING WITH FRANCIS

Pray that Mary will help you recognize the image of God in each person you meet.

Rich and Poor

He would recall, not without tears, what great want surrounded the poor Virgin on that day [of Christ's birth] [Luke 2:7]. Once when he was sitting at dinner, a certain brother talked about the poverty of the Blessed Virgin and recalled the want of Christ, her Son. Francis immediately arose from the table and, with great sighs and many tears, ate the rest of the meal on the bare ground. For this reason he used to say that this virtue that shone forth so eminently in the King and Queen was a royal virtue. And when the brothers were discussing at a gathering which virtue does more to make one a close friend of Christ, Francis, as though making known to them a secret of his heart, answered: "Know, my sons, that poverty is the special way to salvation; its fruit is manifold, but it is really well known only to a few." (Celano, Second Life of St. Francis, 200)

LIVING AS FRANCIS DID

Poverty for the sake of the kingdom of God has always been a hard sell. As people acquire more, they are tempted to think that their success reflects God's special blessing. On the other hand, people who are poor can easily be judged as lazy. Life is not that simple. Wealth does not automatically signify virtue, and poverty does not indicate that a person is cursed by God. Think of Jesus and Mary, who were both poor and virtuous.

GROWING WITH FRANCIS

What is your greatest richness? Your most virtuous poverty?

MAY 21

Devotion and Respect

When he had finished there [rebuilding San Damiano], he came to a place called the Portiuncula where there was an old church dedicated to the Virgin Mother of God which was now abandoned with no one to look after it. Francis had great devotion to the Queen of the world and when he saw that the church was deserted, he began to live there constantly in order to repair it. He heard that the angels often visited it, so that it used to be called St. Mary of the Angels, and he decided to stay there permanently out of reverence for the angels and love for the Mother of Christ. He loved this spot more than any other in the world. It was here that he began his religious life in a very small way; it was here that he made such extraordinary progress, and it was here that he came to a happy end. (Bonaventure, Major Life of St. Francis, II, 8)

LIVING AS FRANCIS DID

St. Mary of the Angels is now a large basilica enclosing the original chapel of that title and the small chapel built over the nearby spot where St. Francis died. The victory over self that Francis won early in his conversion process when he embraced a leper continued at St. Mary of the Angels as Francis dealt with the virtues and sinfulness of his friars.

GROWING WITH FRANCIS

Speak respectfully to everyone you meet today.

Taught by the Spirit

After this, at God's prompting, Francis brought his little flock of twelve friars to St. Mary of the Portiuncula. It was there that the Order of Friars Minor had been founded by the merits of the Mother of God, and it was there, too, that it would grow to maturity by her intercession.

From the Portiuncula, Francis set out as a herald of the Gospel to preach the kingdom of God in the towns and villages in the vicinity, "not in such words as human wisdom teaches, but in words taught him by the Spirit" (1 Corinthians 2:13). To those who saw him he seemed like a man from another world as, with his gaze fixed on heaven where his heart always dwelt, he tried to lift their thoughts on high. As a result of his efforts the supernatural vineyard of Christ began to put forth shoots which gave out a pleasing fragrance before God and produced fruit in abundance, lush and rich. (Bonaventure, Major Life of St. Francis, IV:5)

LIVING AS FRANCIS DID

Opening one's heart wider and wider to God's grace is not accomplished in the blink of an eye. The praying that Francis did at St. Mary of the Angels and elsewhere helped him to be a more faithful and generous disciple of Jesus. In this, Francis was following the example of Mary.

GROWING WITH FRANCIS

What is your next step in growth as a disciple?

MAY 23

Carrying Baggage

The memory of the poverty felt by Christ and his Mother often reduced him to tears and he called poverty the Queen of the Virtues because it was so evident in the life of the King of Kings and of the Queen, his Mother. When the friars asked him privately what virtue made one dearest to Christ, he replied as if revealing his closest secret, "Believe me, my brothers, poverty is the special way of salvation. It is the source of humility and the root of all perfection and its fruit is manifold, though unseen. This is the treasure hidden in the field in the Gospel to buy which we must sell all—and anything that cannot be sold should be abandoned for love of it." (Bonaventure, Major Life of St. Francis, VII:1)

LIVING AS FRANCIS DID

Poverty can be grinding and dehumanizing, turning people into objects to be manipulated for someone else's advantage. Francis opposed that type of poverty but readily embraced a poverty for the sake of the kingdom of God, one that never interfered with the preaching of Jesus's Good News.

Jesus told the apostles to travel light so that they would not lose focus on their mission. Francis wanted the same from his brothers. *Impedimenta* is the Latin word for baggage, what prevents the feet from moving. All baggage, whether physical or emotional, can interfere with the freedom that Jesus's disciples need.

GROWING WITH FRANCIS

Are you carrying emotional baggage that interferes with your life as a disciple of Jesus?

MAY 24

Love Everlasting

He embraced the Mother of our Lord Jesus with indescribable love because, as he said, it was she who made the Lord of majesty our brother, and through her we found mercy. After Christ, he put all his trust in her and took her as his patroness for himself and his friars. In her honor he fasted every year from the feast of Saints Peter and Paul until the Assumption. He had an unshakeable love for the Angels who burn with a marvellous fire, so that they are taken out of themselves to God and long to inflame the souls of the elect. Each year he fasted and prayed in their honor for forty days from the feast of the Assumption. In his ardent zeal for the salvation of souls he was particularly devoted to St. Michael the Archangel because it is his task to bring souls before God. (Bonaventure, Major Life of St. Francis, IX, 3)

LIVING AS FRANCIS DID

Francis observed a type of Lent between the feast of Sts. Peter and Paul (June 29) and the feast of Mary's assumption (August 15). These were times of extra prayer and fasting, not used as leverage for obtaining something from God but practiced as a sign of gratitude. Francis easily linked Mary to angels as special signs of God's loving mercy; he had a special devotion to St. Michael the Archangel, as well.

GROWING WITH FRANCIS

Our love and mercy can feel exhausted or spent at times, but God's love and mercy never run out.

MAY 25

My All

[At the canonization of St. Francis,] the day was bright and colored with more splendid rays than usual. There were green olive branches there and fresh branches of other trees. Brightly glittering festive attire adorned all the people, and the blessing of peace filled the minds of those who had come there with joy. Then the happy Pope Gregory [IX] descended from his lofty throne, and going by way of the lower steps, he entered the sanctuary to offer the vows and voluntary oblations (Numbers 29:39); he kissed with his happy lips the tomb that contained the body that was sacred and consecrated to God. He offered and multiplied his prayer and celebrated the sacred mysteries [the Mass]. A ring of his brethren (Sirach 50:13) stood about him, praising, adoring, and blessing Almighty God who had done great things in all the earth (Sirach 50:24). (Celano, First Life of St. Francis, 126)

LIVING AS FRANCIS DID

Celano makes no explicit reference here to Mary, but the rite of canonization cites Mary first among the saints. Francis would not have been officially recognized as a saint if he had not followed Mary's example of generous discipleship. She may never have prayed "My God and My All" (a favorite prayer of Francis), but she lived that prayer all her life.

GROWING WITH FRANCIS

What part of your "all" are you not yet ready to surrender to God's love and mercy? Why?

MAY 26

Live Humbly

A friar once accompanied Francis to pray in an abandoned church. The friar had a vision of heavenly thrones and one that was particularly beautiful. Then he heard a voice telling him, "That throne belonged to one of the fallen angels. Now it is being kept for the humble Francis." When the friar came back to himself, he followed the saint out of the church as usual. As they continued on their journey conversing together about God, the friar remembered his vision and discreetly asked the saint what he thought of himself. "It seems to me," Francis replied, "that I must be the greatest of all sinners. When his companion reproached him, declaring that could not possibly say that with a good conscience, or really believe it, Francis continued, "If Christ had shown such mercy toward the greatest criminal in the world, I am convinced that he would be much more grateful to God than I am." At the sight of such extraordinary humility, his companion was convinced of the truth of his vision. (Adapted from Bonaventure, Major Life of St. Francis, VI, 6)

LIVING AS FRANCIS DID

Genuine humility is knowing who you are before God and in relation to other people. It never requires that people lie to themselves or to others. Mary beautifully expressed this quality, and lived it out in faithfulness to God.

GROWING WITH FRANCIS

Live humbly before God and in relation to others today.

MAY 27

No Entitlement

Another time [Francis] told his companion, "I should not regard myself as a Friar Minor unless I were prepared to behave like this. Suppose I were a superior and I went to a chapter where I addressed the friars and gave them some advice. But then, when I have finished, they all say, 'You are not the right superior for us. You have no education and you are not a good speaker. Besides, you are illiterate and inexperienced.' Then I am thrown out ignominiously and despised by them all. I tell you, if I were not prepared to take all that without being disturbed or without losing my peace of mind, with a firm determination to use it all for my own sanctification, I should not be a Friar Minor." And he continued, "The office of superior may lead to a fall, and praise is a dangerous precipice, but the lowly position of a subject contains great benefit for the soul. Why are we more anxious to run risks than to gain merit? Time has been given us only so that we can gain merit." (Bonaventure, Major Life of St. Francis, VI:5)

Living as Francis Did

Mary's *fiat* ("Let it be done as you have said") in Nazareth is really the basis for what Francis describes here. An office is not a possession to which someone is entitled; it is a service that eventually someone else may be better suited to render.

Growing with Francis

Serve generously and without a sense of entitlement.

MAY 28

Immersed in Scripture

Come and ransom my life; as an answer for my enemies, redeem me (Psalm 68:19).

You have been my guide since I was first formed, my security at my mother's breast. To you I was committed at birth, from my mother's womb you are my God. Be not far from me (Psalm 21:10–12).

You know my reproach, my shame and my ignominy; before you are all my foes.

Insult has broken my heart, and I am weak; I looked for sympathy, but there was none; for comforters, and I found none (Psalm 68:20–21).

O God, the haughty have risen up against me, and the company of fierce men seeks my life, nor do they set you before their eyes (Psalm 85:14).

You are my most holy Father, my King and my God.

Make haste to help me, O Lord my salvation! (Psalm 37:23).

(Office of the Passion)

LIVING AS FRANCIS DID

Francis knew the Psalms by heart; so did Mary. How could all these things recounted in the Psalms be true? What connection did they have to Mary's life? To Francis's life? That was the work of their prayer.

GROWING WITH FRANCIS

Take time today to reflect on the verses above, choosing one that speaks to you in a particular way. Hold that verse in your heart for the day.

MAY 29

Jagged Edges

Shout joyfully to God, all you on earth, sing praise to the glory of his name; proclaim his glorious praise.

Say to God, "How tremendous are your deeds! For your great strength your enemies fawn upon you.

Let all the earth worship and sing praise to you, sing praise to your name!" (Psalm 65:1–4).

Bless our God, you people, loudly sound his praise (Psalm 65:8).

In him shall all the tribes of the earth be blessed; all the nations shall proclaim his happiness.

Blessed be the Lord, the God of Israel, who alone does wondrous deeds.

And blessed forever be his glorious name; may the whole earth be filled with his glory. Amen. Amen (Psalm 71:17–19).

(Office of the Passion, Terce for Sunday in Ordinary Time)

LIVING AS FRANCIS DID

The Psalms reflect the entire gamut of human emotion in relation to God and refute the common assumption that prayer must always start from a mood of serenity and contentment. Prayer can have jagged edges! Many Psalms begin in anger and frustration but end by confessing God's overall control of the world—even though it is sometimes not exercised according to our standards. Honest prayer is not always pretty, but then, it is a work in progress.

GROWING WITH FRANCIS

Make sure your prayer today is honest.

MAY 30

Pray Scripture

I will give thanks to you, O Lord, most holy Father, King of heaven and earth; that you have comforted me (Psalm 85:12,17).

You are God my savior (Psalm 24:5); I will act with confidence and have no fear (Isaiah 12:2).

My strength and my courage is the Lord, and he has been my savior (Psalm 117:14).

Your right hand, O Lord, has mightily shown its power, your right hand, O Lord, has struck the enemy; in your plenteous glory you have put down my adversaries (Exodus 15:6–7).

See, you lowly ones, and be glad; you who seek God, may your hearts be merry! (Psalm 68:33).

Let the heavens and the earth praise him, the seas and whatever moves in them! (68:35)

For God will save Sion and rebuild the cities of Judah. They shall dwell in the land and own it, and the descendants of his servants shall inherit it, and those who love his name shall inhabit it (Psalm 68:36–37).

(Office of the Passion)

Living as Francis Did

Certainly Mary used some of these same biblical passages in her spoken and unspoken prayers. They echo her deep belief that God's goodness is everlasting.

Growing with Francis

Look up one of these Psalms or biblical passages and pray it in context.

MAY 31

Glory and Praise

Sing joyfully to God our strength (Psalm 80:2); cry jubilee to the Lord, the true and living God, with a voice of exultation.

For the Lord, the Most High, the awesome, is the great King over all the earth (Psalm 46:3).

Our most holy Father of heaven, our King, before time was, sent his beloved Son from on high and he was born of the blessed and holy Virgin Mary.

He shall say of me, "You are my father," and I will make him the first-born, highest of the kings of the earth (Psalm 88:27–28).

By day the Lord bestows his grace, and at night I have his song (Psalm 41:9).

This is the day the Lord has made; let us be glad and rejoice in it (Psalm 117:24).

Glory to God in the highest, and on earth peace among men of good will (Luke 2:14).

Let the heavens be glad and the earth rejoice, let the sea and what fills it resound; let the plains be joyful and all that is in them (Psalm 95:11–12).

Sing to the Lord a new song; sing to the Lord, all you lands (Psalm 95:1).

For great is the Lord and highly to be praised; awesome is he, beyond all gods (Psalm 95:4).

Give to the Lord, you families of nations, given to the Lord glory and praise; give to the Lord the glory due his name! (Psalm 95:7–8).

(Office of the Passion)

Eucharist

When Francis was twenty-three, Lateran Council IV met for a month in Rome. Devotion to the Eucharist was one of its major concerns, leading to a decree that Catholics must receive Holy Communion at least once a year during the Easter season. This was considered an important step forward because Catholics who received the Eucharist at Christmas, Easter, and several other major feasts were then considered "frequent communicants." The Council also officially adopted the term *transubstantiation* to describe how the bread and wine are transformed into the Body and Blood of Jesus.

Thomas of Celano wrote that Francis had three great devotions: the birth of Jesus in Bethlehem, the Lord's passion and death and resurrection, and then the Eucharist. Francis wrote several letters urging greater respect for the Blessed Sacrament as shown through the cleanliness of churches, plus altar linens, vessels, and vestments that are worthy of their special use.

The Albigensian Christians were popular at that time in southern France and in much of Italy. Because they felt that all things material were evil, they were scandalized by all the sacraments because Catholics used material goods (water, wine, oil, and so on) in a very positive way. They were also sympathetic to the much older Donatist heresy that taught a sacrament's effectiveness depended on the holiness of its minister. Ultimately, that cast doubt on the validity of every sacramental celebration because a good priest could have been ordained by a bishop who was not in the state of grace when that priest was ordained.

Lateran IV directed that bishops pay more attention to the training of priests and that the word of God be preached regularly to the people. Both decisions eventually influenced the growth of Francis's brotherhood, the Order of Friars Minor.

Regularly joining in the celebration of the Mass helped Francis to know and pray over the Gospels. The Eucharist led Francis to give his friars many of the Admonitions cited in this chapter and to write his Letter to a General Chapter that is also quoted several times. Lay men and women who became members of the Secular Franciscan Order were encouraged to receive Holy Communion more often than was common for many of their contemporaries. Francis encouraged them to confess their sins often.

Francis directed that when his friars entered a church or even saw one from afar they should pray together: "We adore you, most holy Lord Jesus Christ, here and in all your churches throughout the world because by your holy cross you have redeemed the world." The church building was made holy by the Eucharist and the other sacraments that were celebrated there.

In heaven there will be no need for altars or the Eucharist because God will be everything for everyone there. Here and now, the Eucharist is a pledge of heavenly glory.

JUNE 1

Christ Present

God inspired me, too, and still inspires me with such great faith in priests who live according to the laws of the holy Church of Rome, because of their dignity, that if they persecuted me, I should still be ready to turn to them for aid. And if I were as wise as Solomon and met the poorest priests of the world, I would still refuse to preach against their will in the parishes in which they live. I am determined to reverence, love and honor priests and all others as my superiors. I refuse to consider their sins, because I can see the Son of God in them and they are better than I. I do this because in this world I cannot see the most high Son of God with my own eyes, except for his most holy Body and Blood which they receive and they alone administer to others. (Testament)

LIVING AS FRANCIS DID

Francis participated in the Mass whenever he could and received the Eucharist more often than did many of his contemporaries. Francis was an observant man; he realized perfectly well that priests are also sinners trying to open themselves to God's grace, trying to accept God's values. The Eucharist makes Christ present in a unique way for us as it did for Francis.

GROWING WITH FRANCIS

Read today's Scripture readings—or this coming Sunday's. Many parish bulletins carry the references, or go to www.catholicmatters.com.

JUNE 2

Spirit and Life

Above everything else, I want this most holy Sacrament [the Eucharist] to be honored and venerated and reserved in places which are richly orna-mented. Whenever I find his most holy name or writings containing his words in an improper place, I make a point of picking them up, and I ask that they be picked up and put aside in a suitable place. We should honor and venerate theologians, too, and the ministers of God's word, because it is they who give us spirit and life. (Testament)

LIVING AS FRANCIS DID

Francis had a very deep sense of Jesus's Incarnation. That sense caused him to be especially concerned that everything used for the Eucharist should be clean and suitable for praising God. Francis also venerated the words of Scripture and the humble theologians who opened up the treasures of God's word. There was a famine of good preaching in Francis's day, and the Eucharist strengthened Francis to respond to that hunger.

It is hard to imagine that the adult Francis ever complained that the Mass was boring or that he got nothing out of it. Every Mass drew him closer to Christ and to Christ's boundless love.

GROWING WITH FRANCIS

The next time you participate at Mass, ask God to help you appreciate its benefits and deal with distractions.

JUNE 3

Be Transformed

Sacred Scripture tells us that the Father dwells in light inaccessible (1 Timothy 6:16) and that God is spirit (John 4:24), and St. John adds, "No one has ever seen God" (John 1:18). Because God is a spirit he can be seen only in spirit; "It is the spirit that gives life; the flesh profits nothing" (John 6:63). But God the Son is equal to the Father and so he too can be seen only in the same way as the Father and the Holy Spirit.... In the same way now, all those are damned who see the sacrament of the Body of Christ which is consecrated on the altar in the form of bread and wine by the words of our Lord in the hands of the priest, and do not see or believe in spirit and in God that this is really the most holy Body and Blood of our Lord Jesus Christ. It is the Most High himself who has told us, "This is my body...and blood of the new covenant" (Mark 14:22–24), and, "Those who eat my flesh and drink my blood abide in me and I in them" (John 6:55). (Admonition I)

LIVING AS FRANCIS DID

Allow yourself to be transformed as much as the bread and wine used at Mass. Write down any changes you experience in yourself and give God thanks.

GROWING WITH FRANCIS

Take extra time before and after receiving the Eucharist to contemplate its deepest meaning in your life.

JUNE 4

Indwelling Spirit

And so it is really the Spirit of God who dwells in his faithful who receive the most holy Body and Blood of our Lord. Anyone who does not have this Spirit and presumes to receive him eats and drinks judgment to himself (1 Corinthians 11:29).… Every day he humbles himself just as he did when he came from his heavenly throne (Wisdom 18:15) into the Virgin's womb; every day he comes to us and lets us see him in abjection, when he descends from the bosom of the Father into the hands of the priest at the altar. He shows himself to us in this sacred bread just as he once appeared to his apostles in real flesh. With their own eyes they saw only his flesh, but they believed that he was God, because they contemplated him with the eyes of the spirit. We, too, with our own eyes, see only bread and wine, but we must see further and firmly believe that this is his most holy Body and Blood, living and true. In this way our Lord remains continually with his followers, as he promised, "Remember, I am with you always, to the end of the age" (Matthew 28:20). (Admonition I)

LIVING AS FRANCIS DID

At Emmaus, two disciples recognized Jesus in "the breaking of the bread," the Eucharist (Luke 19:13–35). Do we?

GROWING WITH FRANCIS

Where and when do you experience Jesus most deeply? Talk to him about that.

JUNE 5

Live Right Side Up

Try to realize the dignity God has conferred on you. He created and formed your body in the image of his beloved Son, and your soul in his own likeness (Genesis 1:26). And yet every creature under heaven serves and acknowledges and obeys its Creator in its own way better than you do. Even the devils were not solely responsible for crucifying him; it was you who crucified him with them and you continue to crucify him by taking pleasure in your vices and sins. (Admonition V)

LIVING AS FRANCIS DID

The Eucharist is a constant reminder of the dignity that is ours through God's gift. God who sent Jesus as a permanent and unmistakable sign of divine love left the Eucharist to benefit people like ourselves who have not seen Jesus with their own eyes but who have seen him present among his followers, especially when they gather to celebrate the Eucharist joyfully yet humbly.

In some ways, we live in a world that is upside down: sin and vice present themselves as more realistic and trustworthy than God's values. The Eucharist helps to turn our world right side up for us and those whom God loves and for whom Jesus died and rose. It can set our hearts afire as Jesus did when he spoke to two disciples on the road to Emmaus and celebrated the Eucharist with them.

GROWING WITH FRANCIS

How do you revere the Eucharist?

JUNE 6

Source of All Good

St. Paul tells us, No one can say Jesus is Lord, except in the Holy Spirit (1 Corinthians 12:3) and, There is none who does good, no, not even one (Romans 3:12). And so when a man envies his brother the good God says or does through him, it is like committing a sin of blasphemy, because he is really envying God, who is the only source of every good. (Admonition VIII)

LIVING AS FRANCIS DID

The Eucharist can keep us honest, or we can use it as a way to reinforce a self-righteous blindness. Week after week, the Eucharist reminds us that God is the source of every good. Thus, Francis saw jealousy as a form of blasphemy because it refuses to admit the connection between God and the gift we think someone else does not deserve. If we could snatch that gift from the other person, would it produce equally good effects in us?

If some church had a sign giving that parish's name and the words "Where only the best Christians pray," would you feel at home joining in the Eucharist in that setting? Probably not; you would rightly sense that people were using the Mass to reinforce their illusions about themselves and about others not being worthy to join them.

GROWING WITH FRANCIS

At Mass, we hear the word of God and try to open ourselves more deeply and widely to it. How does your church welcome Christians of other denominations?

JUNE 7

True Love

Our Lord says in the Gospel, Love your enemies (Matthew 5:44). A man really loves his enemy when he is not offended by the injury done to himself, but for love of God feels burning sorrow for the sin his enemy has brought on his own soul, and proves his love in a practical way. (Admonition IX)

LIVING AS FRANCIS DID

We truly love a person when we want for him or her everything that God desires. We don't have to be at Mass to feel such love, but we cannot participate regularly in the Eucharist without experiencing a positive effect during hours outside of Mass.

The Eucharist helped Francis draw his brothers away from their mistaken securities and into the bracing adventure of God's love. Apart from the Eucharist, people can set themselves up as judge, jury, and executioner (figuratively!) of other people's sins or failings. The Eucharist should lead us, as it led Francis, into greater compassion, to acts of mercy and compassion.

GROWING WITH FRANCIS

Borrow a missalette from your parish this week if necessary. Pray with one of the Eucharistic Prayers of the Mass, allowing it to stretch you and enrich you. Notice the praise for God's goodness and the acknowledgement that *we* need to be transformed as well as the bread and wine. Are there resentments of family members or other people that need to be set aside to allow us to make that Eucharistic Prayer an expression of our own prayer?

JUNE 8

The Blame Game

Many people blame the devil or their neighbor when they fall into sin or are offended. But that is not right. Everyone has his own enemy in his power and this enemy is his lower nature which leads him into sin. Blessed the religious who keeps this enemy a prisoner under his control and protects himself against it. As long as he does this no other enemy, visible or invisible, can harm him. (Admonition X)

LIVING AS FRANCIS DID

At first reading, it might seem that the passage above has no direct connection to the Eucharist. In fact, everything that Francis says in his Admonitions comes from two sources: his experience of living with his brothers and his experience of what God was trying to communicate to him during Mass. Based on that, private prayer is reinforced.

Being offended by the sins of others, some people pride themselves on not being the hypocrites that they say other Christians are. Those most intent on avoiding hypocrisy often see it everywhere except in themselves. The sins of others can harm us, but the sins we refuse to see in ourselves will almost always cause the greater damage.

GROWING WITH FRANCIS

Allow your participation in the Eucharist—or your private prayer before the Blessed Sacrament—to lead you to see more accurately the deepest truths about God, yourself, and others. Once you do that, it will be difficult to sustain anger as a characteristic habit.

JUNE 9

Radical Transparency

We can be sure that a man is a true religious and has the spirit of God if his lower nature does not give way to pride when God accomplishes some good through him, and if he seems all the more worthless and inferior to others in his own eyes. Our lower nature is opposed to every good. (Admonition XII)

LIVING AS FRANCIS DID

Again, this quote might not seem to have a direct connection to the Eucharist. In fact, this wisdom did not come to Francis out of the blue. It came through prayerful reflection on the gifts and the blind spots present among his brothers.

Laywomen and laymen who were drawn to Francis were attracted by the radical transparency of his life. The Eucharist nurtured that transparency and moved Francis to deal with any part of his life that was still resisting God's grace, God's values.

In Francis's day, there was one friar whom many other friars considered a holy man. When Francis told that friar to confess his sins, the friar refused, indicating that he did not wish to break his silence. What seemed a virtue turned out to be an elaborate mask for sinful pride. That friar soon left the brotherhood.

GROWING WITH FRANCIS

Be willing to admit your sins and accept God's grace to live as God wants you to live. View others through the lens of the Eucharist and see what a difference that makes in your acceptance of others.

JUNE 10

Holy Searching

Blessed are the clean of heart, for they shall see God (Matthew 5:8). A man is really clean of heart when he has no time for the things of this world but is always searching for the things of heaven, never failing to keep God before his eyes and always adoring him with a pure heart and soul. (Admonition XVI)

LIVING AS FRANCIS DID

Francis did not simply dream about what being "clean of heart" might mean. In passages from the Old Testament and the New Testament, Francis received both positive and negative examples about people who were clean of heart. Hearing these passages at Mass with other Christians contributed to Francis's ongoing conversion.

Every Eucharist is a foretaste of heaven, a glimpse of a banquet where God will be everything in all those who are present. Gone will be the jealousies that this person received on earth more than he or she deserved. Gone will be any temptation to one-up other guests at the same banquet.

GROWING WITH FRANCIS

Over time, the Eucharist redefines what "normal" means to us. God's ways can initially seem awkward and not completely trustworthy. Sharing in the Eucharist regularly should lessen the awkwardness and put any doubts in proper perspective.

Am I allowing the Eucharist to redefine my sense of "normal"? Do I confine its effects to the time that I spend participating at Mass, perhaps anxious to get back to a more real world outside?

JUNE 11

Holy Listening

Blessed that religious who finds all his joy and happiness in the words and deeds of our Lord and uses them to make people love God gladly. Woe to the religious who amuses himself with silly gossip, trying to make people laugh. (Admonition XXI)

LIVING AS FRANCIS DID

What Francis praises here is the natural result of allowing the Eucharist to have its full effects in a person's life. What Francis criticizes is possible only if someone has set up very strict boundaries within which the Eucharist can have an effect but outside of which it is not really welcome. Francis did not become more honest, compassionate, and transparent *in spite of* his devotion to the Eucharist but *because of* that devotion.

He did not set himself on a path of self-improvement or self-fulfillment apart from God. No, Francis's life became more and more rooted in God in large part through his private prayer before the Blessed Sacrament and through participation in public Masses.

GROWING WITH FRANCIS

We do not need to encourage or coach the Eucharist to have its beneficial effect in our lives. No, we simply need to follow its lead, allowing any self-deception to be recognized for what it is. In a sense, the Eucharist is a huge gift exchange where we surrender our paltry treasures for the much bigger ones that God wants to give us.

The Eucharist leads us to holy listening for direction in our lives.

Discovering One's Real Self

Blessed that person who is just as unassuming among his subjects as he would be among his superiors. Blessed the religious who is always willing to be corrected. A man is a faithful and prudent servant (Matthew 24:45) when he is quick to atone for all his offences, interiorly by contrition, exteriorly by confessing them and making reparation. (Admonition XXIV)

LIVING AS FRANCIS DID

The Eucharist kept Francis grounded, rooted in the threefold truth about God, himself, and others. With such a basis, Francis could hardly allow the day's events (whether positive or negative) to throw him off course for long. The Eucharist helped Francis to remain the faithful and prudent servant praised in the quote above.

Without some false persona to defend, Francis could lead his friars into honesty about the gifts God had given them and how they, from time to time, got in the way of those same gifts. In our terms, Francis was a low-maintenance person, making him increasingly available for the Lord's work, especially encouraging his brothers in humble service—whether as leaders within the brotherhood or as true brothers to the other friars.

GROWING WITH FRANCIS

Are you a high-maintenance or a low-maintenance person? Whichever way you describe yourself, how is that working for you? How is that working for your daily witness to the kingdom of God? Be ready to make whatever adjustments may be needed in order for your life to reflect Gospel values more intensely.

JUNE 13

Keep Priests in Prayer

Blessed is that servant of God who has confidence in priests who live according to the laws of the holy Roman Church. Woe to those who despise them. Even if they fall into sin, no one should pass judgement on them, for God has reserved judgement on them to himself. They are in a privileged position because they have charge of the Body and Blood of our Lord Jesus Christ, which they receive and which they alone administer to others, and so anyone who sins against them commits a greater crime than if he sinned against anyone else in the whole world. (Admonition XXVI)

LIVING AS FRANCIS DID

Francis knew very well that some priests in his day were far from living up to their vocation. Even so, he chose to leave the task of judging them to God. For better or for worse, they exercise a vital ministry in breaking open the word of God at Mass and of consecrating the bread and wine into the Body and Blood of Jesus.

For Francis, the mysteries of Jesus's Incarnation and the Eucharist were intricately connected. Francis could not admire a distant Jesus and look down (as many of his contemporaries did) on an all-too-human Church, one that still needed conversion at all levels.

GROWING WITH FRANCIS

The next time you are at Mass, pray for the priest and for all other priests—that they may be worthy of the vocation that God has given them for service to God's people. If you witness serious error in a priest's life, pray for discernment in helping him to return to the Lord's ways.

JUNE 14

Body Building

Blessed the religious who treasures up for heaven (Matthew 6:20) the favors God has given him and does not want to show them off for what he can get out of them. God himself will reveal his works to whomsoever he pleases. Blessed the religious who keeps God's marvelous doings to himself. (Admonition XXVIII)

LIVING AS FRANCIS DID

Francis could have become a carnival sideshow all by himself if he had failed to foster the attitude described above. Whatever good we accomplish is due much more to God's grace and mercy than to our talents and cleverness. This spirit prompted Francis to keep his stigmata a secret as best he could. Many people probably would have given Francis too much credit and God too little credit for this unique gift.

A friar who seeks adulation can never succeed because that desire is a form of appropriation (taking for oneself what belongs to God alone). To Francis's way of thinking, that was and is the primary sin.

GROWING WITH FRANCIS

As St. Paul reminded the Christians in Corinth, every spiritual gift is given in order to build up the Body of Christ. Any other use of that gift would be as misguided as using the handle of a screwdriver as though it were a hammer. It might get the job done partially—but not very well and at a steep price.

Refer every blessing back to God and pray to use it for God's glory and for building up the Body of Christ.

JUNE 15

Living in Eucharistic Freedom

And moreover, we should confess all our sins to a priest and receive from him the Body and Blood of our Lord Jesus Christ. The man who does not eat his flesh and drink his blood cannot enter into the kingdom of God (John 6:54). Only he must eat and drink worthily because "all who eat and drink without discerning the body, eat and drink judgment against themselves" (1 Corinthians 11:29); that is, if he sees no difference between it and other food.

Besides this, we must bring forth "fruits worthy of repentance" (Luke 3:8) and love our neighbors as ourselves. Anyone who will not or cannot love his neighbor as himself should at least do him good and not do him any harm. (Letter to All the Faithful)

LIVING AS FRANCIS DID

Francis was addressing laymen, laywomen, and diocesan priests who were attracted by the way he lived out the Gospel of Jesus. They were not, however, to imitate Francis slavishly. Rather, they were to allow God to show them how live in the divine freedom in which they were created. The Eucharist was the most important way that God would teach them how to live in that freedom—and thus as genuine sisters and brothers to all people everywhere.

GROWING WITH FRANCIS

Allow the Eucharist to have its full power in your life—not through self-serving display but through humble service.

JUNE 16

God Works through Imperfection

We are also bound to fast and avoid vice and sin, taking care not to give way to excess in food and drink, and we must be Catholics. We should visit churches often and show great reverence for the clergy, not just for them personally, for they may be sinners, but because of their high office, for it is they who administer the most holy Body and Blood of our Lord Jesus Christ. They offer It in sacrifice at the altar, and it is they who receive It and administer It to others. We should realize, too, that no one can be saved except by the Blood of our Lord Jesus Christ and by the holy words of God, and it is the clergy who tell us his words and administer the Blessed Sacrament. (Letter to All the Faithful)

LIVING AS FRANCIS DID

Some of the people to whom this letter was addressed may have been tempted look down on the Eucharist because it is so material, so fleshy, and because its ministers were still sinners. The first part of that temptation is not nearly as strong today, but the second part is. Francis did not lie to himself about the presence of sin among the Church's clerics, but Francis had a deep respect for the fact that God has chosen to work through human beings who constantly fall short of his immense glory.

GROWING WITH FRANCIS

Pray that the Eucharist may build up your parish community as God desires.

JUNE 17

Spiritual Housecleaning

All those who refuse to do penance and receive the Body and Blood of our Lord Jesus Christ are blind, because they cannot see the true light, our Lord Jesus Christ. They indulge their vices and sins and follow their evil longings and desires, without a thought for the promises they made. In body they are slaves of the world and of the desires of their lower nature, with all the cares and anxieties of this life; in spirit they are slaves of the devil. They have been led astray by him and have made themselves his children, dedicated to doing his work. They lack spiritual insight because the Son of God does not dwell in them, and it is he who is the true wisdom of the Father. It is of such men as these that Scripture says, their skill was swallowed up (Psalm 106:27). They can see clearly and are well aware what they are doing; they are fully conscious of the fact that they are doing evil, and knowingly lose their souls. (Letter to All the Faithful)

LIVING AS FRANCIS DID

Though harsh, these words tell us that God does not really need physical space in our lives, but God needs all the psychic space that we can clear out for his values. Otherwise, our lives will gradually be filled with more and more stuff that does not lead us to God.

GROWING WITH FRANCIS

What spiritual housecleaning can you do to make more room for God in your life?

JUNE 18

Life Changing Gift

We clerics cannot overlook the sinful neglect and ignorance some people are guilty of with regard to the holy Body and Blood of our Lord Jesus Christ. They are careless, too, about his holy name and the writings which contain his words, the words that consecrate his Body. We know his Body is not present unless the bread is first consecrated by these words. Indeed, in this world there is nothing of the Most High himself that we can possess and contemplate with our eyes, except his Body and Blood, his name and his words, by which we were created and by which we have been brought back from death to life. (Letter to All Clerics)

LIVING AS FRANCIS DID

Francis felt that he had something worthwhile to say to clerics. This letter and the one to the faithful were part of his "Eucharistic Crusade" after Lateran Council IV (1215) to aid the Church's reform. That council instituted the practice of receiving Holy Communion at least once during the Lent or Easter season—and the custom of confessing any mortal sins previously unconfessed.

Few people received the Eucharist regularly; they were satisfied at Mass to look at the consecrated and elevated host. The people needed to be instructed to show greater reverence for the Eucharist, but the best way of doing this was the good example of clerics when they celebrated Mass.

GROWING WITH FRANCIS

Let your life reflect the change the Eucharist creates in you.

JUNE 19

Helping Hands

Those who are in charge of these sacred mysteries, and especially those who are careless about their task, should realize that the chalices, corporals and altar linens where the Body and Blood of our Lord Jesus Christ are offered in sacrifice should be completely suitable. And besides, many clerics reserve the Blessed Sacrament in unsuitable places, or carry It about irreverently, or receive It unworthily, or give It to all-comers without distinction. God's holy name, too, and his written words are sometimes trodden underfoot, because the sensual man does not perceive the things that are of the Spirit of God (1 Corinthians 2:14).

Surely we cannot be left unmoved by loving sorrow for all this; in his love, God gives himself into our hands; we touch him and receive him daily into our mouths. Have we forgotten that we must fall into his hands? (Letter to All Clerics)

LIVING AS FRANCIS DID

Francis was very concerned that altar linens be kept clean and that churches be swept and ready for divine worship. St. Clare of Assisi shared a similar concern and embroidered many corporals and purificators for use at Mass. Exterior reverence was a sign of these saints' devotion to the Eucharist, which they allowed to transform their lives so that God's values became more and more natural for them.

GROWING WITH FRANCIS

Have you offered your help as a lector, Communion distributor, usher, or sacristan at your parish? Chances are, it has needs in this area.

JUNE 20

Gatherings Can Bond

In the name of the most high Trinity and holy Unity, Father, Son, and Holy Spirit. Amen.

To all the friars, so reverend, so well-beloved; to the Minister General of the Order of Minors and to his successors; to all the ministers and custodes; to the ordinary priests of the Order in Christ, and to all the friars who are obedient and without pretensions, to first and last, Brother Francis, the least of your servants, worthless and sinful, sends greetings in him who redeemed and cleansed us in his precious Blood. At the sound of his name you should fall to the ground and adore him with fear and reverence; the Lord Jesus Christ, Son of the Most High, is his name, and he is blessed for ever. Amen. (Letter to a General Chapter)

LIVING AS FRANCIS DID

Francis was writing to a gathering (chapter) of friars, held outside Assisi each year near the feast of Pentecost. The Eucharist brought the friars together and prevented their differing backgrounds and interests from becoming an obstacle to their communal living of the Gospel.

Gatherings of the faithful—celebrations, parish picnics, song fests, book groups, and prayer gatherings—bond church members.

GROWING WITH FRANCIS

Many people dread meetings. You may be one of them. Consider that sometimes they are necessary to help a group achieve its purpose. Well planned meetings produce results. Be constructive if you have a meeting today.

JUNE 21

Whose Way?

Listen, then, sons of God and my friars, and give ear to my words (Acts 2:14). Give hearing (Isaiah 55:3) with all your hearts and obey the voice of the Son of God. Keep his commandments wholeheartedly and practise his counsels with all your minds. Give thanks to the Lord, for he is good (Psalm 136:1); extol him in your works (Tobit 13:6). This is the very reason he has sent you all over the world, so that by word and deed you might bear witness to his message and convince everyone that there is no other almighty God besides him (Tobit 13:4). Be well disciplined then and patient under holy obedience, keeping your promises to him generously and unflinchingly. God deals with you as with sons (Hebrews 12:7). (Letter to a General Chapter)

Living as Francis Did

At these general (worldwide) chapters, the friars reported on their lives and ministry. Based on what they heard from other friars, they might decide to undertake some new apostolic work. The friars did not necessarily return to the same place from which they came. Anthony of Padua, for example, once came from Sicily to a chapter in Assisi and ended up being assigned to a hermitage near Bologna. The friars showed flexibility because they shared a common zeal for Gospel living.

Growing with Francis

How flexible am I when doing the Lord's work? Ask God to help you recognize the Gospel call—even if it comes in the form of someone else's idea!

JUNE 22

Pray for Workers for Christ

Remember your dignity, then, my friar-priests. You shall make and keep yourselves holy, because God is holy (Leviticus 11:44). In this mystery God has honored you above all other human beings, and so you must love, revere, and honor him more than all others. Surely this is a great pity, a pitiable weakness, to have him present with you like this and be distracted by anything else in the whole world. (Letter to a General Chapter)

LIVING AS FRANCIS DID

In the very beginning, the majority of the friars were not priests. Francis was not a priest. Over time however, the Church began to expect those who preached in its name should have studied first, and many of these friars were ordained as priests. This did not give them special privileges among the friars; it increased need to give good example by their words and their way of life. As long as Francis was present—or they read letters such as this one—they would be faithful to the common life they had vowed to live.

GROWING WITH FRANCIS

The priestly ministry that most Catholics receive comes from their parish priests, who are committed to work within the diocese where they were ordained. The Church's need for holy priests is no less than it was in Francis's day. Pray that priests will truly represent Christ. Pray for all who work for Christ.

JUNE 23

Done by Grace and Mercy

Kissing your feet with all the love I am capable of, I beg you to show the greatest possible reverence and honor for the most holy Body and Blood of our Lord Jesus Christ through whom all things, whether on the earth or in the heavens, have been brought to peace and reconciled with Almighty God (Colossians 1:20). And I implore all my friars who are priests now or who will be priests in the future, all those who want to be priests of the Most High, to be free from all earthly affection when they say Mass, and offer single-mindedly and with reverence the true sacrifice of the most holy Body and Blood of our Lord Jesus Christ, with a holy and pure intention, not for any earthly gain or through human respect or love for any human being, not serving to the eye as pleasers of men (Ephesians 6:6). With the help of God's grace, their whole intention should be fixed on him, with a will to please the most high Lord alone, because it is he alone who accomplishes this marvel in his own way. (Letter to a General Chapter)

LIVING AS FRANCIS DID

All these thoughts about the Eucharist, coming from a single letter, indicate how central this sacrament was to the life and ministry of Francis.

GROWING WITH FRANCIS

Pray for everyone whom God is feeding at the next Mass in which you participate.

JUNE 24

Live Worthily

All of you who are priests should remember what is written of the law of Moses; all those who violated it even in externals "died without mercy" (Hebrews 10:28), by God's own decree. "How much worse punishments do you think will be deserved by those who have spurned the Son of God, profaned the blood of the covenant by through which they were sanctified, and outraged the Spirit of grace?" (Hebrews 10:29). A man despises, defiles, and tramples underfoot the Lamb of God when, as St Paul says, he sees no difference between the bread which is Christ and other food (1 Corinthians 11:29), or between receiving It and any other employment, and receives It unworthily, or even if he is in the state of grace, receives It without faith or proper devotion. God tells us by the Prophet Jeremiah, "Cursed is the one who is slack in doing the work of the Lord" (Jeremiah 48:10). Those spurn the priests who refuse take this to heart with the words, "I will curse your blessings" (Malachi 2:2). (Letter to a General Chapter)

LIVING AS FRANCIS DID

Francis spent much time and energy urging his brother priests to live in a way worthy of their vocation because many priests were giving mixed messages about whether their deepest loyalty was to Jesus or to some other person or group.

GROWING WITH FRANCIS

Today pray especially for friends, relatives, and coworkers who may be in special need.

JUNE 25

Pray Privately and Publicly

Our whole being should be seized with fear, the whole world should tremble and heaven rejoice, when Christ the Son of the living God is present on the altar in the hands of the priest. What wonderful majesty! What stupendous condescension! O sublime humility! O humble sublimity! That the Lord of the whole universe, God and the Son of God, should humble himself like this and hide under the form of a little bread, for our salvation. Look at God's condescension, my brothers, and pour out your hearts before him (Psalm. 62:8). Humble yourselves that you may be exalted by him (1 Peter 5:6). Keep nothing for yourselves, so that he who has given himself wholly to you may receive you wholly. (Letter to a General Chapter).

LIVING AS FRANCIS DID

On anyone else's lips, expressions such as "sublime humility" and "humble sublimity" could seem like tongue twisters. From Francis they were supreme spiritual superlatives. The Eucharist gave Francis strength to try again when he might easily have given in to discouragement. It had its full effect in Francis's life because he was ready to make the connections that God wanted him to make. For that, private prayer was also needed. Otherwise, Francis might miss what God very much wanted to give him.

GROWING WITH FRANCIS

Do you feel that public prayer such as the Eucharist is all that you need? Does such prayer allow you to avoid deeper conversion? Pray publicly *and* privately.

JUNE 26

Sincere Reverence

With everything I am capable of and more, I beg you to ask the clergy with all humility, when it is called for and you think it is a good idea, to have the greatest possible reverence for the Body and Blood of our Lord Jesus Christ, together with his holy name and the writings which contain his words, those words which consecrate his body. They should set the greatest value, too, on chalices, corporals, and all the ornaments of the altar that are related to the holy Sacrifice. If the Body of our Lord has been left in a poverty-stricken place, they should put It somewhere that is properly prepared for It, according to Church law, so that It will be kept safe. They should carry It about with the greatest reverence and be discreet in administering It to others. If the name of God or the writings that contain his words are found lying in the dust, they should be picked up and put in a suitable place. (Letter to All Superiors of the Friars Minor)

LIVING AS FRANCIS DID

This particular writing was addressed to the ministers (leaders) of the friars. It echoes many of the concerns expressed in Francis's Letter to a General Chapter. Reverence for the Eucharist and the printed words of Scripture were of paramount importance in keeping the friars' lives focused.

GROWING WITH FRANCIS

What in your own life do you revere?

JUNE 27

Live with Integrity

In all your sermons you shall tell the people of the need to do penance, impressing on them that no one can be saved unless he receives the Body and Blood of our Lord [John 6:54]. When the priest is offering sacrifice at the altar or the Blessed Sacrament is being carried about, everyone should kneel down and give praise, glory, and honor to our Lord and God, living and true. (Letter to Superiors of the Order)

LIVING AS FRANCIS DID

Francis never tired of reminding the friars that their apostolic work and their lives together would prosper only if they were centered on God, uniquely present to them in the Eucharist. Sermons should invite people to repent, not try to scare them into repenting. Fear doesn't work as a long-term strategy. Drawing closer to God's immense love is its own reward. Nowhere is that more clear than in the celebration of the Eucharist.

GROWING WITH FRANCIS

What is the best sermon that you have ever heard? Was it moving simply because the preacher was a good public speaker who worked in interesting stories? Or was it good because his life consistently supported his words? Live with as much integrity as you would like to see in those who preach to you.

JUNE 28

Reconcile and Receive

They are to make a confession of their sins three times a year and to receive Communion at Christmas, Easter, and Pentecost. They are to be reconciled with their neighbors and to restore what belongs to others. They are to make up for past tithes and pay future tithes. (Rule of Third Order, 5)

LIVING AS FRANCIS DID

For over one hundred years, frequent Communion at Sunday or weekday Masses has been common. Many people can still recall Communion Sundays in which some organization within a parish gathered at the same Mass and received Holy Communion. First Friday devotions also encouraged at least monthly reception of the Eucharist.

In St. Francis's day, the Eucharist was not received so often. In 1215, Lateran Council IV felt it necessary to decree that Catholics must receive Holy Communion at least once a year, having confessed any mortal sins that they may have committed in the previous year. In this context, the directive that Secular Franciscans are to confess their sins and receive Holy Communion three times year is notable. The Eucharist is to be shared, not simply adored from afar. Francis linked reception of Holy Communion to reconciliation with one's neighbors and the paying of tithes. The Eucharist clearly impacts a person's public life.

GROWING WITH FRANCIS

Does the Eucharist sufficiently impact your public life? The stories you repeat or don't repeat? The organizations that you join or don't join? The groups and causes that you voluntarily support financially?

JUNE 29

Adoration in Prayer

Francis burned with a love that came from his whole being for the sacrament of the Lord's body, and he was carried away with wonder at the loving condescension and the most condescending love shown there. Not to hear at least one Mass each day, if he could be there, he considered no small contempt. He frequently received Holy Communion, and he did so with such devotion that he made others devout. Showing toward that sacrament deserving of all reverence he could, he offered a sacrifice of all his members; and receiving the Lamb that was offered [1 Peter 1:18–19], he immolated his own spirit with the fire that burned always upon the altar of his heart. (Celano, Second Life of St. Francis, 201)

LIVING AS FRANCIS DID

This month's quotations show that Francis had a great devotion to the Eucharist. In these days, Eucharistic adoration is becoming more common in some parishes, scheduled times for people to pray privately before the Blessed Sacrament. In such moments of praise and honesty, a person's conversion might go deeper and wider. A major life decision may be seen in a new light. A vocational choice might take a step forward. A decision to reconcile—or at least to forgive someone—could be made.

GROWING WITH FRANCIS

Whether you participate in scheduled Eucharistic adoration or pray before the Blessed Sacrament apart from such a program, you are acknowledging that the Eucharist influences your life far beyond the hours that you devote to public worship.

JUNE 30

Encouraging Vocations

He loved France as a friend of the Body of the Lord, and he longed to die there because of its reverence for sacred things. He wished at one time to send his brothers through the world with precious pyxes, so that wherever they should see the price of our redemption kept in an unbecoming manner, they should place it in the very best place. He wanted great reverence shown to the hands of priests, for to these has been given authority from God over the consecrated bread and wine. Often he would say: "If it should happen that I would meet at the same time some saint from heaven and any poor priest, I would first show honor to the priest and quickly go to kiss his hands. And I would say to the other: 'Wait, St. Lawrence, for the hands of this one touch the Word of Life [1 John 1:1], and have something about them that is more than human.'" (Celano, Second Life of St. Francis, 201)

LIVING AS FRANCIS DID

Francis could never separate the Eucharist from the ordained priests who were so vital in its celebration. He knew that, being human, they fell prey to failures and shortcomings, yet he also held them in high esteem as those who were the ordained ministers of Christ in the world.

GROWING WITH FRANCIS

How would you react if a family member expresses interest in a priestly vocation? Encouraging? Cautious? Dismissive?

Fraternal Charity

A few years after Francis's conversion and his decisive break with his former way of life, men began to ask to be admitted into his brotherhood. Women began to follow St. Clare, a close friend of Francis, into a radically new form of monastic life that did not depend on extensive land holdings. Lay women and men (most of them married) began to follow Francis in what became known as the Secular Franciscan Order. Franciscan orders continue to call men and women to follow Francis as he followed Jesus.

All these people began with great zeal. But soon many friars discovered that other friars were still sinners and could get on their nerves. Likewise, not everyone who became a Secular Franciscan was already a saint. In fact, no one was!

Religiously zealous people can succumb to the temptation to rank other people in terms of their zeal. In the real world many are found wanting, and being perpetually scandalized over the sins of others can unintentionally become a way of life. A dishonest zeal such as Jesus described (seeing the speck in another person's eye while ignoring the plank in one's own eye) quickly begins to feed upon itself, leading people farther and farther from the very Gospel they claim as their reason for following Francis.

Also, religiously motivated people can easily become self-righteous. Because Francis was acutely aware of the possibility of such a "look how good I am" attitude, he gave his brother friars many exhortations about fraternal charity. A similar spirit was needed among the Poor Clares and Secular Franciscans if they were to avoid the factionalism that has caused many religious groups that have begun well to end badly.

That same spirit of fraternal charity can guide all Christians in their interpersonal relationships. Francis would support today's appeals for servant leaders, for men and women as ready to wash the feet of others as to issue commands and directives. Francis was concerned that leadership positions not become possessions that could be appropriated as if the office holder had an indefinite right to that office.

Leadership positions are for service. In Francis's view, they were never to become some type of ladder indicating the next higher position to be desired and then achieved. Francis even introduced the possibility that the leader of the Friars Minor might later be judged unfit for that office. In that case, the leader could be voted out of office.

Fraternal charity was relatively easy when there were few friars and all of them knew Francis personally. It became more challenging when the friars became more numerous and diverse in nationality and social class. Francis lived in a very status-conscious society where a person's background forever indicated who is important and who is not.

The brotherhood of Francis's followers would eventually challenge the commitment of each of its members. Only a deep fraternal charity would allow them to continue to witness to Jesus's Good News.

JULY 1

Actions Above Words

"It is a fearful thing to fall into the hands of the living God" (Hebrews 10:31), and so the ministers must keep close watch over their own souls and those of their friars. A friar is not bound to obey if a minister commands anything that is contrary to our life or his own conscience, because there can be no obligation to obey if it means committing sin....

If a friar is clearly determined to live according to the flesh and not according to the spirit [Romans 8:6], no matter where he is, the others are bound to warn, instruct and correct him with humble charity. (Rule of 1221, chapter 5)

LIVING AS FRANCIS DID

Because Francis was devoted to helping the friars shape their lives to that of the Lord, his writings often address them directly. Many of these messages apply equally to the laity. When a fellow Christian is observed living in a manner harmful to his spiritual life, Francis would suggest that that person's companions in the faith bring to his attention in a loving manner what they observe.

GROWING WITH FRANCIS

It takes courage to address what appears to be damaging the life of a Christian friend. More than that, it takes serious self-examination and prayer before entering such a conversation. Most often, however, our own lifestyle speaks more lovingly and loudly than our words.

A "Step Down" Society

The friars who cannot observe the Rule, no matter where they are, must have recourse to their minister as soon as possible and tell him all about it. The minister should do his best to provide for them as he would like provision to be made for himself, if he were in similar circumstances.

No one is to be called "Prior." They are all to be known as "Friars Minor" without distinction, and they should be prepared to wash one another's feet. (Rule of 1221, chapter 6)

LIVING AS FRANCIS DID

Francis wanted friar leaders to be servant leaders, explicitly citing here the example of Jesus at the Last Supper, as recorded in the Gospel of John (13:1–10). A position of leadership is not some rung on a career or social ladder; it is a chance to imitate Jesus in a new way.

Status was very important in Francis's society, as it is in our own. Someone born a noble would always be a noble—no matter how poor or politically marginal that person might become. Another person born into the merchant or serf class rarely passed into the nobility. The first followers of Francis were making radical choices by the standards of their contemporaries as they chose humbly to step down in their society.

GROWING WITH FRANCIS

Are you prepared to wash another's feet? Those of a homeless man on the streets? Of an elderly woman in a nursing home?

JULY 3

Work Is Honorable

The friars who are engaged in the service of lay people for whom they work should not be in charge of money or of the cellar. They are forbidden to accept positions of authority in the houses of their employers, or to take on any job which would give scandal or make them lose their own souls. They should be the least and subordinate to everyone in the house.

The friars who have a trade should work at it, provided that it is no obstacle to their spiritual progress and can be practised without scandal. The Psalmist tells us, "You shall eat the fruit of the labor of your hands; you shall be happy, and it shall go well with you" (128:2)]; and St. Paul adds, "Anyone unwilling to work should not eat" (2 Thessalonians 3:10b). Everyone should remain at the trade and in the position in which he was called. In payment they may accept anything they need, except money. If necessary, they can go for alms like the rest of the friars. They are allowed to have the tools which they need for their trade. (Rule of 1221, chapter 7)

LIVING AS FRANCIS DID

Work for friars should not mean social advancement. Honesty and hard work could tempt employers to move them into places of esteem, but this was not in keeping with Francis's Rule.

GROWING WITH FRANCIS

Do you over-identify with your work? Does it define you completely? If so, how can you change that?

Idleness Invites Temptation

All the friars must work hard doing good, as it has been said, "Always be doing something worthwhile; then the devil will always find you busy" [St. Jerome, Letter 125], and, "Idleness is the enemy of the soul" [Anselm, Letter 49]. And so those who serve God should be always busy praying or doing good.

No matter where they are, in hermitages or elsewhere, the friars must be careful not to claim the ownership of any place, or try to hold it against someone else. Everyone who comes to them, friend or foe, rogue or robber, must be made welcome.

And all the friars, no matter where they are or in whatever situation they find themselves, should, like spiritually minded men, diligently show reverence and honor to one another "without complaining" (1 Peter 4:9). They should let it be seen that they are happy in God, cheerful and courteous, as is expected of them, and be careful not to appear gloomy or depressed like hypocrites. (Rule of 1221, chapter 7)

LIVING AS FRANCIS DID

Francis and his followers were not born saints. Friction with fellow members of the Franciscan family was always possible, and still is. Brotherly or sisterly charity is always needed, no matter with whom we live.

GROWING WITH FRANCIS

The more honestly a person lives, the less time and energy she or he needs to maintain a false self-image. Be humble by choice.

JULY 5

Caring for the Sick

If a friar falls ill, no matter where he is, the others may not leave him, unless someone has been appointed to look after him as they should like to be looked after themselves....

I beg the friar who is sick to thank God for everything; he should be content to be as God wishes him to be, in sickness or in health, because it is those who were "destined for eternal life" (Acts 13:48) that God instructs by sickness and affliction and the spirit of compunction. He tells us himself, "I reprove and discipline those whom I love" (Revelation 3:19). But if the sick friar lets his illness upset him and becomes angry with God or with the other friars, always looking for medicine in an effort to relieve the body that is soon to die and is the enemy of the soul, it is a result of evil in him and a sign that he is a carnal person; he does not seem to be a real friar, because he cares more for his body than for his soul. (Rule of 1221, chapter 10)

LIVING AS FRANCIS DID

Life on the road, going in pairs or small groups, increases the number of times friars might have to care for a sick friar. Yet caring for the sick is essential in Francis's eyes.

GROWING WITH FRANCIS

How willing are you to care for a sick relative? Visit one in the hospital?

Discard the Unnecessary

As they go about the country, the friars are to "take nothing with them for [their] journey, no staff, nor bag, nor bread, nor money" (Luke 9:3). When they enter a house, they are to say first of all, "Peace to this house!" (Luke 10:5). And they should "remain in the same house, eating and drinking whatever they provide" (Luke 10:7).

They should not offer resistance to injury; if a man strikes them on the right cheek, they should turn the other cheek also towards him (Matthew 5:39). If a man would take away their cloak, they should not grudge him their coat along with it. They should give to every man who asks, and if a man takes what is theirs, they should not ask him to restore it (Luke 6:29–30). (Rule of 1221, chapter 14)

LIVING AS FRANCIS DID

Francis saw his friars as living more like the apostles on a missionary journey while Jesus was with them than like a community living in one place and witnessing to God there. The friars' mobility demanded that they have few possessions; otherwise, they might be tempted to settle down and do whatever work could be done without moving around. Possessions could tend to accumulate under such circumstances.

GROWING WITH FRANCIS

How many possessions do you need? Which emotional attachments do you require? Clean a desk or a closet today, and pray as you work.

JULY 7

Gather Together

Each year, on the feast of St. Michael the Archangel, the ministers and their friars may hold a chapter wherever they wish, to treat of the things of God. All the ministers are bound to attend the chapter at St. Mary's of the Portiuncula at Pentecost, those from overseas or beyond the Alps once every three years, and the others once each year, unless the Minister General, who is the servant of the whole Order, has made some other arrangements. (Rule of 1221, chapter 18)

LIVING AS FRANCIS DID

In the earliest days, all the friars returned to Assisi once a year to celebrate a chapter, to learn what God was doing in their lives, and to open them to what else God might be asking of them. By 1221, the date of this quote, the number of friars had become too large for all friars to come to Assisi every year. Ministers (leaders) were to call their friars together annually to engage in the same type of prayer and reflection that characterized the chapters in Assisi.

Christians need to listen to each other. Once they do that, they have a better foundation for knowing what God might be asking of them in the future. This is true for all members of the Franciscan family as well as for people inspired by the example of Francis.

GROWING WITH FRANCIS

How good a listener are you? Would better listening strengthen your witness as a follower of Jesus Christ?

JULY 8

Respect for Others

All the friars are bound to be Catholics, and live and speak as such. Anyone who abandons the Catholic faith or practice by word or deed must be absolutely excluded from the Order, unless he repents. We must regard all other clerics and religious as our superiors in all that concerns the salvation of the soul and is not contrary to the interests of our religious life. We must respect their position and office, together with their ministry. (Rule of 1221, chapter 19)

Living as Francis Did

Just as iron filings are drawn to a magnet, sometimes people unhappy with aspects of the Catholic Church were drawn to St. Francis. He did not send them away, but insisted that they must be Catholic if they were to join his family. Then and today Franciscans do not deny the bad example of some Church members; the hope of the glorious Church in heaven must be balanced with the reality of the life and ministry of the Church on earth.

Today Catholic Franciscans respect and sometimes gather with Franciscans of other Christian faiths, including The Order of Ecumenical Franciscans, The Society of St. Francis, and the Third Order Society of St. Francis.

Growing with Francis

Being charitable without lying to oneself or enabling someone else's destructive choices is sometimes difficult. Is there a difficult person or situation you might be able to mentor to help achieve harmony in the community?

JULY 9

Sin Is Real

We must hate our lower nature with its vices and sins; by living a worldly life, it would deprive us of the love of our Lord Jesus Christ and of eternal life, dragging us down with it into hell. By our own fault we are corrupt, wretched, strangers to all good, willing and eager only to do evil, as our Lord says in the Gospel: "For it is from within, from the human heart that evil intentions come: fornication, theft, murder, adultery, avarice, wickedness, deceit, licentiousness, envy, slander, pride folly. All these evil things come from within, and they defile a person" (Mark 7:21–23).

We have left the world now and all we have to do is to be careful to obey God's will and please him. (Rule of 1221, chapter 22)

LIVING AS FRANCIS DID

Francis's warning about our lower nature makes sense. Francis was not retreating from his gratitude for God's creation; Francis was simply pointing out that we may not always read it correctly. Sin is alive and well. You have only to read the morning newspaper or listen to news on radio, watch TV, or read on the Internet to realize that God's standards or values can be portrayed as idealistic but unrealistic. We are sometimes like people trying to find medicine in a pharmacy where all the labels have been switched; everything is not what it seems.

GROWING WITH FRANCIS

People pride themselves on being realistic. Are you realistic about sin? Your own sin? About God's grace?

JULY 10

Divest, Divest!

If anyone wants to profess our Rule and comes to the friars, they must send him to their provincial minister, because he alone, to the exclusion of others, has permission to receive friars into the Order. The ministers must carefully examine all candidates on the Catholic faith and the sacraments of the Church. If they believe all that the Catholic faith teaches and are prepared to profess it loyally, holding by it steadfastly to the end of their lives, and if they are not married; or if they are married and their wives have already entered a convent or after taking a vow of chastity have by the authority of the bishop of the diocese been granted this permission; and the wives are of such an age that no suspicion can arise concerning them: let the ministers tell them what the holy Gospel says (Matthew 19:21), that they should go and sell all that belongs to them and endeavour to give it to the poor. If they cannot do this, their good will is sufficient. (Rule of 1223, chapter 2)

LIVING AS FRANCIS DID

Material possessions can be blockades to the spiritual life, and Francis wanted his followers to be as unencumbered as possible. Before they could enter the community, they were to divest of their goods and give them to the poor; that was to be their first Franciscan practice.

GROWING WITH FRANCIS

Do you live in the freedom that God created for us? If not, what is holding you back?

JULY 11

Motivated Living

When this has been done, the ministers should clothe the candidates with the habit of probation, namely, two tunics without a hood, a cord and trousers, and a caperon reaching to the cord, unless the ministers themselves at any time decide that something else is more suitable. After the year of the novitiate, they should be received to obedience, promising to live always according to this life and Rule. It is absolutely forbidden to leave the Order, as his holiness the Pope has laid down. For the Gospel tells us, "No one who puts his hand to the plow and looks back is fit for the kingdom of God (Luke 9:62).... All the friars are to wear poor clothes and they can use pieces of sackcloth and other material to mend them, with God's blessing. (Rule of 1223, chapter 2)

LIVING AS FRANCIS DID

Experience showed Francis that vocations to his brotherhood needed to be tested, not because those coming to him were consciously deceitful but because their motivation might not be enough to sustain a life of Gospel living as friars. In the beginning, friars professed vows of poverty, chastity, and obedience immediately. Now they have a year's novitiate and at least three years of temporary profession before they make those vows for life. Secular Franciscans also have extended periods of formation to determine their vocation.

GROWING WITH FRANCIS

Do you have a passion for the Franciscan life? If so, how might you express that?

JULY 12

Plank or Speck

If any of the friars, at the instigation of the enemy, fall into mortal sin, they must have recourse as soon as possible, without delay, to their provincial ministers, if it is a sin for which recourse to them has been prescribed for the friars. If the ministers are priests, they should impose a moderate penance on such friars; if they are not priests, they should see that a penance is imposed by some priest of the Order, as seems best to them before God. They must be careful not to be angry or upset because a friar has fallen into sin, because anger or annoyance in themselves or in others makes it difficult to be charitable. (Rule of 1223, chapter 7)

LIVING AS FRANCIS DID

Those who became friars in Francis's day—and today, as well—were still sinners. Hopefully they avoided the most serious sins, but Francis needed to outline how the friars should handle such situations.

Mark Twain once said that nothing is so enjoyable as examining another person's conscience. Religious people must use caution to avoid being judgmental, as Jesus himself did. Not all anger is righteous or justified anger. Anger can be used to deflect attention from oneself onto someone else.

GROWING WITH FRANCIS

Are you ever tempted to notice the speck in someone else's eye but miss the plank in your own? If so, what can you do about it?

JULY 13

Prayerful Elections

The friars are always bound to have a member of the Order as Minister General, who is the servant of the whole fraternity, and they are strictly bound to obey him. At his death the provincial ministers and the custodes [officials who assist the provincial ministers] are to elect a successor at the Pentecost Chapter, at which the provincial ministers are bound to assemble in the place designated by the Minister General. This chapter should be held once every three years, or at a longer or shorter interval, if the Minister General has so ordained.

If at any time it becomes clear to all the provincial ministers and custodes that the Minister General is incapable of serving the friars and can be of no benefit to them, they who have the power to elect must elect someone else as Minister General. (Rule of 1223, chapter 8)

LIVING AS FRANCIS DID

Francis assumed that the Minister General would die in office, but he explained what should happen if the majority decided that the Minister General should be replaced. In medieval society, almost no one could be voted out of office! Yet Francis was wise enough to know that a leader could become incapable of serving the community to its benefit. He himself made the choice to leave as head of the Franciscans when he felt he was no longer effective in that role.

GROWING WITH FRANCIS

Prayer is essential to guide any elections, religious or civil. Pray for God-directed leadership in the world.

JULY 14

Maintaining Harmony

When God gave me some friars, there was no one to tell me what I should do, but the Most High himself made it clear to me that I must live the life of the Gospel. I had this written down briefly and simply and his holiness the Pope confirmed it for me. Those who embraced this life gave everything they had to the poor. They were satisfied with one habit which was patched inside and outside, and a cord, and trousers. We refused to have anything more. (Testament)

LIVING AS FRANCIS DID

Only God's grace and a strong sense of fraternal charity made a life as brothers possible. The mixture of social classes, nationalities, and educational backgrounds could have led to factions, each side claiming it was more closely attuned to God's ways than the other factions.

Although God's grace is never lacking, fraternal charity can dry up. It must be nurtured constantly through countless deeds of generosity. Francis submitted his proposed way of life (Rule) to the Church for its approval. In that sense, he was not a free agent who saw himself as somehow apart from the Church.

GROWING WITH FRANCIS

Sometimes groups doing good work run into trouble when egos become overinflated and siphon off the groups' physical or spiritual resources. Do you have the courage to be a voice of reason and charity within any group when you perceive that such trouble looms?

JULY 15

Moving On

The friars must be very careful not to accept churches or poor dwellings for themselves, or anything else built for them, unless they are in harmony with the poverty which we have promised in the Rule; and they should occupy these places only as strangers and pilgrims.

In virtue of obedience, I strictly forbid the friars, wherever they may be, to petition the Roman Curia, either personally or through an intermediary, for a papal brief, whether it concerns a church or any other place, or even in order to preach, or because they are being persecuted. If they are not welcome somewhere, they should flee to another country where they can lead a life of penance, with God's blessing. (Testament)

LIVING AS FRANCIS DID

Just as Jesus told his disciples to move on when their preaching was not accepted, Francis of Assisi admonished his friars that when their preaching was not accepted, they should go elsewhere to "lead a life of penance, with God's blessing." Other responses risked making the disciples or the friars the main issue; they could endlessly defend their honor and complain that they were misunderstood. God knows the truth of each situation; that should be enough.

GROWING WITH FRANCIS

When have you wasted time and energy defending yourself in situations that really did not matter? Seek the wisdom to know when to move on to serve others rather than yourself.

JULY 16

Obedient Living

Our Lord tells us in the Gospel, "None of you can be my disciple if you do not give up all your possessions" (Luke 14:33), and, "Those who want to save their life will lose it, and those who lose their life for my sake will find it" (Matthew 16:25). A man takes leave of all that he possesses and loses both his body and his life when he gives himself up completely to obedience in the hands of his superior. Any good that he says or does which he knows is not against the will of his superior is true obedience. A subject may realize that there are many courses of action that would be better and more profitable to his soul than what his superior commands. In that case he should make an offering of his own will to God, and do his best to carry out what the superior has enjoined. This is true and loving obedience which is pleasing to God and one's neighbor. (Admonition III)

LIVING AS FRANCIS DID

For Francis, obedience was not as much a matter of fulfilling commands given by one's leader as it was a state of living in harmony with the others. Francis sometimes spoke of friars who lived "outside obedience" (in communion with their own egos perhaps, but not in communion with the other friars).

GROWING WITH FRANCIS

By our baptismal vows, we are committed to obedience to God. How are you living that commitment?

JULY 17

Conscientious Decision Making

If a superior commands his subject anything that is against his conscience, the subject should not spurn his authority, even though he cannot obey him. If anyone persecutes him because of this, he should love him all the more, for God's sake. A religious who prefers to suffer persecution rather than be separated from his confreres certainly perseveres in true obedience, because he lays down his life for his brethren (John 15:13). There are many religious who under the pretext of doing something more perfect than what their superior commands look behind and go back to their own will that they have given up (Proverbs 26:11). People like that are murderers, and by their bad example they cause the loss of many souls. (Admonition III)

LIVING AS FRANCIS DID

Conscience issues are always serious. Wearing this pair of shoes or another pair is a matter of personal preference—not of conscience. If someone knew that a product results from forced child labor or dehumanizing adult labor, buying it or not could be a matter of conscience. Conscience could prevent someone from obeying a legitimate superior. Such a decision must be reached after trying every means to explain why that order cannot be obeyed. Conscience reveals to us who we are in a unique way; the integrity of life apart from the issue under dispute matters greatly.

GROWING WITH FRANCIS

What was the last decision of conscience you made? Over what issue?

JULY 18

Be Holy

Look at the Good Shepherd, my brothers. To save his sheep he endured the agony of the cross. They followed him in trials and persecutions, in ignominy, hunger, and thirst, in humiliations and temptations, and so on. And for this God rewarded them with eternal life. We ought to be ashamed of ourselves; the saints endured all that, but we who are servants of God try to win honor and glory by recounting and making known what they have done. (Admonition VI)

LIVING AS FRANCIS DID.

Saints should spur us to strive to become living examples of the virtues we honor them for living. Saints are unique examples of integrity. In his early twenties, St. John XXIII wrote in his *Journal of a Soul* that if he were to be a saint, it would have to be according to his God-given talents and deeds. "If St. Aloysius [Gonzaga] were as I am, he would have become a saint in a different way." That does not take anything away from the holiness of St. Aloysius. Angelo Roncalli (the future St. John XXIII) certainly understood this admonition—even if he never linked it to Francis of Assisi. No one becomes a saint by thinking that holiness is easier in some other century, another country, or a different line of work or family situation.

GROWING WITH FRANCIS

Holiness is possible for anyone, at any time. To be holy is to be fully human. How can you be more human?

JULY 19

Judge Not

Nothing should upset a religious except sin. And even then, no matter what kind of sin has been committed, if he is upset or angry for any other reason except charity, he is only drawing blame upon himself. A religious lives a good life and avoids sin when he is never angry or disturbed at anything. Blessed the man who keeps nothing for himself, but "gives to the emperor the things that are the emperor's, and to God the things that are God's" (Matthew 22:21b). (Admonition XI)

LIVING AS FRANCIS DID

It is possible to live in a state of high anxiety, always terribly disappointed because of someone else's sins while never truly facing one's own sin. When we want for another person what God wants for that person, then charity will prevail. Francis is not telling the friars to lie to themselves about the destruction that someone else's bad example can bring. But the motivation is not a sense of personal entitlement; the humble motivation is that God deserves better from that person—and from us.

Francis could see sin as well as anyone else—in fact, better than most people. But that did not give him the right to attempt to pass God's final judgment on anyone—not even upon himself.

GROWING WITH FRANCIS

How do you tell the difference between genuine charity and enabling another person's self-destructive behavior? What helps you maintain perspective in those situations?

JULY 20

Patience Prepares Us

Blessed the religious who takes no more pride in the good that God says and does through him, than in that which he says and does through someone else. It is wrong for anyone to be anxious to receive more from his neighbor than he himself is willing to give to God. (Admonition XVII) Blessed the man who is patient with his neighbor's shortcomings as he would like him to be if he were in a similar position himself. (Admonition XVIII)

LIVING AS FRANCIS DID

Francis had a strong sense of fairness. If I consider someone else's gifts as a threat to my own, I'm probably not being completely honest about my gifts...or theirs. At the Easter Vigil, if I pass my candle's flame to the next person, I am in no way diminished by that act. I am helping someone turn a potential light into a real light. Why should I feel threatened by another person's gift? Doesn't it ultimately point back to God, the giver of every gift?

No one is born patient; Francis certainly wasn't. He learned patience through honesty and humility. Impatient people try to convince others that they had no other option than to be impatient. Patient people know there are options—some better than others.

GROWING WITH FRANCIS

Who is the most patient person you know personally? Did that person have an easy life? What can you learn from that person?

JULY 21

Key to Happiness

And the holy one [St. Francis] said to them: "Brothers, in order that we may give thanks to the Lord our God faithfully and devoutly for all his gifts, and that you may know what kind of life the present and future brothers are to live, understand the truth of the things that are to come. We will find now, at the beginning of our life, fruits that are extremely sweet and pleasant to eat; but a little later some that are less sweet and less pleasant will be offered; and lastly, some that are full of bitterness will be given, which we will not be able to eat, for because of their bitterness they will be inedible to all, though they will manifest some external fragrance and beauty. (Celano, First Life of St. Francis, 28)

LIVING AS FRANCIS DID

People sometimes speak of Francis as unrealistic. It's easy to allow another person's blind spots to keep us in continuous agitation: "If only so-and-would do such and such," we may say. The key to our happiness is not in someone else's hands but in ours. The more honestly and humbly we live, the more we will rejoice in someone else's gifts and the more ready we will be to recognize our own.

GROWING WITH FRANCIS

Do you feel threatened by someone else's gifts? Would greater honesty about your gifts make you feel less threatened?

JULY 22

Honesty and Humility

"Thanksgiving and the voice of song" (Isaiah 51:3b) resounded everywhere so that many put aside worldly cares and gained knowledge of themselves from the life and teaching of the most blessed Francis, and they longed to attain love and reverence for their Creator. Many of the people, both noble and ignoble, cleric and lay, impelled by divine inspiration, began to come to St. Francis, wanting to carry on the battle constantly under his discipline and under his leadership. All of these the holy man of God, like a plenteous river of heavenly grace, watered with streams of gifts; he enriched the field of their hearts with flowers of virtue, for he was an excellent craftsman; and, according to his plan, rule, and teaching, proclaimed before all, the Church is being renewed in both sexes, and the threefold army of those to be served is triumphing [reference to the three Orders that Francis helped to found]. To all he gave a norm of life. (Celano, First Life of St. Francis, 37)

Living as Francis Did

People don't feel threatened by humble people; these folks don't require a great deal of "maintenance." Francis's honesty and humility drew people to him; they wanted some of the treasure of the field he had discovered. Francis appealed to diverse peoples. He encouraged them to live honestly and generously, true to themselves and to God.

Growing with Francis

In what areas could you use a measure of honesty? Humility?

JULY 23

Obedience Wins

Since they despised all earthly things and did not love themselves with a selfish love, pouring out their whole affection on all the brothers, they strove to give themselves as the price of helping one another in their needs. They came together with great desire; they remained together with joy; but separation from one another was sad on both sides, a bitter divorce, a cruel estrangement. But these most obedient knights dared put nothing before holy obedience; before the command of obedience was even uttered, they prepared themselves to fulfill the order; knowing not how to misinterpret the commands, they put aside every objection and hastened to fulfill what was commanded. (Celano, First Life of St. Francis, 39)

LIVING AS FRANCIS DID

In civil society or in the Catholic Church, reform groups often begin strong but splinter because of strong personalities or divisive issues. The obedience and fraternal charity described here usually prevented that from happening among people inspired by Francis. The obedience Celano describes is not a situation in which one person wins only because every else loses. No, everyone wins with such obedience because the focus remains on sharing the Good News of Jesus Christ.

If differences arise, face them openly. In time, an individual or group must make a decision that the rest of the group follows. That decision can be revisited and revised later if necessary.

GROWING WITH FRANCIS

Consider ways to focus groups on God's will in decision-making situations.

JULY 24

Patience Is a Virtue

The virtue of patience so took hold of them that they sought rather to be where they might suffer persecution of their bodies than where they might be lifted up by the favor of the world, when their holiness was known or praised. For many times when they were insulted and ridiculed, stripped naked, beaten, bound, imprisoned, they did not protect themselves by means of anyone's patronage, but they bore all things so courageously that nothing but the voice of praise and thanksgiving resounded in their mouths. Scarcely at all, or really never, did they let up in their praise of God and in their prayers; but recalling by constant discussion what they had done, they gave thanks to God for what they had done well; for what they had neglected or incautiously committed, they poured forth groans and tears. (Celano, First Life of St. Francis, 40)

LIVING AS FRANCIS DID

Mutual charity is often the first casualty when a group of people runs into trouble. What if problems arise because group members are being faithful to what they have promised? The friars learned to praise God even in these circumstances. They were not to fight to justify themselves; doing so would make *them* the center of the dispute. The friars needed patience with one another; they needed to pray that their persecutors would open their hearts to God's grace.

GROWING WITH FRANCIS

How do you deal with people who persecute you? With patience and love, or in other ways?

JULY 25

Develop Alternatives

The servant of the Most High God, Francis, leaving the sea, walked over the land, and ploughing it up with the word, he sowed the seed of life and brought forth blessed fruit. For immediately quite a few good and suitable men, clerics and lay, fleeing from the world and manfully crushing the devil, followed Francis devoutly in his life and purpose through the grace and the will of the Most High. (Celano, First Life of St. Francis, 56)

LIVING AS FRANCIS DID

People noticed the good example set by Francis and followed him. Even so, he resisted every attempt to promote a "cult of personality" that would draw attention to himself and away from God. He referred every good gift back to its author. Some people thought Francis in later life was being insincere when he referred to himself as a great sinner. Yet the closer he drew to God, the more conscious Francis was of the huge gap between himself and God.

Not long before he died, Francis told the friars, "I have done what was mine to do; may the Lord teach you what you must do." Only a truly patient and humble person could make such a statement.

GROWING WITH FRANCIS

Learning patience is usually not a personal goal such as learning a new language. People learn patience by reacting differently to situations that once automatically made them angry.

When you get upset, how do you explore ways you could handle the situation?

JULY 26

The Challenge of Conversion

So great was the faith of the men and women, so great their devotion toward the holy man of God, that he pronounced himself happy who could but touch his garment. When he entered any city, the clergy rejoiced, the bells were rung, the men were filled with happiness, the women rejoiced together, the children clapped their hands; and often, taking branches from the trees, they went to meet him singing. The wickedness of heretics was confounded, the faith of the Church exalted; and while the faithful rejoiced, the heretics slipped secretly away.... In the midst of all these things and above everything else, Francis thought that the faith of the holy Roman Church was by all means to be preserved, honored, and imitated, that faith in which alone is found the salvation of all who are to be saved. (Celano, First Life of St. Francis, 62)

LIVING AS FRANCIS DID

Not everyone was enthralled with Francis or converted immediately because of his words or deeds. Genuine conversion is costly because it never involves trivial matters. Life will be different after conversion; that can be scary. Celano did not exaggerate how much Francis saw the Church of his day, with all its imperfections, as announcing and living God's Good News.

GROWING WITH FRANCIS

Fraternal charity, like every virtue, is built up day by day through Christian community. What community encourages your spiritual growth?

JULY 27

Be a Blessing

Indeed, he was extremely steadfast, and he paid no attention to anything except what pertained to the Lord. For when he so very often preached the word of God to thousands of people, he was as sure of himself as though he were speaking with a familiar companion. He looked upon the greatest multitude of people as one person and he preached to one as he would to a multitude. Out of the purity of his mind he provided for himself security in preaching a sermon and, without thinking about it beforehand, he spoke wonderful things to all and things not heard before. When he did give some time to meditation before a sermon, he at times forgot what he had meditated upon when the people had come together, and he knew nothing else to say. Without embarrassment he would confess to the people that he had thought of many things but could remember nothing at all of them; and suddenly he would be filled with such great eloquence that he would move the souls of the hearers to admiration. At times, however, knowing nothing to say, he would give a blessing and dismiss the people, feeling that from this alone they had received a great sermon. (Celano, First Life of St. Francis, 72)

LIVING AS FRANCIS DID

Francis did not bluff his way through situations. If all he could do was to give a blessing, he was happy to do that.

GROWING WITH FRANCIS

Who might you bless today with words or presence?

JULY 28

Departing

A certain brother, however, from among those standing about, whom the saint loved with a great affection, in his anxiety for all the brothers, said to him, when he saw these things and recognized that Francis was approaching his end: "Kind Father, alas, your sons are now without a father and are deprived of the true light of their eyes. Remember therefore your orphan sons whom you are now leaving; forgive them all their faults and give joy to those present and absent with your holy blessing." And the saint said to him: "Behold, my son, I am called by God; I forgive my brothers, both present and absent, all their offenses and faults, and, in as far as I am able, I absolve them; I want you to announce this to them and to bless them all on my behalf." (Celano, First Life of St. Francis, 109)

Living as Francis Did

When Jesus told the apostles at the Last Supper that he was going away from them, they protested that he was leaving them orphans. He responded by saying that he was giving them the Holy Spirit to guide them. If Francis's work was simply the result of a personality cult, then it would collapse after he died. It didn't because it was deeply rooted in God's love and the need for ongoing conversion.

Growing with Francis

We continue to learn from Francis of Assisi even though his world and ours differ greatly. What can you learn from Francis today?

JULY 29

Genuine Silence

There was a certain brother of extraordinary sanctity, as far as could be seen outwardly, outstanding in his life, yet quite singular. He spent all his time in prayer and he observed silence with such strictness that he was accustomed to confess not with words but with signs. He derived great ardor from the words of Scripture, and, after hearing them, he relished them with wonderful sweetness. Why should we give many details? He was considered thrice holy by all. The blessed father happened to come to that place and happened to see that brother and hear him called a saint. But when all were commending him and praising him, the father replied: "Leave off, brothers, and do not praise the things the devil has fashioned in him. Know in truth that it is a temptation of the devil and a fraudulent deception. I am convinced of this and the greatest proof of it is that he does not want to confess." (Celano, Second Life of St. Francis, 28)

Living as Francis Did

Francis knew that the acid test of that friar's sincerity would be his willingness to confess his sins, to admit that he was a sinner. If that friar valued silence over confessing his sins, that revealed the motivation for his silence.

Growing with Francis

Anything that is from God will stand the test of time. Be cautious about people who seem too good to be true. Sometimes they are neither. What is disingenuous in you?

Soul Cleansing

The brothers took this ill, especially the vicar of the saint [Brother Elias]. "And how could it be true," they inquired, "that the workings of fraud could be concealed under so many signs of perfection?" The father said to them: "Let him be admonished to confess twice or once a week; if he does not do this, you will know that what I have said is true." The vicar took him aside and first joked familiarly with him, then commanded him to confess. He refused, and putting his finger into his ear and shaking his head, he indicated that he would not by any means confess. The brothers were silent, fearing the scandal of a false saint. After not many days, he left religion of his own accord, went back to the world, returned to his vomit [Proverbs 26:11]. Finally, redoubling his crimes, he was deprived at the same time of repentance and of life. Singularity is always to be avoided, for it is nothing else but a lovely precipice.... Attend, on the other hand, to the power of devout confession, which not only makes a person holy, but also manifests his holiness. (Celano, Second Life of St. Francis, 28)

LIVING AS FRANCIS DID

Francis's strategy with this friar worked. Everyone else came to see what Francis already knew.

GROWING WITH FRANCIS

A willingness to confess one's sins shows that the person knows God's grace does not have sufficient room within to operate. Repentance creates room. Search your soul today for what you might need to confess.

JULY 31

God Provides

When Francis was staying in a certain hermitage near Rieti, a doctor visited him daily to take care of his eyes. But one day the saint said to the brothers: "Invite the doctor and give him something very good to eat." The guardian answered him, saying: "Father, we blush to say that we are ashamed to invite him, because we are now so poor." The saint replied, saying: "Do you want me to tell you again?" The doctor, who was standing by, said: "Dearest brothers, I will consider your poverty a real delicacy." The brothers hurried and placed upon the table all they had in their store-room, namely, a little bread, not much wine, and, that they might eat a bit more sumptuously, the kitchen provided some vegetables. Meanwhile the table of the Lord had compassion on the table of his servants. There was a knock at the door and it was answered quickly. Behold, a certain woman offered them a basket full of fine bread, fishes and lobster pies, honey and grapes…. At length they were satisfied, but the miracle gave them greater satisfaction than the banquet…. The poor man is provided with a more abundant table than the tyrant, in as much as God is more generous in his gifts than man. (Celano, Second Life of St. Francis, 44)

LIVING AS FRANCIS DID

God looks after Francis's followers.

GROWING WITH FRANCIS

Live as you know God wants you to live; give as you know God wants you to give.

Poverty and Simplicity

How much stuff does someone need in order to do God's work? Friars and Poor Clares obviously need less than kings and queens, many of whom were attracted to Francis's ways of life during his lifetime. In fact, St. Elizabeth of Hungary, born a princess, and St. Louis IX of France, who became king in 1226, are the patrons of the Secular Franciscan Order. They used their positions and their possessions for service to others and not selfishly.

As the conversion of Francis grew deeper and wider, he found that he needed fewer and fewer things. He regarded even those things that he had as simply on loan. When the bishop of Assisi urged Francis and the brothers to own more goods as a matter of prudence, Francis pointed out that the more the friars owned, the more they would need arms to protect those possessions.

Not every possession, however, is physical. Resentments can be guarded as zealously as a miser guards money. The miser's loyalties are pretty clear. That is not the case with someone who is externally poor but internally treasures feelings of resentment at not receiving one's due, not having one's importance recognized, and so on.

As we just read in the quotes for July 29 and 30, there was a friar in Francis's community who had a great reputation for holiness and for silence. When Francis ordered that friar to confess his sins, the friar refused—seemingly in order to preserve his silence. The friar left the brotherhood shortly after that incident, considering it more important to maintain a false image of himself as sinless than to admit what he shared with the rest of humanity.

St. Paul praised Jesus who became poor for our sake so that we might become rich in what matters to God. The more honest a person is, the smaller will be her sacrifice to become poor and simple. If someone operates out of an inflated sense of self, every movement toward poverty and simplicity will seem to be a step in the wrong direction.

Physical stuff can clutter up our lives while never truly fulfilling us because every prized possession will eventually look paltry in comparison with what someone else has. People who over-identify with their possessions cannot be truly happy because their security is always at risk. Likewise, people who nurture destructive attitudes as a form of self-protection cannot be genuinely secure.

Jesus told his apostles that they must travel light—both in physical goods and in the attitudes they bring to the people whom they encounter. When the Good News of Jesus stops stretching us, then it is no longer the Good News but has become a more subtle method of social or political advancement.

Francis understood well that poverty and simplicity were virtues essential to those who seek to do the work of God.

AUGUST 1

Grow Through Sacrifice

If anyone is inspired by God to live our life and comes to our brothers, they should welcome him; and if they see that he is determined to profess our Rule, they should bring him to their minister as soon as possible, being very careful not to interfere in his temporal affairs in any way. The minister, for his part, should receive him kindly and encourage him and tell him all about our way of life. When that has been done, the candidate should sell all his possessions and give the money to the poor, if he is willing and able to do so in conscience and without hindrance. The friars and their ministers, however, should be careful not to interfere in his affairs in any way; they must not accept any money from him, either personally or through an intermediary. But if they are in want, the friars could accept other material goods for their needs, just like the rest of the poor, but not money. (Rule of 1221, chapter 2)

LIVING AS FRANCIS DID

Men wanting to become friars were to be welcomed into the brotherhood; selling their possessions and giving the money to the poor indicated their sincerity. Francis instructed the friars, however, not to interfere in the process. In this way it would assure that the decision to give all away was made freely.

GROWING WITH FRANCIS

What are you willing to sacrifice to become a more faithful follower of Jesus?

Being Obedient

If anyone who seeks admission to the Order cannot dispose of his property without hindrance, although he is spiritually minded to do so, he should leave it all behind him, and that is enough.

No candidate may be received contrary to the norms and prescriptions of the Church.

The friars who have already made their profession of obedience may have one habit with a hood and, if necessary, another without a hood. They may also have a cord and trousers. All the friars must wear poor clothes and they can patch them with pieces of sackcloth and other material, with God's blessing. As our Lord tells us in the Gospel, "Those who put on fine clothing and live in luxury are in royal palaces" (Luke 7:25b). And even though people may call them hypocrites, the friars should never cease doing good. (Rule of 1221, chapter 2)

LIVING AS FRANCIS DID

Franciscans do not live for themselves alone; they live to witness Gospel values within a Church always marked by human sin. The Church had a legitimate right to ensure that the friars lived what they professed. In some ways, the first Franciscans were a destabilizing influence in their society. What if everyone tried to live the way they did?

GROWING WITH FRANCIS

Many friars found giving up their material goods easier than vowing to live "in obedience." Which would be more challenging for you, and why?

AUGUST 3

Love and Care

The friars should have no hesitation about telling one another what they need, so that they can provide for one another. They are bound to love and care for one another as brothers, according to the means God gives them, just as a mother loves and cares for her son.... In case of necessity the friars, no matter where they are, can eat any ordinary food, just as our Lord asks: "Have you never read what David did when he and his companions were hungry and in need of food? He entered the house of God, when Abiathar was high priest, and ate the bread of Presence, which it is not lawful for any but the priests to eat, and he gave some to his companions" (Mark 2:25–26). And they should remember those other words of the Lord: "Be on guard so that your hearts are not weighed down with dissipation and drunkenness and the worries of this life, and that day catch you unexpectedly, like a trap. For it will come upon all who live on the face of the whole earth" (Luke 21:34–35). (Rule of 1221, chapter 9)

LIVING AS FRANCIS DID

The poverty that Francis expected of his followers would not be bearable apart from the fraternal charity that Francis modeled for them.

GROWING WITH FRANCIS

When have you experienced a time of deprivation made easier by the love of others? Have you shown such love to others?

Resolve Anger

Far from indulging in detraction or disputing in words (2 Timothy 2:14), the friars should do their best to avoid talking, according as God gives them the opportunity. There must be no quarrelling among themselves or with others, and they should be content to answer everyone humbly, saying, "We are worthless slaves" (Luke 17:10b). They must not give way to anger because the Gospel says: "If you are angry with a brother or sister, you will be liable to judgment; and if you insult a brother or sister, you will be liable to the council; and if you say, 'You fool,' you will be liable to the hell of fire" (Matthew 5:22b).

The friars are bound to love one another because our Lord says, "This is my commandment, that you love one another as I have loved you" (John 15:12). And they must prove their love by deeds, as St. John says, "Let us not love in word or speech, but in truth and action" (1 John 3:18). (Rule of 1221, chapter 11)

LIVING AS FRANCIS DID

Poverty and simplicity are as much a matter of attitude as of physical possessions. A person can have few earthly goods while retaining a sense of entitlement, a bottomless pit of self-pity that their talents have not been sufficiently recognized.

GROWING WITH FRANCIS

What makes you angry? Can you envision yourself reacting out of love instead the next time this situation arises?

AUGUST 5

Judge Not

I warn all the friars and exhort them not to condemn or look down on people whom they see wearing soft or gaudy clothes and enjoying luxuries in food or drink; each one should rather condemn and despise himself. (Rule of 1223, chapter 2)

LIVING AS FRANCIS DID

In some ways, this is the key to Franciscans' gift to the Church: to live in joyful poverty without denouncing people who enjoy a higher standard of living or have more influence socially or politically. Otherwise, that could become a full-time and exhausting job. Envy feeds on itself. Other sins eventually lead to exhaustion, at least for a short time, but envy never tires. The temptation to denounce and feel self-righteous is a strong one that must be resisted constantly; the more honest we are with ourselves, the easier it is to resist this temptation.

There were many people in Francis's day who felt that the Church needed to give better witness to Christ's self-emptying than to accumulating wealth as a sign of success. Francis succeeded in large part because he lived the crucial advice that he gives in this quote. Where his followers have failed to live by that advice, they have not borne fruit; they have not been powerful witnesses of God's grace and mercy.

GROWING WITH FRANCIS

How can you avoid appropriating a self-righteous attitude that leaves you with no time or energy for anything more worthwhile?

A Virtuous Treasure

The friars are to appropriate nothing for themselves, neither a house, nor a place, nor anything else. As "aliens and exiles" (1 Peter 2:11) in this world, who serve God in poverty and humility, they should beg alms trustingly. And there is no reason why they should be ashamed, because God made himself poor for us in this world. This is the pinnacle of the most exalted poverty, and it is this, my dearest brothers, that has made you heirs and kings of the kingdom of heaven, poor in temporal things, but rich in virtue. This should be your portion, because it leads to the land of the living. And to this poverty, my beloved brothers, you must cling with all your heart, and wish never to have anything else under heaven, for the sake of our Lord Jesus Christ. (Rule of 1223, chapter 6)

LIVING AS FRANCIS DID

Francis tells the friars to work hard to provide for their own needs, plus the needs of friars who may be ill or no longer able to work as they once did. Only if their hard work did not supply for their most basic needs were the friars permitted to beg.

We can appropriate objects for personal use, but we can also attempt to appropriate virtues that do not reflect where our treasure is. For example, humility must be deeply rooted in honesty. It cannot grow in any other soil, for it then becomes an exercise in self-congratulation.

GROWING WITH FRANCIS

Where is your treasure? What virtues can you cultivate to guard it?

AUGUST 7

Ideal or Real?

I, little Brother Francis, wish to live according to the life and poverty of our most high Lord Jesus Christ and his most holy Mother and to persevere in this to the last. And I beseech you, my Ladies, and I exhort you to live always in this most holy life and poverty. Keep close watch over yourselves so that you never abandon it through the teaching or advice of anyone. (St. Francis's Form of Life and Last Will for St. Clare)

LIVING AS FRANCIS DID

In Francis's day, Church members spoke more readily about the power and majesty of Jesus and Mary than of their poverty and humility. Believers thought they were honoring Jesus and Mary in this way. Holy people such as Francis and Clare tend to make us nervous. What do they know that we do not?

It's easier to dismiss holy people as idealists, people whose grip on reality isn't as strong as ours. Many Church leaders thought that Clare was asking too much of her sisters. These leaders felt that their prudence could protect the Poor Clares from their misguided zeal. Besides, who ever heard of every level of society living peacefully side by side as the Poor Clares obviously did?

GROWING WITH FRANCIS

Poverty, simplicity, love: it is possible to have all three together, but that is a house always under construction. How might you build one in your community?

AUGUST 8

Washing Feet

"The Son of Man came not to be served but to serve" (Matthew 20:28a), our Lord tells us. Those who are put in charge of others should be no prouder of their office than if they had been appointed to wash the feet of their confreres. They should be no more upset at the loss of their authority than they would be if they were deprived of the task of washing feet. The more they are upset, the greater the risk they incur to their souls. (Admonition IV)

Living as Francis Did

"Upward mobility" is not an invention of our times. Francis lived in a world that tended to judge people by the kind of work they did and the highest office they attained. No office was ever relinquished voluntarily except for a higher office. In such a world, Francis was clearly revolutionary. When he heard the story of Jesus washing his disciples' feet at the Last Supper, Francis understood that servant leadership is the only kind that lasts and is truly fruitful.

St. Clare used to wash the feet of the "extern" sisters who begged on behalf of San Damiano when the work of the sisters and donations from the people did not provide all the sisters needed. Clare came from a noble family; the extern sisters probably did not.

Growing with Francis

What is one way that you serve, washing the feet of others?

AUGUST 9

Recognize Illusion

"Blessed are the poor in spirit, for theirs is the kingdom of heaven" (Matthew 5:3). There are many people who spend all their time at their prayers and other religious exercises and mortify themselves by long fasts and so on. But if anyone says as much as a word that implies a reflection on their self-esteem or takes something from them, they are immediately up in arms and annoyed. These people are not really poor in spirit. A person is really poor in spirit when he hates himself and loves those who strike him in the face (Matthew 5:39). (Admonition XIV)

LIVING AS FRANCIS DID

Francis doesn't use the word "hypocrite" here, but that's what he is describing. Prayer and fasting can lead some people deep into self-righteousness, rather than into the love of God and neighbor. They pride themselves on their humility—until it is put to the smallest test.

Entitlement tends to grow on its own—like an invasive vine. Humility must be nurtured. Community living, married life, a generous single life help humility grow—but not always gently. The deeper a person lives in illusion, the more difficult it is to recognize illusion for what it is. Humble people do not write off all opposition as the work of the devil; sometimes it's a clumsy invitation to live more truthfully.

GROWING WITH FRANCIS

Under what illusions are you living? Begin the process toward seeing clearly.

AUGUST 10

Virtues Challenge

Hail, Queen Wisdom! The Lord save you,
  with your sister, pure, holy Simplicity.
Lady Holy Poverty, God keep you,
  with your sister, holy Humility.
Lady Holy Love, God keep you,
  with your sister, holy Obedience.
All holy virtues,
  God keep you,
  God, from whom you proceed and come.
In all the world there is not a man
  who can possess any one of you
  without first dying to himself.
The man who practices one and does not offend against the others
  possesses all;
The man who offends against one,
  possesses none and violates all.
Each and every one of you
  puts vice and sin to shame. (Praises of the Virtues)

LIVING AS FRANCIS DID

Francis saw how the virtues are connected, how they support each other.
No virtue can be pursued in isolation from its partners.

GROWING WITH FRANCIS

Which pair of virtues is hardest for you to understand? Pray about that.

AUGUST 11

Virtue vs. Vice

Holy Wisdom puts satan
  and all his wiles to shame.
Pure and holy Simplicity puts
  all the learning of this world,
  all natural wisdom, to shame.
Holy Poverty puts to shame
  all greed, avarice,
  and all the anxieties of this life.
Holy Humility puts pride to shame,
  all the inhabitants of this world
  and all that is in the world.
Holy Love puts to shame all the temptations
  of the devil and the flesh
  and all natural fear.
(Praises of the Virtues)

LIVING AS FRANCIS DID

The virtues cited above shame their opposite vices because the virtues lead us more deeply into the truth about God, ourselves, and others.

GROWING WITH FRANCIS

What truth have your virtues helped you to see?

AUGUST 12

Sharing God's Life

Holy Obedience puts to shame
    all natural and selfish desires.
It mortifies our lower nature
    and makes it obey the spirit
    and our fellow men.
Obedience subjects a man
    to everyone on earth,
And not only to men,
    but to all the beasts as well
    and to the wild animals,
So that they can do what they like with him,
    as far as God allows them.
(Praises of the Virtues)

LIVING AS FRANCIS DID

Every genuine virtue is a sharing in God's life. Because of that, we see every sinful appropriation for what it is and seek to avoid it.

GROWING WITH FRANCIS

Are you ready to follow God's life (God's grace) wherever it leads you? If not, what are you afraid must be left behind?

AUGUST 13

Dressing Down

The men belonging to this brotherhood shall dress in humble, undyed cloth, the price of which is not to exceed six Ravenna soldi in all, unless for evident and necessary cause a temporary dispensation be given. And breadth and thinness of the cloth are to be considered in said price.

They shall wear their outer garments and furred coats without open throat, sewed shut or uncut but certainly laced up, not open as secular people wear them; and they shall wear their sleeves closed. (Secular Franciscan Rule, 1–2)

LIVING AS FRANCIS DID

Many contemporaries of Francis of Assisi saw the Gospel come alive in the way he, the other friars, St. Clare, and the Poor Clares lived. Having already made commitments in marriage, as single people, or as diocesan priests, they had obligations that other members of the Franciscan family did not have. A lay order of Franciscans was born. They were not to wear fancy clothing or the most popular styles. Following Christ after the example of Francis was more than changing a person's way of thinking. It lead to external choices, such as clothing.

In some ways, Secular Franciscan men anticipated Amish customs about simplicity of clothing and referring to one another as "brother." Both customs helped them maintain their focus on Gospel living.

GROWING WITH FRANCIS

What kind of image do you try to present by your clothing choices? Is this in keeping with the values you hold dear?

AUGUST 14

Simplicity in Style

The sisters in turn shall wear an outer garment and tunic made of cloth of the same price and humble quality; or at least they are to have with the outer garment a white or black underwrap or petticoat, or an ample linen gown without gathers…. They are not to wear silken or dyed veils and ribbons.

And both the brothers and the sisters shall have their fur garments of lamb's wool only. They are permitted to have leather purses and belts sewed in simple fashion without silken thread, and no other kind. Also other vain adornments they shall lay aside at the bidding of the Visitor. (Secular Franciscan Rule, 3–4)

When anybody wishes to enter this brotherhood, the ministers shall carefully inquire into his standing and occupation, and they shall explain to him the obligations of the brotherhood, especially that of restoring what belongs to others. And if he is content with it, let him be vested according to the prescribed way, and he must make satisfaction for his debts, paying money according to what pledged provision is given. They are to reconcile themselves with their neighbors and to pay up their tithes. (Secular Franciscan Rule, 29)

LIVING AS FRANCIS DID

Simplicity of clothing applies to all members of the Franciscan Order—brothers, sisters, or lay members.

GROWING WITH FRANCIS

How might you clean your closet in order to more authentically reflect a Franciscan life?

AUGUST 15

Stripped Down

He [Francis] rose up, therefore, fortified himself with the sign of the cross, got his horse ready and mounted it, and taking with him some fine cloth to sell, he hastened to the city called Foligno. There, as usual, he sold everything he had with him, and, successful as a merchant, he left behind even the horse he was riding, after he had received payment for it; and, free of all luggage, he started back, wondering with a religious mind what he should do with the money. Soon, turned toward God's work in a wondrous manner, and accordingly feeling that it would be a great burden to him to carry that money even for an hour, he hastened to get rid of it, considering the advantage he might get from it as so much sand. When, therefore, he neared the city of Assisi, he discovered a certain church along the way that had been built of old in honor of St. Damian but which was now threatening to collapse because it was so old. (Celano, First Life of St. Francis, 8)

LIVING AS FRANCIS DID

Selling cloth in Foligno and giving the money to the church of San Damiano seemed like a good idea to Francis. When his father protested to the bishop of Assisi, the bishop agreed that Francis did not have the right to do that. Francis then stripped himself naked and returned his clothes to Pietro Bernardone.

GROWING WITH FRANCIS

Try not to define yourself as much by external possessions as by loving relationships.

Staying True

And then, coming back, he said with joy to his brothers: "Be strengthened, dear brothers, and rejoice in the Lord" [Ephesians 6:10 and Philippians 3:1] and do not be sad because you seem so few; and do not let either my simplicity or your own dismay you, for, as it has been shown me in truth by the Lord, God will make us grow into a very great multitude and will make us increase to the ends of the world. For your profit I am compelled to tell you what I have seen, though I would much rather remain silent, were it not that charity urges me to tell you. (Celano, First Life of St. Francis, 27)

LIVING AS FRANCIS DID

This incident occurred shortly after Francis and eleven friars went to Rome in 1209 in order to seek the approval of Pope Innocent III for their Gospel way of life. The temptation to measure their success (or lack thereof) by their numbers was still present, and Francis assured them that their numbers would grow. In a short time, Francis's followers had the opposite problem: Many men had joined them, but how deeply committed were they to the Gospel life that had initially attracted them? Any small group with a weak sense of identity is in danger of seeking to become more popular by imitating values that are, in fact, foreign to the group's reason for existing.

GROWING WITH FRANCIS

What is the source of your deepest values? How do you stay true to them?

AUGUST 17

Stretchability

"I [Francis] saw a great multitude of men coming to us [the friars] and wanting to live with us in the habit of our way of life and under the rule of our blessed religion. And behold, the sound of them is in my ears as they go and come according to the command of holy obedience. I have seen, as it were, the roads filled with their great numbers coming together in these parts from almost every nation. Frenchmen are coming, Spaniards are hastening, Germans and Englishmen are running, and a very great multitude of others speaking various tongues are hurrying." When the brothers had heard this, they were filled with a salutary joy, both because of the grace the Lord God gave to his holy one and because they were ardently thirsting for the advantages to be gained by their neighbors, whom they wished to grow daily in numbers and to be saved thereby. (Celano, First Life of St. Francis, 27)

LIVING AS FRANCIS DID

Francis came from Umbria in central Italy, but soon his way of Gospel living attracted people in other parts of Italy, then in other parts of Europe, and eventually people from every continent. That required extraordinary flexibility on his part and that of the other friars. The same dynamic would be true of the Poor Clares and Secular Franciscans. Every member of the Franciscan family will be stretched by other Franciscans.

GROWING WITH FRANCIS

How willing am I to be stretched by Francis? By Jesus?

AUGUST 18

Brother? Sister?

Immediately, however, four other good and suitable men were numbered among them and they followed the holy man of God [Francis].... There was indeed at that time a great rejoicing and a singular joy among St. Francis and his brothers whenever one of the faithful, no matter who he might be or of what quality, rich or poor, noble or ignoble, despised or valued, prudent or simple, cleric or unlettered or lay, led on by the spirit of God, came to put on the habit of holy religion. There was also great wonder among the people of the world over all these things and the example of humility led them to amend their way of life and to do penance for their sins. Not even lowness of birth or any condition of poverty stood in the way of building up the work of God in those in whom God wished to build it up, God who delights to be with the outcasts of the world and with the simple. (Celano, First Life of St. Francis, 31)

LIVING AS FRANCIS DID

People unlikely to call one another "brother" or "sister" readily did so in Francis's day once they became part of the Franciscan family, which soon crossed boundaries of social class and nationality. Many people outside this family, however, found this mixing of people foolish at best, or worse, a threat to the stability of society.

GROWING WITH FRANCIS

Do you consider each person a gift from God?

AUGUST 19

Expect Surprises

[The friars] began therefore to have in that place commerce with holy poverty; and comforted exceedingly in the absence of all things that are of this world, they resolved to cling to poverty everywhere just as they were doing here. And because once they had put aside solicitude for earthly things, only the divine consolation gave them joy, they decreed and confirmed that they would not depart from its embraces no matter by what tribulations they might be shaken or by what temptations they might be led on. But, though the pleasantness of that place, which could contribute not a little toward a weakening of their true strength of mind, did not detain their affections, they nevertheless withdrew from it, lest a longer stay might entangle them even in some outward show of ownership; and, following their happy father, they went at that time to the Spoleto valley. (Celano, First Life of St. Francis, 35)

LIVING AS FRANCIS DID

This quote described Francis's first followers immediately after they had been turned out of Rivo Torto, a very modest dwelling on the plain below Assisi, because a farmer wanted to use it to shelter his pigs. The voluntary poverty that Francis's followers embraced could easily become a burden unless it was matched by a generous fraternal spirit. God had other work for them to do.

GROWING WITH FRANCIS

Be on the lookout for God's unexpected invitations today.

Saintly Inspiration

And indeed they were lesser brothers, who, being subject to all, always sought a place that was lowly and sought to perform a duty that seemed in some way to be burdensome to them so that they might merit to be founded solidly in true humility and that through their fruitful disposition a spiritual structure of all virtues might arise in them. Truly, upon the foundation of constancy a noble structure of charity arose, in which the living stones, gathered from all parts of the world, were erected into a dwelling place of the Holy Spirit. O with what ardor of charity the new disciples of Christ burned! How great was the love that flourished in the members of this pious society! For whenever they came together anywhere, or met one another along the way, as the custom is, there a shoot of spiritual love sprang up, sprinkling over all love the seed of true affection. (Celano, First Life of St. Francis, 38)

LIVING AS FRANCIS DID

Franciscan poverty and simplicity inspire great trust on the part of others. For this reason, Francis cautioned the friars that they were not to accept the position of steward in anyone's household. Both Sts. Francis and Dominic had to resist pressures that their priestly followers might make good bishops. The Church needed poor and holy shepherds like the friars to reflect a Gospel way of living.

GROWING WITH FRANCIS

Which saints inspire you and why?

AUGUST 21

Facing Challenges

Followers of most holy poverty, because they had nothing, loved nothing, they feared in no way to lose anything. They were content with one tunic, patched at times within and without; in it was seen no refinement, but rather abjectness and cheapness, so that they might seem to be completely crucified to the world. Girt with a cord, they wore poor trousers, and they had the pious intention of remaining like this, and they wished to have nothing more. They were, therefore, everywhere secure, kept in no suspense by fear; distracted by no care, they awaited the next day without solicitude, nor were they in anxiety about the night's lodging, though in their journeyings they were often placed in great danger. For, when they frequently lacked the necessary lodging amid the coldest weather, an oven sheltered them, or at least they lay hid for the night humbly in grottos or caves.(Celano, First Life of St. Francis, 39)

LIVING AS FRANCIS DID

Medieval society had a static sense of social class and valued physical stability. Franciscan life was a challenge on both counts. When the bishop of Assisi advised Francis that friars should be more open to accepting properties and buildings, Francis replied that friars would then need weapons to defend those gifts. In Francis's mind, this was counter to Gospel living.

GROWING WITH FRANCIS

Are you as flexible as God wants you to be?

One Spirit

For holy simplicity had so filled them, innocence of life was so instructing them, purity of heart so possessed them, that they knew nothing of duplicity of mind. For, as there was one faith in them, so was there one spirit in them, one will, one love; there was unity of souls among them, harmony of behavior, the practice of virtues, conformity of minds, and piety of actions. (Celano, First Life of St. Francis, 46)

LIVING AS FRANCIS DID

The smaller the group, the more easily its members can maintain the spirit described above. Members of a larger group can allow it to stumble over petty differences of opinion. People living in close quarters, as the friars did, can easily get on one another's nerves! Astronauts on the International Space Station are selected not only for their technical skills but also for their ability to live under those unique circumstances.

External simplicity in food, clothing, lodging, and means of transportation will almost inevitably be abandoned unless it is reinforced by an internal simplicity of mind and will.

GROWING WITH FRANCIS

Reflect on the various voluntary groups to which you currently belong. Does your behavior in those groups reflect the generous spirit described by Celano? How do you contribute to a more healthy spirit in your groups?

AUGUST 23

Open to God

About midnight, when some of the brothers were resting and some were praying in silence with great devotion, a most splendid fiery chariot entered through the door of the house and turned around two or three times here and there inside the house; a huge globe of light rested above it, much like the sun, and it lit up the night. The watchers were dazed, and those who had been asleep were frightened; and they felt no less a lighting up of the heart than a lighting up of the body. Gathering together, they began to ask one another what it was; but by the strength and grace of that great light each one's conscience was revealed to the others. Finally they understood and knew that it was the soul of their holy father that was shining with such great brilliance and that, on account of the grace of his understanding purity and his great tenderness for his sons, he merited to receive such a blessing from God. (Celano, First Life of St. Francis, 47)

LIVING AS FRANCIS DID

This incident happened when Francis was preaching in Assisi while the other friars were at St. Mary of the Angels on the plain below Assisi. The fiery chariot recalls how the prophet Elijah was taken from this earth. He left behind a successor, Elisha, to continue the prophetic work. Francis inspired others to cooperate generously with the grace of God.

GROWING WITH FRANCIS

Be open to whatever God wishes to accomplish through you today.

AUGUST 24

Servant Leaders

For he saw many pursuing offices of authority, and despising their rashness, he sought to recall them from this pestilence by his example. He used to say that it was a good and acceptable thing before God to exercise the care of others and that it was becoming that they should undertake the care of souls who would seek in it nothing of themselves but who would attend always to the divine will in all things. Those, namely, who would put nothing ahead of their own salvation and who would pay no heed to the applause of their subjects but only to their advancement; who would seek not display before men, but glory before God; who do not strive after a prelacy, but who fear it; who are not puffed up by such a thing when they have it, but are humbled, and who are not dejected when it is taken away, but are filled with joy. (Celano, First Life of St. Francis, 104)

LIVING AS FRANCIS DID

In an era when leadership positions tended to be for life, Francis insisted on a rotating leadership because offices were not for life—not even the office of general minister of the friars. Having renounced upward mobility in business, social standing, or government, the friars could seek a higher status (especially as a religious superior) for seemingly more spiritual motives. Servant leadership was the only effective response to the temptation of upward mobility.

GROWING WITH FRANCIS

Be a servant leader today.

AUGUST 25

Greater Sacrifice

When he was on a pilgrimage to Rome, he [Francis] put off his fine garments out of love of poverty, clothed himself with the garments of a certain poor man, and joyfully sat among the poor in the vestibule before the church of St. Peter, where there were many poor, and considering himself one of them, he ate eagerly with them. Many times he would have done a similar thing had he not been held back by shame before those who knew him. Astounded when he came to the altar of the prince of the apostles that the offerings of those who came there were so meager, he threw down a handful of coins at that place, thus indicating that he whom God honored above the rest should be honored by all in a special way. (Celano, Second Life of St. Francis, 8)

Living as Francis Did

This incident happened in the basilica of St. Peter, built by the Emperor Constantine in the fourth century and pulled down in the sixteenth century to make room for the present basilica of St. Peter in Rome. Francis was early in his conversion and quite ready to show that his generosity was greater than that of other pilgrims. By the end of his life, Francis had a greater and more interior sense of poverty and simplicity. In time, he would sacrifice much more than money to honor St. Peter.

Growing with Francis

Allow God's grace to touch your life in a new place today.

AUGUST 26

Love Softens

When he had been changed from a person of extreme delicacy to a lowly and patient laborer, the priest to whose care the church pertained, seeing that Francis was worn down by constant labor and moved to pity, began to give him daily some special food, though it was not dainty since he was poor. Commending the discretion of the priest and welcoming his kindness, Francis nevertheless said to himself: "You will not find a priest everywhere to provide these things always for you. This is not the life of a man who professes poverty. It is not proper for you to get accustomed to such things; gradually you will return to the things you have despised, and you will run again after delicacies. Arise now without delay, and beg from door to door for foods of mixed kinds." He therefore begged for prepared foods from door to door throughout Assisi, and when he saw his bowl full of all kinds of scraps, he was struck with horror; but mindful of God and conquering himself, he ate the food with joy of spirit. Love softens all things and makes every bitter thing sweet. (Celano, Second Life of St. Francis, 14)

LIVING AS FRANCIS DID

"Love softens all things and makes every bitter thing sweet." Celano's words could have been those of Francis.

GROWING WITH FRANCIS

Perhaps love can soften some challenge you now face.

AUGUST 27

All God's Children

"Francis," he [Christ] said, "speak thus to the pope. A certain woman who was poor but very beautiful lived in a certain desert. A certain king loved her because of her very great beauty; he gladly married her and begot very handsome sons by her. When they had grown to adulthood and been brought up nobly, their mother said to them: 'Do not be ashamed, my loved ones, in that you are poor, for you are all sons of that king. Go gladly to his court and ask him for whatever you need.' Hearing this they were in admiration and rejoiced, and buoyed up by the assurance of their royal origin, they regarded want as riches, knowing that they would be heirs. They boldly presented themselves to the king and they did not fear the face of him whose likeness they bore. Recognizing his own likeness in them, the king wondered and asked whose sons they were. When they said they were the sons of that poor woman living in the desert, the king embraced them and said: 'You are my sons and heirs; fear not....'" The saint was made happy and glad by the parable and reported the holy message to the pope. (Celano, Second Life of St. Francis, 16)

LIVING AS FRANCIS DID

Jesus's words reminded Francis that all God's children bear his resemblance.

GROWING WITH FRANCIS

Who do I have difficulty respecting as much as I respect others? What can I do to remedy that?

Rich in Virtue

This woman was Francis, because he was fruitful in many sons, not because of any softness in his actions. The desert was the world, untilled and barren at that time in the teaching of virtues. The handsome and numerous progeny of sons was the great multitude of brothers adorned with every virtue. The king was the Son of God, to whom they bore a resemblance by their holy poverty. And they received nourishment at the table of the king, despising all shame over their meanness; for, content with imitating Christ and living by alms, they knew they would be happy amid the reproaches of the world. (Celano, Second Life of St. Francis, 17)

LIVING AS FRANCIS DID

In 1209, Francis and eleven friars met Pope Innocent III to ask his approval for their way of life. Yesterday's quote described a parable that Francis told the pope; today's quote explains it. Poverty was hardly foreign to Christ, and except for Matthew, the tax collector, the apostles were not wealthy men. Even he soon learned the richness of a life focused on imitating Christ. Both the apostles and Francis's first followers were rich in virtue— without becoming self-righteous. Their virtues prepared them to do the Lord's work under any circumstances.

GROWING WITH FRANCIS

Perform one of the corporal works of mercy—feed the hungry, give drink to the thirsty, clothe the naked, shelter the homeless, visit the sick, visit the imprisoned, or bury the dead—today or within the next week.

AUGUST 29

Nurture Virtues

At that time when the holy Francis returned from beyond the sea with Brother Leonard of Assisi as his companion, it happened that, weary and fatigued from the journey, he was riding on a donkey for a while. But his companion was following behind him, and not a little tired, he [Brother Leonard] began to say within himself, giving way to a bit of humanness: "This man's parents and mine were not accustomed to play together as equals. Yet he is riding and I on foot am leading the donkey." While he was thinking this, the holy man got down from the donkey and said: "Brother, it is not right that I should ride, and you go on foot, for you were more noble and more powerful than I in the world." That brother was astounded at this and, filled with shame, he knew that he had been found out by the holy man. He cast himself at his feet and, bathed in tears, he made known his thought to him and begged his pardon. (Celano, Second Life of St. Francis, 31)

LIVING AS FRANCIS DID

Before this event, Brother Leonard probably considered himself a poor and simple friar, yet when weary, he reverted to his pre-conversion way of thinking about social status as indicating a person's worth. Old habits die only with great difficulty. Our thoughts nurture certain virtues and make others more unlikely.

GROWING WITH FRANCIS

Is God's grace trying to find a foothold in your life?

Descend to Grace

The blessed Francis frequently said that a true Friar Minor should not be long without going out to beg alms. "And the more noble my son is," he said, "the more ready should he be to go, for in this way will merits be heaped up for him." There was a certain brother in a certain place who never went out for alms but always ate more than several together at table. When the saint observed that he was a friend of the belly, one who shared the fruits without sharing the labor, he once said to him: "Go your way, brother fly, for you want to eat the sweat of your brothers and to do nothing in God's work. You are like brother drone who wants to first to eat the honey, though he does not do the work of the bees." When that carnal man saw that his gluttony was discovered, he went back to the world that he had not as yet given up. (Celano, Second Life of St. Francis, 75)

LIVING AS FRANCIS DID

A jarring event may show us that we are not as far advanced in a particular virtue as we might like to believe. In a sense, we do not *advance* in virtue; we *descend* into it by accepting God's grace at a deeper level and acting accordingly. We need not a spirituality of addition but one of subtraction.

GROWING WITH FRANCIS

Be as honest with yourself and others today as you can be.

AUGUST 31

What's Yours to Do?

Humility is the guardian and the ornament of all virtues. If the spiritual building does not rest upon it, it will fall to ruin, though it seems to be growing. This virtue filled Francis in a more copious abundance, so that nothing should be wanting to a man adorned with so many gifts. In his own opinion, he was nothing but a sinner, despite the fact that he was the ornament and splendor of all sanctity. He tried to build himself up upon this virtue, so that he would lay the foundation he had learned from Christ [Matthew 11:29]. Forgetting the things he had gained, he set before his eyes only his failings in the conviction that he lacked more than he had gained. (Celano, Second Life of St. Francis, 140)

LIVING AS FRANCIS DID

Humility is basic to every virtue: it never forgets that every gift comes from God, and it is always open to growth. In his early twenties Francis kissed a leper; the poor man of Assisi's humility was even greater in his mid-forties. He told the friars that he had done what was his to do, and he assured them that the Lord would teach them what was theirs to do.

GROWING WITH FRANCIS

As the years piled up, Francis became poorer and more simple because he increasingly aligned his prayers and his works with God's grace. Do the same.

Service to the Poor

Francis understood Jesus's washing the feet of his disciples at the Last Supper at a very deep level. He did not need encouragement to be a servant leader; no other way of leading would have made sense to him. Not everyone in the brotherhood came to that conclusion as quickly as he did, but he patiently led them to accept the Lord's style of servant leadership. Before he got off his horse one day and embraced a leper as a brother in Christ, Francis probably had thrown a few coins to lepers from a very safe distance. Bonaventure later wrote that Francis's service to God began with a victory over himself. In fact, this incident helped Francis to see that what he had previously regarded as very bitter was, in fact, truly sweet.

Francis did not need the assurance of success in order to throw himself into service. During the year that he was a prisoner of war in Perugia, Francis decided to reach out to an embittered man shunned by his fellow prisoners.

As Francis's conversion went deeper and wider, he had fewer things (physical or otherwise) that needed to be protected. This made him increasingly open to the needs of other people. When and where he could help, he always did so. Regardless of his resources at any given moment, Francis could always treat those in need as people created and loved by God.

Most people do not feel threatened by someone who lives God's truth at a very deep level; that's why most men and women felt comfortable around Francis. His humility and simplicity led quickly to generous service. Early on, Francis resolved never to refuse what he could offer if someone asked for help "for the love of God."

The healings and other miracles that Francis worked during his lifetime were never done to enhance his status; they were simply part of being a servant leader. If other people were tempted to measure Francis's actions by some other yardstick, he gently but effectively helped them understand his true motivation.

At times, Francis acted as a servant leader to people who were rich or politically very powerful. He was not afraid to call them to conversion as well, to confess their sins, to serve Christ among people who lacked life's most basic necessities.

Many rich and powerful people were converted to the Lord's ways by Francis's humble service on behalf of poor people. When the bishop of Assisi and its mayor were in a very bitter dispute, Francis invited them to a meeting and sent two friars to sing about the need to forgive.

When a peasant once cautioned Francis to be as good as people said he was, Francis could easily have taken offense at these words. Instead, he was genuinely grateful for this reminder.

SEPTEMBER 1

Using God's Measure

This is how God inspired me, Brother Francis, to embark upon a life of penance. When I was in sin, the sight of lepers nauseated me beyond measure; but then God himself led me into their company, and I had pity on them. When I had once become acquainted with them, what had previously nauseated me became a source of spiritual and physical consolation for me. After that I did not wait long before leaving the world. (Testament)

Living as Francis Did

Francis was steeped in knowledge of the Bible; here he is probably alluding to St. Paul's words: "Yet whatever gains I have, these I have come to regard as loss because of Christ. More than that, I regard everything as loss because of the surpassing value of knowing Christ Jesus my Lord. For his sake I have suffered the loss of all things, and I regard them as rubbish, in order that I may gain Christ and be found in him." (Philippians 3:7–9)

We tend to pride ourselves on not wasting time and energy. Before this chance meeting, Francis probably did not consider anyone suffering from leprosy as a person loved by God. That day, life changed for Francis. He did not have a blueprint for his entire life, but Francis would never return to the self-serving belief that the leper was cursed by God.

Growing with Francis

There are many ways of calculating loss and gain. Today, use God's way of measuring them.

Victory over Self

Then the holy lover of complete humility went to the lepers and lived with them, serving them most diligently for God's sake; and washing all foulness from them, he wiped away also the corruption of the ulcers, just as he said in his Testament: "When I was in sins [sic], it seemed extremely bitter to me to look at lepers, and the Lord himself led me among them and I practiced mercy with them." So greatly loathsome was the sight of lepers to him at one time, he used to say, that, in the days of his vanity, he would look at their houses only from a distance of two miles and he would hold his nostrils with his hands. But now, when by the grace and the power of the Most High he was beginning to think of holy and useful things, while he was still clad in secular garments, he met a leper one day and, made stronger than himself, he kissed him. From then on he began to despise himself more and more, until, by the mercy of the Redeemer, he came to perfect victory over himself. (Celano, First Life of St. Francis, 17)

LIVING AS FRANCIS DID

Serving the poor required Francis to achieve victory over himself, a victory over the conventional wisdom of his times about who counts and who doesn't. God's grace opened for Francis a new world of what God was asking of him.

GROWING WITH FRANCIS

Rejoice in any victory over yourself that may present itself today.

SEPTEMBER 3

Walk the Walk

Of other poor, too, while he yet remained in the world and still followed the world, he was the helper, stretching forth a hand of mercy to those who had nothing, and showing compassion to the afflicted. For when one day, contrary to his custom, for he was a most courteous person, he upbraided a certain poor man who had asked an alms of him, he was immediately sorry; and he began to say to himself that it was a great reproach and a shame to withhold what was asked from one who had asked in the name of so great a King. He therefore resolved in his heart never in the future to refuse any one, if at all possible, who asked for the love of God. This he most diligently did and carried out, until he sacrificed himself entirely and in every way; and thus he became first a practicer before he became a teacher of the evangelical counsel: To him who asks of thee, he said, give; and from him who would borrow of thee, do not turn away [Matthew 5:42]. (Celano, First Life of St. Francis, 17)

LIVING AS FRANCIS DID

Francis may have congratulated himself for initially refusing this request, perhaps rationalizing that the man was not truly in need. Francis walked the walk, refusing to recommend virtues he practiced sparingly. He was the real deal.

GROWING WITH FRANCIS

Be courteous to everyone who seeks help—even if you cannot alleviate their immediate need.

Serve the Marginalized

During the day, those who knew how labored with their hands, staying in the houses of lepers, or in other decent places, serving all humbly and devotedly. They did not wish to exercise any position from which scandal might arise, but always doing what is holy and just, honest and useful, they led all with whom they came into contact to follow their example of humility and patience. (Celano, First Life of St. Francis, 39)

LIVING AS FRANCIS DID

If PR companies had existed in Francis's day, he would not have hired one to publicize what he and his brothers were doing. God knew how they were serving; nothing more was needed. Wordless sermons are ultimately the best ones. No one can argue with good example and integrity. The good example of a holy life makes any preacher's words all the more powerful.

Members of the Franciscan family still minister to people suffering from Hansen's disease, but they also minister to people who may be marginalized in society in other ways: day laborers, immigrants, poor people, those in prison, men and women who are no longer healthy, orphans, widows, and…well, you know who they are in your society. Conventional wisdom rarely reflects God's judgment.

GROWING WITH FRANCIS

Strive to change any actions that contradict Francis's words in favor of serving God's people in need.

SEPTEMBER 5

God Heals

Once when the holy man of God Francis was going about through various regions to preach the kingdom of God, he came to a certain city called Toscanella. There, when he was sowing the seed of life [Luke 8:11–15] in his usual way, a certain soldier of that city gave him hospitality; he had an only son who was lame and weak of body. Though he was a young child, he had passed the years of weaning; still he remained in a cradle. When the father of the boy saw the great sanctity of the man of God, he humbly cast himself at his feet, begging from him health for his son. But Francis, who considered himself useless and unworthy of such great power and grace, refused for a long time to do this. But finally overcome by the insistence of his petitions, he prayed and then put his hand upon the boy and, blessing him, raised him up. Immediately, with all present looking on and rejoicing, the boy arose completely restored and began to walk here and there about the house. (Celano, First Life of St. Francis, 65)

LIVING AS FRANCIS DID

Francis did not cure the boy immediately, perhaps because he feared that those who witnessed such a healing would attribute it to him rather than to God. He restored that young boy to his family but also to the wider society. No one falls beneath God's radar.

GROWING WITH FRANCIS

Today, treat everyone as someone on God's radar.

Caring Heals

A certain woman from the city mentioned just above [Narni], who had been struck blind, merited to receive immediately the sight she desired when the blessed Francis drew the sign of the cross upon her eyes. At Gubbio there was a woman both of whose hands were so crippled that she could do no work at all with them. When she learned that St. Francis had entered the city, she immediately ran to him; and with her face covered with misery and sadness, she showed her crippled hands to him and began to ask him to touch them. Moved to pity he touched her and healed her. Immediately the woman went home full of joy, made a kind of cheese cake with her own hands, and offered it to the holy man. He took a little of it in his kindness and commanded the woman to eat the rest of it with her family. (Celano, First Life of St. Francis, 67)

LIVING AS FRANCIS DID

Both Francis and Clare sometimes traced the sign of the cross on someone who needed a healing. Their action showed that it is God who heals; humans are only the means of that healing. Francis may well have been embarrassed when the healed woman offered him her cheese cake. He took a little of it but directed her to share the rest with her family.

GROWING WITH FRANCIS

Call or write a sick friend or relative. Caring heals.

SEPTEMBER 7

God's in Charge

Also at Città di Castello there was a woman obsessed by the devil. When the most blessed father Francis was in this city, the woman was brought to the house where he was staying. That woman, standing outside, began to gnash her teeth and, her face twisted, she began to set up a great howl, as unclean spirits do. Many people of both sexes from that city came and pleaded with St. Francis in her behalf, for that evil spirit had long tormented and tortured her and had disturbed them with his loud cries. The holy father then sent to her a brother who was with him, wishing to discover whether it was really a devil or deception on the part of the woman. When that woman saw him, she began to deride him, knowing that it was not Francis who had come out. The holy father was inside praying. He came out when he had finished his prayer. But the woman, unable to stand his power, began to tremble and roll about on the ground. St. Francis called to her and said: "In virtue of obedience, I command you, unclean spirit, to go out of her." Immediately he [the unclean spirit] left her, without injuring her, but departing in great anger. (Celano, First Life of St. Francis, 70)

LIVING AS FRANCIS DID

Demonic possession still exists today. Prayer is a key part of any exorcism.

GROWING WITH FRANCIS

Be quick to affirm that God is in charge of this world.

Sharing with the Poor

The father of the poor, the poor Francis, conforming himself to the poor in all things, was grieved when he saw someone poorer than himself, not because he longed for vainglory, but only from a feeling of compassion. And, though he was content with a tunic that was quite poor and rough, he very frequently longed to divide it with some poor person. But that this very rich poor man, drawn on by a great feeling of affection, might be able to help the poor in some way, he would ask the rich of this world, when the weather was cold, to give him a mantle or some furs. And when, out of devotion, they willingly did what the most blessed father asked of them, he would say to them: "I will accept this from you with this understanding that you do not expect ever to have it back again." And when he met the first poor man, he would clothe him with what he had received with joy and gladness. He bore it very ill if he saw a poor person reproached or if he heard a curse hurled upon any creature by anyone. (Celano, First Life of St. Francis, 76)

Living as Francis Did

By seeking and accepting the gift of warm clothing, Francis was reminding people able to do so to provide such clothing as witness to their solidarity with those in need.

Growing with Francis

The weather will soon turn colder. Do you have any warm clothing you could give away?

Avoid Stereotypes

Once it happened that a certain brother uttered a word of invective against a certain poor man who had asked for an alms, saying to him: "See, perhaps you are a rich man and pretending to be poor." Hearing this, the father of the poor, St. Francis, was greatly saddened, and he severely rebuked the brother who had said such a thing and commanded him to strip himself before the poor man and, kissing his feet, beg pardon of him. For, he was accustomed to say: "Who curses a poor man does an injury to Christ, whose noble image he wears, the image of him who made himself poor for us in this world." Frequently, therefore, when he found the poor burdened down with wood or other things, he offered his own shoulders to help them, though his shoulders were very weak. (Celano, First Life of St. Francis, 76)

LIVING AS FRANCIS DID

It's easy to blame poor women, men, and children for being poor. Francis was courteous with everyone because each person has been made in the image and likeness of God. Francis's rebuke of the brother who spoke harshly to a poor man was part of that brother's journey of conversion. It is unlikely that he ever forgot Francis's words on that occasion.

GROWING WITH FRANCIS

Humbly but firmly challenge the next person you hear suggesting that poor people are simply lazy, or whatever stereotype that person is applying to poor people.

Choose a Different Path

Indeed, once when there was a bloody battle between the citizens of Perugia and those of Assisi, Francis was made captive with several others and endured the squalors of a prison. His fellow captives were consumed with sorrow, bemoaning miserably their imprisonment; Francis rejoiced in the Lord, laughed at his chains and despised them. His grieving companions resented his happiness and considered him insane and mad. Francis replied prophetically: "Why do you think I rejoice? There is another consideration, for I will yet be venerated as a saint throughout the whole world." And so it has truly come about; everything he said has been fulfilled.

There was at that time among his fellow prisoners a certain proud and completely unbearable knight whom the rest were determined to shun, but Francis's patience was not disturbed. He put up with the unbearable knight and brought the others to peace with him. Capable of every grace, a chosen vessel of virtues, he poured out his gifts on all sides. (Celano, Second Life of St. Francis, 4)

LIVING AS FRANCIS DID

Francis's saying that he would eventually be recognized as a saint may not interest us as much as the patience he demonstrated with the unbearable knight in this story. He could have joined fellow prisoners in putting down the knight, but chose a different path.

GROWING WITH FRANCIS

Let choosing to be a peacemaker today be your challenge, even if that requires a great deal of patience and you risk being misunderstood.

SEPTEMBER 11

Seek and Find

Freed from his chains a short time later, he became more kindly toward the needy…. One day he met a knight who was poor and well nigh naked; moved by pity, he gave him for Christ's sake the costly garments he was wearing. How did he conduct himself any differently from the way the most holy Martin [of Tours, a saint] conducted himself, except that, while both had the same purpose and both did the same deed, they differed in the way they acted. Francis first gave his garments before the rest of his things; Martin first gave up the rest of his things and then finally his garments. Both lived poor and feeble [Isaiah 16:14] in this world; both entered heaven rich. The latter, a knight, but poor, cut his garment in two to clothe a poor man; the former, not a knight, but rich, clothed a poor knight with his whole garment. Both, having fulfilled the command of Christ [Matthew 5:42], merited to be visited by Christ in a vision; one was praised for his perfection, the other was graciously invited to fulfill what was yet lacking. (Celano, Second Life of St. Francis, 5)

Living as Francis Did

Martin of Tours was one of the first saints who was not a martyr, besides saints such as Mary, Joseph, and the apostle John.

Growing with Francis

Seek out someone who needs a kindness today.

SEPTEMBER 12

Kissing Lepers

For among all the unhappy spectacles of the world Francis naturally abhorred lepers; but one day he met a leper while he was riding near Assisi. Though the leper caused him no small disgust and horror, nevertheless, lest like a transgressor of a commandment he should break his given word, he got off the horse and prepared to kiss the leper. But when the leper put out his hand as though to receive something, he received money along with a kiss. And immediately mounting his horse, Francis looked here and there about him; but though the plain lay open and clear on all sides, and there were no obstacles about, he could not see the leper anywhere.

Filled with wonder and joy as a result, after a few days he took care to do the same thing again. He went to the dwelling places of the lepers, and after he had given each leper some money, he kissed his hand and his mouth. Thus he exchanged the bitter for the sweet, and manfully prepared himself to carry out the rest. (Celano, Second Life of St. Francis, 9)

LIVING AS FRANCIS DID

Celano's second telling of this story is a bit more dramatic, perhaps because some of Francis's companions gave him details that Francis had shared. The suggestion is that this leper was Christ. Francis was willing to recognize people suffering from this disease as his brothers and sisters in Christ.

GROWING WITH FRANCIS

Speak up for some person or group being maligned by others.

SEPTEMBER 13

Offer Compassion

Once when the blessed Francis wanted to go to a certain hermitage that he might devote himself more freely to contemplation there, he obtained an ass from a certain poor man to ride on, because he was not a little weak. Since it was summer, the peasant, following the man of God up the mountain, became fatigued from the difficulty and the length of the trip; and before they had reached the place, he collapsed exhausted by a burning thirst. He called after the saint and begged him to have pity on him; he said he would die unless he would be refreshed by some drink. The holy man of God, who always had compassion on those who were suffering, got down without delay from the ass and kneeling upon the ground, he stretched his hands toward heaven; and he did not let up in his prayers until he felt he had been heard. "Hurry," he said to the peasant, "and you will find living water over there, which Christ has just now mercifully brought from the rock for you to drink."… The peasant drank the water that came from the rock by the power of him who had prayed. (Celano, Second Life of St. Francis, 46)

LIVING AS FRANCIS DID

This incident is recorded in one of Giotto's frescoes in the upper basilica of St. Francis in Assisi.

GROWING WITH FRANCIS

Strike a rock, and see what water flows forth from your prayer.

SEPTEMBER 14

Doing What I Can

What tongue can tell how great was this man's compassion toward the poor? Truly, he had an inborn kindness which was doubled by a kindness given him from on high. Therefore the soul of Francis melted toward the poor, and to those to whom he could not extend a helping hand, he at least showed his affection. Whatever he saw in anyone of want, whatever of penury, he transferred in his mind, by a quick change, to Christ. Thus in all the poor he saw the Son of the poor lady [Blessed Virgin Mary], and he bore naked in his heart him whom she bore naked in her hands. But though he had laid aside all envy, he could not be without envy of poverty. If indeed he saw someone poorer than himself, he was immediately envious, and in the struggle for complete poverty he feared to be outdone by another. (Celano, Second Life of St. Francis, 83)

LIVING AS FRANCIS DID

In Matthew 25:31–46, Jesus describes those who are rewarded for feeding the hungry, clothing the naked, and so on. He goes on to condemn other people who refused this help to their brothers and sisters. They failed to make a vital connection. Once Francis learned to make that connection, he never failed to act on it.

GROWING WITH FRANCIS

Although you cannot feed every hungry person in the world today or respond to every urgent need, that should not prevent you from doing what you can.

SEPTEMBER 15

Free to Give

Another time, when Francis was returning from Siena, he met a certain poor man and said to his companion: "Brother, we must return this mantle to that poor man to whom it belongs. We borrowed it from him until we should meet someone poorer than ourselves." His companion, thinking about his father's need, obstinately refused, lest Francis provide for another by neglecting himself. The saint said to him: "I do not want to be a thief; for it would be considered a theft in us if we did not give to someone who is in greater need than we." The other gave in, and Francis gave over his mantle. (Celano, Second Life of St. Francis, 87)

LIVING AS FRANCIS DID

Francis probably frustrated some of his brothers because he was quick to give away anything that he could—possibly to the injury of his own health. There may have been times when they persuaded Francis to keep what he was about to give away by offering the compassionate service Francis wanted to give. A person with a strong sense of appropriation (I have only what I deserve) would feel threatened by the generosity described here. Because Francis moved beyond that sense, he was free to give whatever he could.

GROWING WITH FRANCIS

Do you think you deserve more than you already have? If so, every act of generosity may lead to a feeling of great loss. However, if you feel that you have more than you deserve, you will be ready to imitate the generosity of Francis.

SEPTEMBER 16

People Matter

Once the mother of two of the brothers came to the saint confidently asking an alms. The holy father had pity on her and said to his vicar, Brother Peter of Catania: "Can we give some alms to our mother?" Francis was accustomed to call the mother of any brother his mother and the mother of all the brothers. Brother Peter answered him: "There is nothing left in the house that could be given her." And he [Peter] added: "We have one New Testament from which we read the lessons at Matins [Office of Readings] since we do not have a breviary." Blessed Francis said to him: "Give the New Testament to our mother that she might sell it to take care of her needs, since we are admonished by it to help the poor [Luke 2:33]. I believe indeed that the gift of it will be more pleasing to God than our reading from it." The book, therefore, was given to the woman, and thus the first Testament that was in the order was given away through this holy kindness. (Celano, Second Life of St. Francis, 91)

LIVING AS FRANCIS DID

So strong was Francis's sense of family that he called the mother of any friar "our mother." Her need was as important as his own mother's need. People were more important than objects for Francis.

GROWING WITH FRANCIS

Do something today to show that people are more important to you than objects.

SEPTEMBER 17

Accepting Truth

Not only did the man of God show himself humble before his superiors; but also among his equals and those beneath him he was more ready to be admonished and corrected than to give admonitions. Wherefore when one day he was riding on an ass, because weak and infirm as he was he could not go by foot, he passed through the field of a peasant who happened to be working there just then; the peasant ran over to him and asked solicitously if he were Brother Francis. When the man of God humbly replied that he was the man he was asking about, the peasant said: "Try to be as good as you are said to be by all men, for many put their trust in you. Therefore I admonish you never to be other than you are expected to be." But when the man of God Francis heard this, he got down from the ass and threw himself before the peasant and humbly kissed his feet, thanking him for being kind enough to give him this admonition. (Celano, Second Life of St. Francis, 142)

LIVING AS FRANCIS DID

Francis was considered a saint by many, and few would have dared to approach him in this way. He "considered himself lowly before God and men," and humbly listened to the man's admonition.

GROWING WITH FRANCIS

How might you react if someone speaks a hard truth to you today that you need to hear?

SEPTEMBER 18

Reach Out to the Sick

Francis had great compassion for the sick, great concern for their needs. When the kindness of secular people sent him choice foods, even though he needed them more than others, he gave them to the rest of the sick. He transferred to himself the afflictions of all who were sick, offering them words of sympathy when he could not give them help. On days of fast he himself would eat, lest the sick should be ashamed to eat; and he was not ashamed to beg meat through the public places of the towns for a sick brother. But he admonished the ill to bear their troubles patiently and not to give scandal when all their wishes were not satisfied. (Celano, Second Life of St. Francis, 175)

LIVING AS FRANCIS DID

There were few social safety nets in Francis's day. Individual Christians and groups of Christians tried to care for people who were sick. This prompted donors to feel confident that their gifts would be well used—not simply for the benefit of the friars but indeed for people in even greater need. Even when Francis could not bring all the relief that he wanted to offer, he urged people not to allow their illness to make them bitter.

GROWING WITH FRANCIS

Whom have you been procrastinating to call or visit: a sick neighbor or relative, someone from church? You cannot take away their pain, but you might take away their sense of loneliness.

SEPTEMBER 19

Anonymous Kindness

Among other words used in ordinary conversation, he could never hear the love of God without a kind of transformation within himself. For immediately upon hearing the love of God, he would become excited, stirred, and inflamed, as though an inner chord of his heart had been plucked by the plectrum [somewhat like a guitar pick] of the outward voice of the speaker. He said that to offer the love of God to get an alms was a noble prodigality, and those who valued it less than money were most foolish men. He himself kept unfailingly to his death the resolution he had made while he was still enmeshed in worldly things, namely, that he would never turn away a poor man who asked an alms for the love of God. For on one occasion when a poor man asked an alms for the love of God and he had nothing, he took a scissors and was going to quickly cut up his tunic. He would have done this too, but he was detected by his brothers, and instead he saw to it that the poor man was provided for by some other means. "The love of him," he said, "who loved us much is much to be loved." (Celano, Second Life of St. Francis, 196)

Living as Francis Did

The generosity of Francis inspired compassion on the part of his brothers.

Growing with Francis

Do something generous today and try hard not to be noticed.

SEPTEMBER 20

Touch Another Life

Even as a young man Francis had an open-handed sympathy for the poor which God had inspired in his heart. This bore him company as he grew up and filled his heart with such generosity that he refused to turn a deaf ear to the Gospel and resolved to give alms to everyone who approached him, especially if it was for the love of God. One time he was caught in a rush of business and, contrary to his custom, he sent away a beggar who had begged an alms for love of God without giving him anything. Then he realized what he had done and he ran after him immediately and gave him a generous alms. There and then he promised God that he would never again refuse anyone who asked for love of him, as long as he had anything to give. (Bonaventure, Major Life of St. Francis, I, 1)

LIVING AS FRANCIS DID

When we talk about someone's conversion, we tend to underestimate the importance of an event such as this one. It was not nearly as dramatic as hearing the San Damiano crucifix speak or kissing a leper along the road, but many genuine conversions involve a promise to oneself, such as Francis made in this story.

GROWING WITH FRANCIS

What promises have you made to yourself? Do others benefit from those promises? Make at least one new promise that touches others' lives.

SEPTEMBER 21

Hidden Needs

Francis had no idea of God's plan for him. He was completely taken up with the affairs of his father's business and his mind was intent on the things of earth because of the corruption of human nature, so that he had never learned to raise his mind to heaven, or acquired a taste for the things of God. Adversity is one of the best means of sharpening a person's spiritual perception and so "the power of the Lord reached out to him and the Most High relented in His dealings with him" (Ezekiel 1:3 and Psalm 76:11). God brought him low with a prolonged illness, in order to prepare his soul to receive the Holy Spirit. When he recovered and was going about dressed as usual in keeping with his position, he met a knight who was of noble birth but very poor, so that he was not properly clad. Francis felt sorry for him and immediately took off his own clothes and gave them to him. At one and the same time he fulfilled the twofold duty of relieving the poverty of the poor and saving a nobleman from embarrassment. (Bonaventure, Major Life of St. Francis, I, 2)

LIVING AS FRANCIS DID

Francis learned to live one day at a time. Later he would be even more generous but on this day he won a small victory over himself, doing something he hadn't intended when he arose that morning.

GROWING WITH FRANCIS

Who has a need to which you have been blind? Try to address it today.

SEPTEMBER 22

Seeing Christ in Others

Francis now developed a spirit of poverty, with a deep sense of humility, and an attitude of profound compassion. He had never been able to stand the sight of lepers, even at a distance, and he always avoided meeting them, but now in order to arrive at perfect self-contempt he served them devotedly with all humility and kindness, because the prophet Isaiah tells us that Christ crucified was regarded as a leper and despised. He visited their houses frequently and distributed alms among them generously, kissing their hands and lips with deep compassion. (Bonaventure, Major Life of St. Francis, I, 6)

LIVING AS FRANCIS DID

After Francis conquered his initial revulsion at the sight of lepers, the other friars began to do likewise, caring for their wounds, providing food, and in other ways showing that people suffering from leprosy were still part of the human family. Some friars came from even wealthier backgrounds than Francis, and showing compassion for lepers may have been a bigger adjustment for them than it was for Francis. Seeing Christ in the people whom he served kept renewing Francis's generosity, especially if those people did not seem very grateful.

GROWING WITH FRANCIS

Be ready to serve even if circumstances make it harder than usual. Seeing Christ in the people you help will be as important for you as it was for Francis. In the long run, we become whatever we choose consistently. Are your choices tending toward greater generosity or away from it?

SEPTEMBER 23

Taking a Risk

When he was approached by beggars, he was not content merely to give what he had—he wanted to give his whole self to them. At times he took off his clothes and gave them away, or ripped or tore pieces from them, if he had nothing else at hand. He came to the aid of priests who were in need, respectfully and devoutly, especially when it concerned the upkeep of the altar. In this way he earned a share in the homage offered to God, while relieving the needs of those who pay homage to him. (Bonaventure, Major Life of St. Francis, I, 6)

LIVING AS FRANCIS DID

As Francis's conversion went deeper and wider, he made connections that must have baffled many of his contemporaries. "What a waste," some of them may have muttered silently, feeling that Francis was throwing his life away on people who did not deserve that kind of attention and generosity. Francis had a sense of loss and gain that did not reflect the conventional wisdom of his day.

He was especially concerned that churches be clean, that altar linens be worthy of their task, and that the liturgy be celebrated in a fitting manner.

GROWING WITH FRANCIS

Does how you measure loss and gain simply reflect the conventional wisdom around you? Have you ever taken a risk for a poor person that seemed to backfire? How did that experience influence your future contacts with poor people?

Do What You Can

He had been taught by a revelation that anyone entering the Order should begin by fulfilling the precept of the Gospel, "If you wish to be perfect, go, sell your possessions, and give the money to the poor" (Matthew 19:21). In obedience to the Gospel and in order to avoid scandal, such as might arise if a friar retained his property, he never received anyone into the Order unless he had renounced everything and kept nothing for himself. When a man asked to be received to the Order in the Marches of Ancona, he told him, "If you want to join Christ's poor, give what you have to the poor in the world." (Bonaventure, Major Life of St. Francis, VII, 3)

Living as Francis Did

Francis would not take goods or money from someone who was becoming a friar for two reasons: first, other friars might deprive truly poor people of these goods; and second, the man entering the friars might be making his own life easier. Those joining the friars should experience a lower standard of living than they had previously. If not, they will be in competition with genuinely poor people.

Growing with Francis:

Many parishes are seeking volunteers this month: to help with catechetical programs, to bring Communion to the sick, to assist with the Rite for the Christian Initiation of Adults, and more. No one can do everything, but everyone can do something. Are you doing what you can?

Big Deal or Not?

At that the candidate went off, but he was influenced by human affection to give his belongings to his relatives, not to the poor. When he came back and told the saint what he had done, Francis reproached him bitterly and said" "On your way, Brother Fly. You never left your home or your family. You gave what you had to your relatives and cheated the poor. You are not worthy of Christ's poor. You tried to begin your religious life by yielding to an earthly attachment and laid a worthless foundation for a spiritual building." The poor fellow immediately returned to his family and demanded his property; he had refused to give it to the poor and so he quickly abandoned the idea of embracing the religious life. (Bonaventure, Major Life of St. Francis, VII, 3)

LIVING AS FRANCIS DID

Motivation can be very complicated and in need of continual purifying. In this case, Francis judged that this would-be friar seriously lacked the proper motivation. It would not take long before his self-serving approach would express itself in some more serious way—to the detriment of the friars and those whom they were sent to serve. Evil is endlessly subtle, banal. It always presents itself as no big deal. If the action in question is truly no big deal, then it should not be difficult to stop insisting on it.

GROWING WITH FRANCIS

How do you evaluate what is a big deal? What is the basis for your judgment?

SEPTEMBER 26

Focus on Jesus

While travelling to a hermitage where he planned to devote himself to prayer, St. Francis rode an ass belonging to a poor laborer because he was weak. It was summertime and, as the owner of the animal followed the saint into the mountains, he was exhausted by the long and gruelling journey. Fainting with thirst, he suddenly cried out after the saint. "I'll die of thirst, if I don't get a drink immediately." Francis dismounted there and then and knelt on the ground with his hands stretched out to heaven, and there he prayed until he knew that he had been heard. When he had finished, he told his benefactor" "Go to that rock and you will find running water. Christ in his mercy has made it flow there for you just now." By God's wonderful condescension which bows so easily to his servants a thirsty human being was able to drink from a rock, quenching his thirst from solid stone, by the power of one man's prayer. Water had never been found at that spot before and none could ever be found there afterwards, although a careful search was made. (Bonaventure, Major Life of St. Francis, VII, 12)

LIVING AS FRANCIS DID

Celano's version of this story was already presented on August 13. Bonaventure chooses to place a greater emphasis on the power of Francis's prayer on this occasion.

GROWING WITH FRANCIS

Model Francis, and give water to a thirsty friend, metaphorically speaking.

SEPTEMBER 27

Respect as Gift

Francis sympathized lovingly and compassionately with those stricken with any physical affliction and he immediately referred to Christ the poverty or deprivation he saw in anyone. He was kind and gentle by nature and the love of Christ merely intensified this. His soul melted at the sight of the poor or infirm and where he could not offer material assistance he lavished his affection. A friar once brusquely refused a beggar who had asked for an alms at an awkward moment. When Francis heard about it, he made the friar take off his habit in his love for the poor, and cast himself at the feet of the beggar, confessing his fault and begging his prayers and forgiveness. The friar obeyed humbly and Francis remarked gently, "My dear brother, when you see a beggar, you are looking at an image of our Lord and his poor Mother. When you see a sick person, remember the infirmities he bore for us." Francis saw Christ's image in every poor person he met and he was prepared to give them everything he had, even if he himself had urgent need of it. (Bonaventure, Major Life of St. Francis, VIII, 5)

LIVING AS FRANCIS DID

Francis often included the Blessed Virgin Mary when he made reference to Christ's poverty. People sometimes allow poverty to embitter them. That was never the case with Jesus, Mary, or Francis.

GROWING WITH FRANCIS

You may not be able to offer whatever someone else needs, but you can, however, always respect them.

SEPTEMBER 28

Spare Nothing

When he was returning from Siena on one occasion, he met a beggar at a time when he himself was wearing a short cloak over his habit because he was not well. At the sight of the poor man's destitution, Francis said to his companion, "We'll have to give this cloak back to that poor beggar, because it belongs to him. We only got it on loan until we found someone in greater need of it." His companion, however, knew well that the saint himself needed the cloak badly and he was reluctant to see him neglect himself while providing for someone else. "But," protested the saint, "God the great Almsgiver will regard it as a theft on my part, if I do not give what I have to someone who needs it more." Whenever he received anything for his needs from a benefactor, he always used to ask permission to give the article away, if he met someone poorer than himself. He spared absolutely nothing—cloaks, habits, books, or altar cloths—…in order to obey the commandment of love; and when he met beggars carrying heavy loads on the road, he often took the weight on his own weak shoulders. (Bonaventure, Major Life of St. Francis, VIII, 5)

LIVING AS FRANCIS DID

Sharing burdens as well as possessions was Francis's mission.

GROWING WITH FRANCIS

Look for a connection between Christ and the needs of someone you meet today.

SEPTEMBER 29

Good Envy

It happened one day when the man of God was going about preaching that he met a certain poor man along the way. When he saw his nakedness, he was struck with compunction, and he turned to his companion, saying: "This man's want brings great shame to us and rebukes our poverty severely." His companion replied: "For what reason, Brother?" And the saint replied with a sad voice: "For my wealth, for my spouse, I chose poverty; but see, poverty shines forth more brightly in this man. Are you ignorant of the fact that the word has gone about the world that we are the poorest of men for Christ's sake? But this poor man proves that the fact is otherwise." O enviable envy! This is not that envy that is grieved over the goods of others; it is not that envy that is darkened by the rays of the sun; not that envy that is opposed to kindness; not that envy that is tortured by spite. Do you think that evangelical poverty has nothing about it to be envied? It has Christ and through him it has all things in all [1 Corinthians 12:6]. (Celano, Second Life of St. Francis, 84)

LIVING AS FRANCIS DID

Francis wasn't being theatrical; he was not focusing on himself or the friars' reputation. Francis desired to live honestly. If the friars could do without something, then it belonged to a poor person who needed it.

GROWING WITH FRANCIS

What goods or time do you have to give?

Honesty in Prayer

He often used to remark, "What a man is before God, that he is and no more." Consequently he was convinced that it was foolish to be elated when people showed him marks of respect; he was upset by praise, but overjoyed when he was insulted. He liked to have people scorn him—that spurred him on to do better—and hated to be praised, which could lead to a fall. When people praised the height of his sanctity, he used to command one of the friars to do the opposite and heap insults upon him. Then, as the friar obeyed reluctantly and called him a boor and a time-server, worthless and good for nothing, he would listen cheerfully and say with a smile, "God bless you, my son. What you say is true. That is the kind of thing the son of Peter Bernardone should have to listen to." (Bonaventure, Major Life of St. Francis, VI, 1)

LIVING AS FRANCIS DID

Francis was always ready to serve the needs of the poor because he always strove to live in the deepest truth about himself. Regular prayer helped ensure that Francis remembered who he was before God and acted accordingly.

GROWING WITH FRANCIS

As Jesus's story about the Pharisee and the tax collector praying in the Temple shows (Luke 18:9–14), prayer can mask dishonesty or express the truth. Make certain that your prayer is as honest as the tax collector's in this story.

Creatures

Perhaps no saint is more famous than Francis of Assisi for stories about harmony with plants, animals, and other humans. He could relate to God the doves, crows, swallows, fish, lambs, worms, falcons, pheasants, sheep, bees, rabbits, cicadas, and the famous wolf of Gubbio.

Francis showed great respect to flowers, rocks, trees, and even "Brother Fire" that was used to cure an eye disease from which he suffered. Francis's harmony with nature was part of the extraordinary inner freedom he demonstrated—even as his external freedom was progressively lessened by disease and illness.

Francis's great "Canticle of the Creatures" put all creation in the context of God's overflowing love. His earliest biographer wrote that Francis made of all creation a ladder by which he might retrace his steps to God, their creator. In the Middle Ages, Christians expected that holy men and women showed a greater harmony with animals than most other people. Saints remind us of the Garden of Eden where Adam and Eve lived peacefully with all creation.

Pope John Paul II's designation in 1979 of Francis as the patron saint of ecology is entirely fitting. Everyone seems at home in Francis's presence. People of deep religious faith and of no explicit faith recognize him as a brother.

While his contemporaries were tempted to prove their worth and importance by accumulating possessions, Francis gradually needed fewer and fewer possessions. Love for God and God's creation was quite enough for Francis. That spirit enabled the Poor Man of Assisi to reach out to people who were often shunned by other members of society. Francis made connections and links where his contemporaries saw only differences and possible threats to themselves.

At their best, all people drawn to the example of Francis live in harmony with creation and thus are naturally peacemakers. Francis's admirers are not Pollyannas, unable to recognize conflict around them or unwilling to deal with it; they simply know that evil never has the last word.

In a sense, holy people always become more transparent, more ready to show creation's inner connections. Knowing such people draws us closer to God, whose goodness was only barely revealed through the life of Francis of Assisi.

We may be tempted to think that Francis lived at a time when holiness was easier. An honest look at his life reveals a very different and grittier story. Through God's grace, Francis learned to make the most of the hand that was dealt to him. He used his talents as best he could, but he knew, as St. Paul had told the Corinthian Christians centuries before, "God gives the growth."

We may be attracted to stories about Francis that we consider winsome. If we met him today, *winsome* would probably be one of the last adjectives we would apply to him. God meant everything to Francis of Assisi; his relationship with creation reflected his relationship with God.

OCTOBER 1

Bless the Lord

Most high, all-powerful, all good, Lord!
  All praise is yours, all glory, all honor
  And all blessing.
To you, alone, Most High, do they belong.
  No mortal lips are worthy
  To pronounce your name.
All praise be yours, my Lord, through all that you have made,
  And first my lord Brother Sun,
  Who brings the day; and light you give to us through him.
How beautiful is he, how radiant in all his splendour!
  Of you, Most High, he bears the likeness.
All praise be yours, my Lord, through Sister Moon and Stars;
  In the heavens you have made them, bright
  And precious and fair.
(The Canticle of Brother Sun)

Living as Francis Did

Francis saw all creation as connected, all of it coming from an all-good God. Praise, blessing, and awe characterized Francis's relationship with all God's creation, including humans.

Growing with Francis

Before you go to bed tonight, look at the sun, moon, and stars, and thank God for all three—and everything else that has blessed your day.

OCTOBER 2

Conserve and Sustain

All praise be yours, my Lord, through Brothers Wind and Air,
  And fair and stormy, all the weather's moods,
  By which you cherish all that you have made.
All praise be yours, my Lord, through Sister Water,
  So useful, lowly, precious and pure.
All praise be yours, my Lord, through Brother Fire,
  Through whom you brighten up the night.
  How beautiful is he, how gay! Full of power and strength.
All praise be yours, my Lord, through Sister Earth, our mother,
  Who feeds us in her sovereignty and produces
  Various fruits with coloured flowers and herbs.
(The Canticle of Brother Sun)

LIVING AS FRANCIS DID

Wind, water, fire, and earth are creation's basic elements that work together to sustain life. Francis knew they held the world together, and praised this holy purpose.

GROWING WITH FRANCIS

Are you committed to reducing your carbon footprint on Mother Earth through more sustainable use of natural resources? What further steps can you take?

OCTOBER 3

Sister Death

Then he spent the few days that remained before his death in praise, teaching his companions whom he loved so much to praise Christ with him. He himself, in as far as he was able, broke forth in this psalm: With my voice, I cry to the Lord with my voice: with my voice I made supplication to the Lord [Psalm 142:1]. He also invited all creatures to praise God, and by means of the words he had composed earlier, he exhorted them to love God. He exhorted death itself, terrible and hateful to all, to give praise, and going joyfully to meet it, he invited it to make its lodging with him. "Welcome," he said, "my sister death." To the doctor he said: "Tell me bravely, brother doctor, that death, which is the gateway of life, is at hand." Then to the brothers: "When you see that I am brought to my last moments, place me naked upon the ground just as you saw me the day before yesterday; and let me lie there after I am dead for the length of time it takes one to walk a mile unhurriedly." The hour therefore came, and all the mysteries of Christ being fulfilled in him, he winged his way happily to God. (Celano, Second Life of St. Francis, 217)

LIVING AS FRANCIS DID

Francis saw "Sister Death" not as a great enemy but as a necessary part of his return to God's embrace.

GROWING WITH FRANCIS

How does this passage affect your feelings about death?

OCTOBER 4

Sending Francis Home

The larks are birds that love the noonday light and shun the darkness of twilight. But on the night that St. Francis went to Christ, they came to the roof of the house, though already the twilight of the night to follow had fallen, and they flew about the house for a long time amid a great clamor, whether to show their joy or their sadness in their own way by their singing, we do not know. Tearful rejoicing and joyful sorrow made up their song, either to bemoan the fact that they were orphaned children, or to announce that their father was going to his eternal glory. The city watchmen who guarded the place with great care, were filled with astonishment and called the others to witness the wonder. (Celano, Treatise on the Miracles of Blessed Francis, 32)

Living as Francis Did

Francis had a special affection for larks; he considered their brown feathers a sign of their closeness to God, of their humility. Thus, it was only fitting that larks should take notice of Francis's death—at twilight, an hour when they are not usually flying around. The harmony of all creation that Francis represented while alive did not end at death. Francis died on the plain below Assisi. The larks' movement attracted the attention of Assisi's watchmen, a thirty-minute walk up the hill.

The larks still swirl through the twilight in Assisi.

Growing with Francis

Be more attentive today to the beauty around you, especially the birds.

OCTOBER 5

For the Birds

When he came one day to a city called Alviano to preach the word of God, he went up to a higher place [Judges 13:16] so that he could be seen by all and he began to ask for silence. But when all the people had fallen silent and were standing reverently at attention, a flock of swallows, chattering and making a loud noise, were building nests in that same place. Since the blessed Francis could not be heard by the people over the chattering of the birds, he spoke to them saying: "My sisters, swallows, it is now time for me to speak, for you have already spoken enough. Listen to the word of the Lord and be silent and quiet until the word of the Lord is finished." And those little birds, to the astonishment and wonder of the people standing by, immediately fell silent, and they did not move from that place until the sermon was finished. When these men therefore saw this miracle, they were filled with the greatest admiration and said: "Truly this man is a saint and a friend of the Most High." And they hastened with the greatest devotion to at least touch his clothing, praising and blessing God [Luke 24:53]. (Celano, First Life of St. Francis, 59)

LIVING AS FRANCIS DID

Francis treated animals kindly because they pointed toward God.

GROWING WITH FRANCIS

Do you allow the animal stories about Francis to point you toward God?

OCTOBER 6

Gone Fishin'

He was moved by the same tender affection toward fish, too, which, when they were caught, and he had the chance, he threw back into the water, commanding them to be careful lest they be caught again. Once when he was sitting in a boat near a port in the lake of Rieti, a certain fisherman, who had caught a big fish popularly called a tinea [part of the carp family] offered it kindly to him. He accepted it joyfully and kindly and began to call it brother; then placing it in the water outside the boat, he began devoutly to bless the name of the Lord. And while he continued in prayer for some time, the fish played in the water beside the boat and did not go away from the place where it had been put until his prayer was finished and the holy man of God gave it permission to leave. For thus did the glorious father Francis, walking in the way of obedience and embracing perfectly the yoke of obedience to God, acquire great dignity in the sight of God in that creatures obeyed him. (Celano, First Life of St. Francis, 61)

LIVING AS FRANCIS DID

The Book of Genesis suggests that Adam and Eve respected all the animals. Disharmony in God's creation came through sin.

GROWING WITH FRANCIS

Many animal stories are connected to the lives of many saints. In your opinion, do those stories remain only at the level of cuteness? Why or why not?

OCTOBER 7

Lamb of God

Francis abounded in the spirit of charity; he was filled with compassion not only toward men in need, but even toward dumb animals, reptiles, birds, and other creatures, sensible and insensible. But, among all the various kinds of animals, he loved little lambs with a special predilection and more ready affection, because in the sacred scriptures the humility of our Lord Jesus Christ is more frequently likened to that of the lamb and best illustrated by the simile of a lamb [Isaiah 16:1; 53:7; Acts 8:32] So, all things, especially those in which some allegorical similarity, to the Son of God could be found, he would embrace more fondly and look upon more willingly. (Celano, First Life of St. Francis, 77)

Living as Francis Did

Lambs have long reminded many people of innocence, of creation's freshness. St. John the Baptist was the first person to call Jesus the "Lamb of God," a term that we continue to use at Mass in the public prayer before we receive Holy Communion. This lamb imagery led John the Evangelist to link the moment of Jesus's death to the very hour when lambs were killed for the feast of Passover.

Jesus recommended that his disciples be as innocent as lambs and as cunning as serpents. He reconciled seeming opposites more readily than we do.

Growing with Francis

Pay special attention today to any animals for which you are responsible.

OCTOBER 8

Filled with Compassion

[Francis once] met a certain man who had two little lambs hanging bound over his shoulder, taking them to the market to sell them. When blessed Francis heard them bleating, he was filled with pity. And he said to the man: "Why are you torturing my brother lambs tied up and hanging like this?" Answering, he said: "I am taking them to the market to sell them, because I need the money." The saint said: "What will happen to them then?" He answered: "Those who buy them will kill them and eat them." "God forbid," replied the saint, "this must not happen. Take the mantle I am wearing as their price and give the lambs to me." He quickly gave him the lambs and took the mantle, for the mantle was of much greater value. Now the saint had borrowed the mantle that day from a certain faithful man to ward off the cold. For the rest, the saint, after receiving the lambs, considered carefully what he should do with them; and, at the advice of his companion, he gave them to that man to take care of them; and he commanded him not to sell them at any time, nor to do them any harm, but to keep them, feed them, and take care of them conscientiously. (Celano, First Life of St. Francis, 79)

LIVING AS FRANCIS DID

We can only hope that this man honored Francis's unusual request.

GROWING WITH FRANCIS

Pray for those who raise sheep.

OCTOBER 9

Even the Worms

O simple piety and pious simplicity! Toward little worms even he glowed with a very great love, for he had read this saying about the Savior: I am a worm, not a man [Psalm 22:6]. Therefore he picked them up from the road and placed them in a safe place, lest they be crushed by the feet of the passersby. What shall I say of the lower creatures, when he would see to it that the bees would be provided with honey in the winter, or the best wine, lest they should die from the cold? He used to praise in public the perfection of their works and the excellence of their skill, for the glory of God, with such encomiums that he would often spend a whole day in praising them and the rest of creatures. For as of old the three youths in the fiery furnace [Daniel 3:1–97] invited all the elements to praise and glorify the Creator of the universe, so also this man, filled with the spirit of God, never ceased to glorify, praise, and bless the Creator and Ruler of all things in all the elements and creatures. (Celano, First Life of St. Francis, 80)

LIVING AS FRANCIS DID

We often pride ourselves on being able to separate things into their proper groupings. Francis rejoiced in recognizing their fundamental similarity as valuable parts of God's creation.

GROWING WITH FRANCIS

What can you do that is helpful for some type of animal in your area?

The Beauty of the Earth

How great a gladness do you think the beauty of the flowers brought to his mind when he saw the shape of their beauty and perceived the odor of their sweetness? He used to turn the eye of consideration immediately to the beauty of that flower that comes from the root of Jesse [Isaiah 11:1] and gives light in the days of spring [Sirach 50:8a] and by its fragrance has raised innumerable thousands from the dead. When he found an abundance of flowers, he preached to them and invited them to praise the Lord as though they were endowed with reason. In the same way he exhorted with the sincerest purity cornfields and vineyards, stones and forests and all the beautiful things of the fields, fountains of water and the green things of the gardens, earth and fire, air and wind, to love God and serve him willingly. (Celano, First Life of St. Francis, 81)

LIVING AS FRANCIS DID

Some people are tempted to roll their eyes at stories of Francis and his relationship with plants and animals, thinking him simply a thirteenth-century Doctor Doolittle. Did Francis discover a harmony in creation that we have overlooked? Are our environmental challenges part of the price that we pay for a false sense of entitlement about the use of earth's resources?

GROWING WITH FRANCIS

A beautiful flower does not need to justify its existence; it praises God simply by being that particular type of flower. Are you willing to acknowledge that? Francis was.

OCTOBER 11

Truly Free?

Finally, he called all creatures brother, and in a most extraordinary manner, a manner never experienced by others, he discerned the hidden things of nature with his sensitive heart, as one who had already escaped into the freedom of the glory of the sons of God [Romans 8:21]. O good Jesus, he is now praising you as admirable in heaven with all the angels, he who on earth preached you as lovable to every creature. (Celano, First Life of St. Francis, 81)

LIVING AS FRANCIS DID

We are quick to describe ourselves as free people, but are we as free as God wants us to be? Have we ever called some form of enslavement "freedom"? Has the pursuit of money, political power, or social status crossed over into enslavement? For ourselves? For other people? Doesn't every addiction present itself as a type of freedom? Don't people begin to break the stranglehold of addiction when they stop lying to themselves and begin describing things as they truly are? In a sense, all twelve-step programs are a means of accepting a new way of recognizing freedom and enslavement —and then acting in increasingly free ways.

Francis's ongoing conversion to the Lord's ways made Francis an increasingly free person. He once thought that despising lepers showed his freedom; eventually he found that freedom in serving them.

GROWING WITH FRANCIS

How integrated is your approach to life? What is keeping you from becoming more integrated, more truly free?

OCTOBER 12

Allow Awe

He embraced all things with a rapture of unheard of devotion, speaking to them of the Lord and admonishing them to praise him. He spared lights, lamps, and candles, not wishing to extinguish their brightness with his hand, for he regarded them as a symbol of Eternal Light. He walked reverently upon stones, because of him who was called the Rock [1 Corinthians 10:4]. When he used this versicle: Thou hast exalted me on a rock [Psalm 61:2], he would say for the sake of greater reverence: Thou hast exalted me at the foot of a rock. (Celano, Second Life of St. Francis, 165)

LIVING AS FRANCIS DID

Francis had a strong sense that all creation was sacramental—not that trees, rivers, flowers, animals, and so forth were gods but that they all came from a single source (God) and could lead attentive readers of all creation back to God. Such a view enabled Francis to read the Scriptures in a way that many people in his day could not. The psalms especially spoke to him because they often reflect a very sacramental view of creation. The imagery of the psalms is extremely concrete as the text above shows.

Francis made connections that many other people could not; he saw God at work where they did not. He was constantly filled with awe whereas many were bored with life.

GROWING WITH FRANCIS

Pick one of the Psalms today and read it. What mental images point you back to God? Count them as a blessing.

OCTOBER 13

Using Nature Gently

He forbade the brothers to cut down the whole tree when they cut wood, so that it might have hope of sprouting again. He commanded the gardener to leave the border around the garden undug, so that in their proper times the greenness of the grass and the beauty of flowers might announce the beauty of the Father of all things. He commanded that a little place be set aside in the garden for sweet-smelling and flowering plants, so that they would bring those who look upon them to the memory of the Eternal Sweetness. (Celano, Second Life of St. Francis, 165)

Living as Francis Did

Again, Francis saw God at work in all of creation. We often see ourselves in competition with creation, trying to find sufficient food, clothing, and shelter, worrying that what others take from creation will deprive us of our rightful share. If indeed creation is a zero-sum proposition, then whatever someone else takes means there will be that much less for me and my loved ones.

Reality TV shows often demonstrate how people act when they are competing for scarce goods. A person with uncommon skills may be highly prized for the moment by people who need those skills to survive. But such loyalties rarely endure, as these shows constantly show us.

Growing with Francis

Is it nature that needs taming? Or do you need to be trained to use nature unselfishly? Use nature gently.

OCTOBER 14

Big Deal?

He removed from the road little worms, lest they be crushed under foot; and he ordered that honey and the best wines be set out for the bees, lest they perish from want in the cold of winter. He called all animals by the name brother, though among all the kinds of animals he preferred the gentle. Who could possibly narrate everything? For that original goodness that will be one day all things in all already shown forth in this saint all things in all [1 Corinthians 12:6]. (Celano, Second Life of St. Francis, 165)

LIVING AS FRANCIS DID

In time, God will be everything in all of us; Francis of Assisi recognized that in his young adult years. He probably saw sin much more clearly than most people. And yet Francis also had a very acute sense of the original goodness of God's creation. The miser seeks happiness by acquiring more and more stuff, but the miser cannot be happy because there is always more stuff beyond his or her reach.

Francis's approach, on the other hand, emphasized that the goods of creation were intended for all people. Yes, there is a natural right of private property, but even that can give people a false sense of security.

GROWING WITH FRANCIS

How many things are a big deal in your life? Would people who know you well be surprised at your list of what belongs in that big deal category?

OCTOBER 15

Blessed Fire

This incident happened prior to the cauterizing of the veins between Francis's eyes and ears: But the blessed father...spoke thus to the fire: "My brother fire, that surpasses all other things in beauty, the Most High created you strong, beautiful, and useful. Be kind to me in this hour, be courteous. For I have loved you in the past in the Lord. I beseech the great Lord who made you that he temper your heat now so that I may bear it when you burn me gently." When his prayer was ended, he made the sign of the cross over the fire and then remained fearless. The doctor took the glowing and hot iron in his hands; all the brothers, overcome by human weakness, fled; and the saint offered himself joyfully and eagerly to the iron. The iron was plunged into the tender flesh with a hiss, and it was gradually drawn from the ear to the eyebrow in its cauterizing. How much pain that fire caused, the words of the saint himself, who knows best, testify. For when the brothers who had fled returned, the father said, smiling: "O fainthearted and weak of heart, why did you flee? In truth I say to you [Luke 4:25], I did not feel either the heat of the fire or any pain in my flesh." (Adapted from Celano, Second Life of St. Francis, 166)

Living as Francis Did

Francis could bless even the fire that was about to singe his flesh!

Growing with Francis

Bless something that you previously feared or scorned.

OCTOBER 16

Be Free

When the blessed Francis was going across the lake of Rieti to the hermitage of Greccio, he was sitting in a certain little boat. A certain fisherman offered him a waterfowl, that he might rejoice over it in the Lord. The blessed father accepted it joyfully, and opening his hands, he gently told it that it was free to fly away. But when it did not wish to leave, but wanted to rest there in his hands as in a nest, the saint raised his eyes and remained in prayer. And returning to himself as from another place after a long while, he gently commanded the bird to go back to its former freedom. So, upon receiving this permission along with a blessing, the bird flew away, showing its joy by a certain movement of the body. (Celano, Second Life of St. Francis, 167)

LIVING AS FRANCIS DID

Francis encouraged this bird to use the physical freedom that God created it to have. He saw things according to their deepest purpose, not according to how he could use them for his advantage. Francis could be extremely free with creatures because he lived in greater freedom than many women and men of his day. His was not freedom of wealth or political influence but freedom of knowing who he was before God—and therefore, who he was in relation to others and in his own eyes.

GROWING WITH FRANCIS

Have you grown in freedom this year? What is holding you back?

OCTOBER 17

Being My Best

When the blessed Francis was staying in a certain hermitage, shunning in his usual way the sight and conversation of men, a falcon that was making its nest in the place attached itself to him in a great bond of friendship. For always during the night it announced with its song and noise the hour at which the saint was accustomed to rise for worship of God. This was very pleasing to the saint of God, in that, by reason of the great solicitude of the bird for him, any delay on his part because of laziness was driven away. But when the saint was afflicted more than usual by illness, the falcon would spare him and not give the signal for the time of the watches. Indeed, as if instructed by God, it would very gently sound the bell of its voice about dawn. Little wonder if all other creatures too venerated this eminent love of the Creator. (Celano, Second Life of St. Francis, 168)

Living as Francis Did

This falcon obviously pointed Francis toward God, reminding Francis when it was time to pray. For that Francis was extremely grateful. God's creatures helped the Poor Man of Assisi live in constant praise and thankfulness, even if Francis did not always have the energy to pray as he wished.

Growing with Francis

Some people tend to bring out the best in us. Do you enjoy their company as much as friends and acquaintances who may not inspire you to be your best?

OCTOBER 18

Drawn to Goodness

A certain nobleman from the commune of Siena sent a pheasant to the blessed Francis while the latter was sick. He accepted it with alacrity, not with the desire of eating it, but, in the way he always rejoiced over such things, out of love for the Creator. And he said to the pheasant: "May our Creator be praised, brother pheasant!" And to the brothers he said: "Let us see now if brother pheasant will stay with us, or if it will go back to its usual and more suitable haunts." One of the brothers took it, at the command of the saint, and placed it at a distance in the vineyard. Immediately, however, it came directly back to the father's cell. Again Francis ordered it placed even farther away; but it came back with the greatest speed to the door of his cell and entered almost by force under the habits of the brothers who were standing at the door. The saint then ordered it to be fed diligently, embracing it and caressing it with soft words. (Celano, Second Life of St. Francis, 170)

LIVING AS FRANCIS DID

This pheasant demonstrates how much Francis was in harmony with all creation. Celano does not tell us that the pheasant stayed with Francis for the rest of his life or the bird's life.

GROWING WITH FRANCIS

Francis teaches us to use things gently and to respect people. At times, we are tempted to respect things and use people. Resist any such temptation today.

OCTOBER 19

Letting Go

When a certain physician who was quite devoted to the saint of God saw this, he begged the pheasant from the brothers, not wanting to eat it, but to raise it out of reverence for the saint. What more? He took it home with him; but the pheasant, as though it had suffered an injury in being separated from the saint, refused absolutely to eat as long as it was away from Francis's presence. The physician was astonished, and immediately taking the pheasant back to the saint, he told him everything just as it had happened. As soon as the pheasant was put upon the ground, it saw its father, and putting off all grief, it began to eat with joy. (Celano, Second Life of St. Francis, 170)

Living as Francis Did

This physician had all the best intentions, but in a sense he held this gift from God too tightly. The man could not become more like Francis by caring for the pheasant of which Francis was so fond. No, the physician became more like Francis by allowing the bird to go back to Francis. Love is not so much about acquiring as about letting go.

Growing with Francis

We sometimes are in danger of smothering the things that we claim to love. The same can be true of people. Today do one thing to nurture someone else's freedom. A compliment on a job well done or saying, "You can do it," could make that person's day. Such generosity is never wasted.

OCTOBER 20

Return to Eden

At these words, as Francis himself used to say and those too who were with him, the birds, rejoicing in a wonderful way according to their nature, began to stretch their necks, extend their wings, open their mouths and gaze at him. And Francis, passing through their midst, went on his way [Luke 4:30] and returned, touching their heads and bodies with his tunic. Finally he blessed them, and then, after he had made the sign of the cross over them, he gave them permission to fly away to some other place. But the blessed father went his way with his companions, rejoicing and giving thanks to God, whom all creatures venerate with humble acknowledgement. But now that he had become simple by grace, not by nature, he began to blame himself for negligence in not having preached to the birds before, seeing that they had listened to the word of God with such great reverence. And so it happened that, from that day on, he solicitously admonished all birds, all animals and reptiles, and even creatures that have no feeling, to praise and love their Creator, for daily, when the name of the Savior had been invoked, he saw their obedience by personal experience. (Celano, First Life of St. Francis, 58)

LIVING AS FRANCIS DID

In some ways, Francis reminded his contemporaries of the harmony of creation before Adam and Eve's sin. That explains why so many animals felt comfortable in his presence.

GROWING WITH FRANCIS

Consider putting up a bird feeder or bird house.

OCTOBER 21

Room for God

Once, when the man of God was traveling from Siena to the Spoleto valley, he came to a certain field on which a rather large flock of sheep was grazing. When he greeted them kindly, as was his custom, they all ran to him, raising their heads and returning his greeting with loud bleating. Francis' vicar noted with very careful attention of his eyes what the sheep did and said to the other companions who were following along behind more slowly: "Did you see what the sheep did to the holy father? Truly he is a great man whom the brutes venerate as their father and, though they lack reason, recognize as the friend of their Creator." (Celano, Treatise on the Miracles of Blessed Francis, 31)

LIVING AS FRANCIS DID

Brother Elias (Francis's vicar) correctly interpreted the event described here, linking the unusual behavior of the sheep back to their Creator. Francis encouraged all creation to praise the God who sustains its existence. Some people admit that God created everything, but they give the impression—or state quite openly—that God has become bored with creation and has more important things to do. Francis never thought or acted that way. God does not need to decrease in order for us to fulfill our destiny. We fulfill our destiny by living in the freedom that God desires for us. Nothing is more valuable.

GROWING WITH FRANCIS

How can you make more room in your life for God today?

All God's Creatures

He came to a certain place near Bevagna where a very great number of birds of various kinds had congregated, namely, doves, crows, and some others popularly called daws [a crowlike bird]. When…Francis saw them, being a man of very great fervor and great tenderness toward lower and irrational creatures, he left his companions in the road and ran eagerly toward the birds. When he was close enough to them, seeing that they were waiting expectantly for him, he greeted them in his usual way. But, not a little surprised that the birds did not rise in flight, as they usually do, he was filled with great joy and humbly begged them to listen to the word of God. Among the many things he spoke to them were these words that he added: "My brothers, birds, you should praise your Creator very much and always love him; he gave you feathers to clothe you, wings so that you can fly, and whatever else was necessary for you. God made you noble among his creatures, and he gave you a home in the purity of the air; though you neither sow nor reap, he nevertheless protects and governs you without any solicitude on your part" [Matthew 6:26 and Luke 12:24]. (Celano, First Life of St. Francis, 58)

Living as Francis Did

We tend to evaluate things according to their usefulness. Francis, however, related every creature back to the Creator.

Growing with Francis

What creature that you consider a nuisance might you learn to appreciate?

OCTOBER 23

Compassion for Creation

Compassion, as St. Paul tells us, is all-availing and it filled the heart of Francis and penetrated its depths to such an extent that his whole life seemed to be governed by it. It was loving compassion which united him to God in prayer and caused his transformation into Christ by sharing his sufferings. It was this which led him to devote himself humbly to his neighbor and enabled him to return to the state of primeval innocence by restoring man's harmony with the whole of creation. (Bonaventure, Major Life of St. Francis, VIII, 1)

LIVING AS FRANCIS DID

Bonaventure, who spent years studying Scripture before he began to teach theology at the University of Paris, saw how the virtue of compassion connected Sts. Paul and Francis of Assisi. Just as envy can easily grow in a person's life, in effect, feeding upon itself, so compassion naturally spreads into all corners of a person's life—that is, unless the person makes an effort to prevent this. Compassion seems obvious when it is person-to-person, but here Bonaventure identifies it as the source of Francis's holistic and life-giving relationship with all of creation.

GROWING WITH FRANCIS

People can be embarrassed by their virtues because others can wrongly judge them not to be genuine. Today try to allow one of your virtues to lead to a decision that shows greater compassion for some part of God's wonderful creation.

OCTOBER 24

Genuine Realists

The realization that everything comes from the same source filled Francis with greater affection than ever and he called even the most insignificant creatures his brothers and sisters, because he knew they had the same origin as himself. However, he reserved his most tender compassion for those creatures which are a natural reflection of Christ's gentleness and are used in Sacred Scripture as figures of him. He often rescued lambs, which were being led off to be slaughtered, in memory of the Lamb of God who willed to be put to death to save sinners. (Bonaventure, Major Life of St. Francis, VIII, 6)

LIVING AS FRANCIS DID

All creation spoke to Francis about God as long as Francis did not try to appropriate any part of it as if he were its true owner. All life comes from God and ultimately returns in some way to God. When people misunderstand their place in creation, they tend to claim ownership whereas they are really only caretakers. Francis was so steeped in the Scriptures that he naturally connected lambs, Jesus, and God the Father. An integrated life is ready to make new connections, ones that go wider and deeper than we previously realized. Unfortunately, people who sometimes use their knowledge selfishly short circuit such connections—all the while claiming that they are being realistic. Saints are the only genuine realists.

GROWING WITH FRANCIS

Let no one convince you that selfishness is more realistic than ever-expanding generosity in response to God's great variety of gifts in creation.

OCTOBER 25

Holy Living

When he was travelling near Siena, St. Francis came upon a large flock of sheep grazing in a field. He greeted them lovingly, as usual, and immediately they stopped grazing and ran to him, standing there with their heads erect and their eyes fastened on him. They showed their appreciation of him so clearly that the shepherds and the other friars were amazed to see the shearlings and even the rams jumping excitedly about him. (Bonaventure, Major Life of St. Francis, VIII, 7)

LIVING AS FRANCIS DID

Again, this is a Francis story that many people are tempted to write off as cute but not important. In some ways, Francis seemed to be a man from another world because his conversion brought him much closer to the state of original innocence than his contemporaries thought possible. People cannot be neutral in the presence of very holy women and men. They either start to want for themselves what these holy people obviously have, or they are determined to prove that there is something fake about this apparent holiness. Holy lives always demand a response.

GROWING WITH FRANCIS

Who are the holiest people whom you have known personally? In fact, weren't they more real, more genuine than the folks who opposed them? Weren't their lives more integrated than the lives of many of their contemporaries? Work toward becoming a more holy person and live in a more integrated, holy way beginning today.

OCTOBER 26

Priorities

Another time he was offered a present of a sheep at the Portiuncula and he accepted it gladly in his love of innocence and simplicity, two virtues which the image of a sheep naturally recalls. He exhorted the animal to give God praise and avoid offending the friars, and the sheep was careful to follow his instructions, just as if it realized the affection he had for it. If it was entering the church and heard the friars singing in the choir, it would go down on one knee spontaneously and bleat before the altar of our Lady, the Mother of the Lamb, as if it were trying to greet her. At the elevation during Mass, it would bow profoundly on bended knees and reproach those who were not so devout by its very reverence, while giving the faithful an example of respect for the Blessed Sacrament. (Bonaventure, Major Life of St. Francis, VIIII, 7)

LIVING AS FRANCIS DID

Francis's priorities influenced even animals he encountered. In this month's quotes and stories, many animals made positive contributions to Francis's prayer and to the prayer of others. This sheep honored Mary, the mother of Jesus, and the presence of Jesus in the Eucharist. Holiness is not simply a matter of having pious ideas; it grows when our gratitude for God's creation continues to find new ways of expressing itself.

GROWING WITH FRANCIS

What are your priorities? Are they obvious to your friends and family members? How might you act more generously on those priorities?

OCTOBER 27

Best Friends

On another occasion while in Rome, St. Francis had a lamb with him which he kept out of reverence for the Lamb of God; and when he was leaving, he gave it to Lady Jacoba di Settesoli to keep. The lamb accompanied its mistress to church and stayed there with her, refusing to leave until she left, just as if the saint had trained it in its spiritual exercises. When she was late getting up in the morning, the lamb nudged her with its horns and roused her with its bleats, urging her to hurry and get to church. She was amazed and became very fond of the animal which had been a disciple of St. Francis and was now a master of the religious life. (Bonaventure, Major Life of St. Francis, VIII, 7)

Living as Francis Did

Lady Jacoba di Settesoli (a widow in Rome) became one of Francis's best women friends. As he lay dying, she arrived with candles, a shroud, and an almond cake that she knew Francis liked very much. He christened her "Brother Jacoba" and allowed her into an area reserved for the friars. Lady Jacoba is buried in the crypt chapel where Francis is buried. The lamb that Francis gave her helped Lady Jacoba to keep praising God in prayer when she might have been distracted by other concerns.

Growing with Francis

Allow God to influence your life 24/7 by making decisions in light of what you know God desires. This road leads to greater, long-lasting freedom.

OCTOBER 28

Reclaim Your Freedom

Another time St. Francis was offered a live hare at Greccio. He put it on the ground and left it free to go where it pleased, but the moment he called it, it jumped into his arms. He held it affectionately and seemed to pity it like a mother. Then, warning it gently not to let itself be caught again, he allowed it to go free. But every time he put it on the ground to let it off, the hare immediately jumped into his arms, as if in some mysterious way it realized the love he had for it. Eventually Francis had the friars bring it off to a safer place in the woods. (Bonaventure, Major Life of St. Francis, VIII, 8)

LIVING AS FRANCIS DID

For a time, the hare used its freedom to stay close to Francis. Eventually, the hare lived freely apart from Francis. Genuinely holy people never seek to make others dependent on them, trying to control them. Saints encourage us to claim and use our freedom to its full extent, not accepting whatever puny caricature Satan is trying to pass off as genuine freedom.

GROWING WITH FRANCIS

Have you allowed other people to exercise undue influence in your life? Are you truly as powerless about this situation or these situations as you may have told yourself? What do you need to do to reclaim the freedom you have mistakenly surrendered? Calmly do one thing today to reaffirm your God-given dignity and freedom.

OCTOBER 29

Setting Free

A cicada used to perch on a fig tree beside St. Francis's cell at the Portiuncula and sing there, inspiring the saint to praise God for its song, because he could admire the glory of the Creator in the most insignificant creature. Then one day he called it and when it hopped on to his hand as if it had been taught by God, he told it, "Sing, my sister cicada. Sing a song of praise to God your Creator." Immediately the cicada started to chirp and never stopped until the saint told it to go back to its usual perch. There it remained for a whole week and it came and went every day, singing at his command. Finally the saint remarked to his companions, "We must give our sister cicada permission to go away. She has given us enough pleasure by her singing and inspired us to praise God for a whole week." Immediately he gave it leave, the cicada disappeared and was never seen there again, as if it did not dare transgress his command in the slightest way. (Bonaventure, Major Life of St. Francis, VIII, 9)

LIVING AS FRANCIS DID

Francis learned to appreciate all of God's creation without infringing on their freedom. This cicada pointed Francis to God, but Francis refused to allow it become an obstacle to God or God's rival. We have seen the same dynamic at work in how he treated people.

GROWING WITH FRANCIS

Set someone or something free today.

Created and Loved

The area around Gubbio was once terrorized by "a fearfully large and fierce wolf which was so rabid with hunger that it devoured not only animals but even human beings.... Consequently everyone in the town was so terrified that hardly anyone dared go outside the city gate. But God wished to bring the holiness of St. Francis to the attention of those people. Francis decided to meet this wolf though the citizens of Gubbio were certain it would attack him. But St. Francis placed his hope in the Lord Jesus Christ who is master of all creatures. Protected not by a shield or a helmet, but arming himself with the Sign of the Cross, he bravely went out of the town....

The wolf came up as if to attack Francis but then laid meekly at his feet. Francis recounted the wolf's attacks on animals and people, saying that the people had a right to try to kill it. "But, Brother Wolf, I want to make peace between you and them, so that they will not be harmed by you any more, and after they have forgiven you all your past crimes, neither men nor dogs will pursue you any more." (Adapted from Little Flowers of St. Francis, 21)

LIVING AS FRANCIS DID

Without denying the harm that people had suffered, Francis recognized that the wolf, the townspeople and their animals were all God's creations.

GROWING WITH FRANCIS

Remember that those with whom you are in conflict are created and loved by God.

OCTOBER 31

Befriend Enemies

The wolf showed by moving its body and tail and ears and by nodding its head that it willing accepted what the Saint had said and would observe it. So St. Francis spoke again: Brother Wolf, since you are willing to make and keep this peace pact, I promise you that I will have the people of this town give you food every day as long as you live, so that you will never again suffer from hunger, for I know that whatever evil you have been doing was done because of the urge of hunger. But, my Brother Wolf, since I am obtaining such a favor for you, I want you to promise me that you will never hurt any animal or man. Will you promise me that?

After the wolf gave its paw to Francis as a sign of acceptance, they went back into the city and repeated this pact in front of the townspeople. They and the wolf honored this peace pact for two years before the wolf died. (Adapted from Little Flowers of St. Francis, 21)

LIVING AS FRANCIS DID

This is perhaps the most famous animal story associated with St. Francis. His contemporaries believed that holiness restored a person to harmony with creation as Adam and Eve had lived before the Fall. Francis could have demonized the wolf; he chose not to.

GROWING WITH FRANCIS

Resist the temptation to demonize individuals or groups with whom you are in conflict.

Gospel

In Francis's day, many people were rediscovering the Gospels as a key part of God's unique revelation through the Scriptures. Francis was part of this rediscovery, but he never treated the Bible as something that he could own or use as a weapon against others.

He learned about the Scriptures through hearing passages read at Mass. Sermons preached on them expanded his understanding of Scripture. He accepted the faith community's judgment about which books were considered the canon, or authoritative books of the Bible, and which were not. He understood that the Scriptures belonged to the faith community long before they belonged to any individual Christian. Francis also had a deep appreciation of the Hebrew Scriptures or the Old Testament, especially the Psalms.

Francis was not a sophisticated theologian, but he knew with every fiber of his being that God's love was uniquely revealed in the person of Jesus Christ. The Gospels told him the truth of God's love; saintly Christians nourished by that truth showed Francis how to cooperate generously with God's grace. *God* does not need to be coaxed to share graced life with us; *we* need to be coaxed to put aside whatever we may consider more important than God's grace. All too often we chase after fools' gold but refuse to recognize it as worthless.

The Scriptures helped to keep Francis grounded and to strengthen him when his preached words or lived example were rejected. What St. Luke says twice of Mary (that she pondered all these events and prayed over them) was certainly true of Francis of Assisi. Pondering the Gospels helped him sort out some of life's most tangled situations.

A very spiritual man, Sultan Malik al-Kamil recognized Francis in early 1220 as a very spiritual person as well. Francis never used the Scriptures as a club to fight the Sultan or to criticize other people. The Bible was for him always a privileged and yet humbling way of knowing an all-good and all-gracious God.

Francis had no problem admitting that he was a sinner. We may be tempted to think that he didn't really mean that. In fact, the closer he seemed to come to God, the more Francis realized his own sinfulness. In all of this, Francis drew on the Scriptures as the surest sign of God's continuing love for the human family. God's mercies were being renewed in every generation by people such as Francis, people who rooted their lives in God's gracious self-revelation through the Scriptures.

Some people may become arrogant as is revealed through the way that they use God for their own purposes. Knowledge of the Bible helped keep Francis humble and extremely grateful for God's presence in his life.

NOVEMBER 1

Love Your Neighbors

Our Lord told his apostles: "See, I am sending you out like sheep into the midst of wolves; so be wise as serpents and innocent as doves" (Matthew 10:16). And so the friars who are inspired by God to work as missionaries among the Saracens and other unbelievers must get permission to go from their minister, who is their servant. The minister, for his part, should give them permission and raise no objection, if he sees that they are suitable; he will be held to account for it before God, if he is guilty of imprudence in this or any other matter. (Rule of 1221, chapter 16)

LIVING AS FRANCIS DID

The Rule of St. Francis was the first rule in Church history to include a section about sending members of religious communities to preach the Gospel to non-Christians. Francis had already visited Egypt and spoken with Sultan Malik al-Kamil when he wrote these words. ("Saracens" refers to anyone who identifies as a member of Islam.)

Much of Spain was under Muslim control in Francis's day. The first friars to go to North Africa went by way of Seville. Five of them were martyred in January 1220. At a time when Christians were fighting Muslims, Francis of Assisi believed that God wanted the friars to preach the Good News of Jesus to them.

GROWING WITH FRANCIS

Love your neighbors who may at times seem to be enemies.

Work and Pray for Peace

The brothers who go [among unbelievers] can conduct themselves among them spiritually in two ways. One way is to avoid quarrels or disputes and "For the Lord's sake accept the authority of every human institution" (1 Peter 2:13), so bearing witness to the fact that they are Christians. Another way is to proclaim the word of God openly, when they see that is God's will, calling on their hearers to believe in God almighty, Father, Son, and Holy Spirit, the Creator of all, and in the Son, the Redeemer and Savior, that they may be baptized and become Christians, because "no one can enter the kingdom of God without being born of water, and the Spirit." (John 3:5).

They may tell them all that and more, as God inspires them, because our Lord says in the Gospel: "Everyone therefore who acknowledges me before others, I also will acknowledge before my Father in heaven" (Matthew 10:32); and: "Those who are ashamed of me and my words, of them the Son of Man will be ashamed when he comes in his glory and the glory of the Father and of the holy angels" (Luke 9:26). (Rule of 1221, chapter 16)

LIVING AS FRANCIS DID

Their good example enabled friars to serve Christian pilgrims visiting the Holy Land. Today friars' schools there teach both Christian and Muslim students.

GROWING WITH FRANCIS

Pray and work for peace in the land where Jesus lived, in whatever way you can.

NOVEMBER 3

A Life's Sermon

No friar may preach contrary to Church law or without the permission of his minister. The minister, for his part, must be careful not to grant permission indiscriminately. All the friars, however, should preach by their example.

The ministers and preachers must remember that they do not have a right to the office of serving the friars or of preaching, and so they must be prepared to lay it aside without objection the moment they are told to do so. In that love which is God (1 John 4:8), I entreat all my friars, whether they are given to preaching, praying, or manual labour, to do their best to humble themselves at every opportunity; not to boast or be self-satisfied, or take pride in any good which God says or does or accomplishes in them or by them; as our Lord himself put it, "Nevertheless, do not rejoice at this, that the spirits are subject to you" (Luke 10:20). (Rule of 1221, chapter 17)

LIVING AS FRANCIS DID

In the earliest days of the Franciscans, friars did not need formal permission from the local bishop in order to preach. After Lateran Council IV, the Church began licensing preachers to speak in its name. Eventually, permission to preach was linked to formal study of Scripture so that enthusiasm and zeal were not being substituted for knowledge.

GROWING WITH FRANCIS

Make sure that your life is a sermon drawing others to Christ.

NOVEMBER 4

Gospel Life

Whenever they see fit, my friars may exhort the people to praise God with words like these: Fear him and honor him, praise him and bless him, thank and adore him, the Lord almighty, in Trinity and Unity, Father, Son, and Holy Spirit, Creator of all. "Repent, for the kingdom of heaven has come near" (Matthew 3:2); remember we must soon die. "Forgive, and you shall be forgiven; give, and it shall be given to you" (Luke 6:38); "if you do not forgive, neither will your Father in heaven forgive you your [trespasses]" (Mark 11:26). Confess all your sins.

It is well for those who die repentant; they shall have a place in the kingdom of heaven. Woe to those who die unrepentant; they shall be children of the devil whose work they do, and they shall go into everlasting fire. Be on your guard and keep clear of all evil, standing firm to the last. (Rule of 1221, chapter 21)

LIVING AS FRANCIS DID

In Francis's day, many people preached that the Church's wealth and social influence proved that it was unfaithful to Jesus's command to preach the Good News to everyone. Yet it is easy to idealize the Church in the first century, thus making the Church in every other century seem to betray Christ's original intention.

GROWING WITH FRANCIS

Your challenge is to live the Gospel life without thinking of yourself as holier than anyone else.

NOVEMBER 5

A Dwelling Place

In that love which is God (1 John 4:16), I entreat all my friars, ministers and subjects, to put away every attachment...and serve, love, honor, and adore our Lord and God with a pure heart and mind.... We should make a dwelling place within ourselves where he can stay, he who is the Lord God almighty, Father, Son, and Holy Spirit.... "Be alert at all times, praying that you may have the strength to escape all these things that will take place, and to stand before the Son of Man" (Luke 21:36). "When you stand praying" (Mark 11:25), say "Our Father in heaven" (Matthew 6:9). Let us adore him with a pure heart for we must pray always and not lose heart (Luke 18:1).... "God is spirit, and [those] who worship him must worship in spirit and truth" (John 4:24). We should turn to him as to the shepherd and guardian of our souls (1 Peter 2:25). He says, "I am the good shepherd" (John 10:11). I feed my sheep and "I lay down my life for my sheep" (John 10:15). "You are all students. And call no one your father on earth; for you have one Father, who is in heaven. (Matthew 23:8b–9). (Rule of 1221, chapter 22)

Living as Francis Did

Detachment from objects, from individuals, doesn't mean abandonment. For Francis detachment was the way to truly focus on God.

Growing with Francis

Create a dwelling place within yourself for Father, Son, and Holy Spirit.

NOVEMBER 6

Faith-Filled Preaching

The friars are forbidden to preach in any diocese, if the bishop objects to it. No friar should dare to preach to the people unless he has been examined and approved by the Minister General of the Order and has received from him the commission to preach.

Moreover, I advise and admonish the friars that in their preaching, their words should be examined and chaste. They should aim only at the advantage and spiritual good of their listeners, telling them briefly about vice and virtue, punishment and glory, because our Lord himself kept his words short on earth. (Rule of 1223, chapter 9)

LIVING AS FRANCIS DID

Like everyone else, bishops need conversion as much as friar preachers do; both groups must work to build up Christ's Church. Both bishops and all Christians must render an account to God for what they have done and what they have failed to do.

A friar's preaching was aimed at promoting conversion among listeners, not displaying the preacher's public speaking skills and thus stroking his ego. Such preaching requires not many words (appealing to "ears itching" as St. Paul put it) but good example outside times of formal preaching. The most effective Franciscan preachers were always accompanied by friar priests to hear the confessions of people who were moved to a conversion of life.

GROWING WITH FRANCIS

Pray that preachers will be both effective and humble.

NOVEMBER 7

Live the Word

St. Paul tells us, "The letter kills, but the Spirit gives life" (2 Corinthians 3:6). A man has been killed by the letter when he wants to know quotations only so that people will think he is very learned and he can make money to give to his relatives and friends. A religious has been killed by the letter when he has no desire to follow the spirit of Sacred Scripture, but wants to know what it says only so that he can explain it to others. On the other hand, those have received life from the spirit of Sacred Scripture who, by their words and example, refer to the most high God, to whom belongs all good, all that they know or wish to know, and do not allow their knowledge to become a source of self-complacency. (Admonition VII)

Living as Francis Did

Francis considered it sacrilegious to turn God's generous self-revelation into a commodity that could be traded for personal profit. With such an attitude, someone might try to gain a monopoly! Scripture gives life to everyone who receives it humbly, allowing it to lead that person back to Scripture's ultimate author, God. In Francis's day, the study of theology was primarily the study of the Bible, both the Hebrew Scriptures (Old Testament) and the New Testament.

Growing with Francis

Dedicate fifteen minutes every day to praying with the Bible, learning more about it as an aid to prayer.

Holy Actions, Holy Words

"Whoever is from God hears the words of God" (John 8:47a), and so we who are called to serve God in a more special way are bound not merely to listen to and carry out what he commands; we must give proof in ourselves of the greatness of our Creator and of our subjection to him by keeping the liturgical books and anything else which contains his holy words with great care. I urge all my friars and I encourage them in Christ to show all possible respect for God's words wherever they may happen to find them in writing. If they are not kept properly or if they lie thrown about disrespectfully, they should pick them up and put them aside, paying honor in his words to God who spoke them. God's words sanctify numerous objects, and it is by the power of the words of Christ that the sacrament of the altar is consecrated. (Letter to a General Chapter)

LIVING AS FRANCIS DID

Francis had a very incarnational approach to life. His concern was never for gaudy display but always for promoting genuine conversion. At general chapters, friars shared the good things God was doing through them; these were also times to accept correction for actions or attitudes that were undermining their witness to Jesus's Good News.

GROWING WITH FRANCIS

Identify ways your actions might contradict your good words about Jesus.

NOVEMBER 9

Change Me, Lord

To Brother Anthony, my bishop, Brother Francis sends greetings.

It is agreeable to me that you should teach the friars sacred theology, so long as they do not extinguish the spirit of prayer and devotedness over this study, as is contained in the Rule. Farewell. (Letter to St. Anthony)

LIVING AS FRANCIS DID

Anthony of Padua, an Augustinian canon in Portugal, was named Fernando before joining the Friars Minor; then he was called Anthony, in honor of St. Anthony of Egypt, one of the founders of monastic life in the East. His preaching talent was revealed when he had to preach on short notice at an ordination. The friars assigned him to teach Scripture in Bologna to future friar preachers. The letter above places that ministry in proper context. Anthony's superiors then sent him to preaching among Albigensians in southern France. The friars' theology school in Bologna is still under St. Anthony's patronage.

Anthony was very knowledgeable about Scripture but resisted every temptation to use it for personal advantage. His knowledge was so great that he was asked to prepare a manual to help preachers carry out their ministry effectively. He completed a set of sermon notes on the Sunday readings and half of the feasts of the most important saints on the Church calendar.

GROWING WITH FRANCIS

Do you allow your heart to be touched by God's word? Make any changes needed as a result of that encounter.

NOVEMBER 10

Tame Me!

But when on a certain day the Gospel was read in that church [feast of St. Matthias, February 24], how the Lord sent his disciples out to preach, the holy man of God, assisting there, understood somewhat the words of the Gospel; after Mass he humbly asked the priest to explain the Gospel to him more fully. When he had set forth for him in order all these things, the holy Francis, hearing that the disciples of Christ should not possess gold or silver or money; nor carry along the way bag, or wallet, or bread, or a staff; that they should not have shoes, or two tunics [Matthew 10:9; Luke 10:4; Mark 6:8; Luke 9:3]; but that they should preach the kingdom of God and penance [Luke 9:2; Mark 6:12], immediately [Francis] cried out exultingly: "This is what I wish, this is what I seek, this is what I long to do with all my heart." Then the holy father, "overjoyed in all our affliction" (2 Corinthians 7:4), hastened to fulfill that salutary word he had heard, and he did not suffer any delay to intervene before beginning devoutly to perform what he had heard. (Celano, First Life of St. Francis, 22)

LIVING AS FRANCIS DID

Francis heard the Gospel in Latin at a weekday Mass. He sought to understand it more deeply, then to act on it.

GROWING WITH FRANCIS

Resist temptation to squeeze God's word into space available after life's so-called priorities are established. Allow God's word to tame you.

NOVEMBER 11

Full Power Ahead

He immediately put off his shoes from his feet, put aside the staff from his hands, was content with one tunic, and exchanged his leather belt for a small cord. He designed for himself a tunic that bore a likeness to the cross, that by means of it he might beat off all temptations of the devil; he designed a very rough tunic so that by it he might crucify the flesh with all its vices and sins [Galatians 5:24]; he designed a very poor and mean tunic, one that would not excite the covetousness of the world. The other things that he had heard, however, he longed with the greatest diligence and the greatest reverence to perform. For he was not a deaf hearer of the Gospel, but committing all that he had heard to praiseworthy memory, he tried diligently to carry it out to the letter. (Celano, First Life of St. Francis, 22)

LIVING AS FRANCIS DID

Here Francis takes very directly Jesus's words that the apostles should travel light on their journeys. All baggage is not physical. For example, people can carry around and nurse resentment and envy for months and years. Clothing will eventually wear out, but well-tended resentment never does. Francis's exterior conversion matched an interior conversion to the Lord's ways.

GROWING WITH FRANCIS

God's word in Scripture can be domesticated to the point of never challenging a person. Let God's word have full power in your life.

Rule of Life

When Blessed Francis saw that the Lord God was daily adding to their number [Acts 2:47], he wrote for himself and his brothers, present and to come, simply and with few words, a form of life and rule, using for the most part the words of the holy Gospel, for the perfection of which alone he yearned. But he did insert a few other things that were necessary to provide for a holy way of life. He then came to Rome [in 1209] with all the aforementioned brothers, desiring very much that what he had written should be confirmed by the Lord Pope Innocent III. (Celano, First Life of St. Francis, 32)

LIVING AS FRANCIS DID

"The Rule and life of the Friars Minor is to observe the holy Gospel by living in obedience, in chastity, and without anything of one's own."

Scripture cannot be properly interpreted without help from the faith community to which it was given. For this reason, Francis sought papal confirmation that he was interpreting the word of God correctly. If the meaning of every biblical passage were self-evident, the disciples on the road to Emmaus would have needed no help from Jesus. Interpretation goes beyond words; it extends to daily choices.

GROWING WITH FRANCIS

When you read the Bible, also read the introductions, cross-references, and notes to gain a fuller understanding of the text.

NOVEMBER 13

Humility Wins

While they were going along the way [back from Rome], they talked with one another about the number and the quality of the gifts the most kind God had bestowed upon them, and about how they had been received most kindly by the vicar of Christ, the lord and father of the whole Christian world; about how they might be able to fulfill his admonitions and commands; about how they could sincerely observe the rule they had taken upon themselves and keep it without failure; about how they should walk in all sanctity and religion before the Most High; and finally, about how their life and conduct might be an example to their neighbors by an increase of holy virtues. (Celano, First Life of St. Francis, 34)

LIVING AS FRANCIS DID

Francis and the first friars rejoiced at Pope Innocent III's verbal approval of their way of life in 1209. Proof of its authenticity would come from their daily choices. Many groups before and after Francis have started well and burned with zeal to live the Gospel. Some of them gave in to the temptation to look down on other Christians who seemed less zealous than the group's members. The friars' common life would foster the humility that would enrich their ministry. Without that humility, they would inevitably fail.

GROWING WITH FRANCIS

Anyone can choose to live in a perpetual state of resentment that all the Church's members are not yet saints. Let humility remind you that most of us are not yet saints.

Scripture Speaks

Brother Anthony [of Padua] was also present at this chapter [meeting of the friars in Provence, France], he whose mind the Lord opened [Luke 24:24] that he might understand the Scriptures and speak among all the people words about Jesus that were sweeter than syrup or honey from the comb [Psalm 19:10]. While he was preaching very fervently and devoutly to the brothers on this topic, "Jesus of Nazareth, King of the Jews" [John 19:19b], the aforementioned Brother Monaldo looked toward the door of the house in which there were many other brothers gathered and he saw there with his bodily eyes Blessed Francis raised up into the air, his arms extended as though upon a cross, and blessing the brothers. And they all were seen to be filled "with the comfort of the Holy Spirit" (Acts 9:31), and, from the joy of salvation they felt, what they were told concerning the vision and the presence of their most glorious father seemed entirely believable. (Celano, First Life of St. Francis, 48)

LIVING AS FRANCIS DID

The friars felt Francis's presence though he was far away. They all prayed and were nourished by the word of God. Celano cites a moment in the Church's life when Jesus was no longer present as he had been yet was encountered through Scripture, the sacraments, and life together.

GROWING WITH FRANCIS

Read chapters 9 and 10 of Acts of the Apostles. What is God saying to you?

NOVEMBER 15

Walk the Talk

Cardinal Hugolino once arranged for Francis to preach in Rome before Pope Honorius. But confident of the mercy of the Almighty, which in the time of need never fails those who trust in it, the bishop brought Francis before the lord pope and the reverend cardinals; and standing before such great princes, after receiving their permission and blessing, he began to speak fearlessly. Indeed, he spoke with such great fervor of spirit, that, not being able to contain himself for joy, when he spoke the words with his mouth, he moved his feet as though he were dancing, not indeed lustfully, but as one burning with the fire of divine love, not provoking laughter, but drawing forth tears of grief. For many of them were pierced to the heart [Acts 2:37] in admiration of divine grace and of such great constancy in man. But the venerable lord bishop of Ostia was kept in suspense by fear and he prayed with all his strength to the Lord that the simplicity of the blessed man would not be despised, since the glory of the saint would reflect upon himself as would his disgrace, in as much as he had been placed over Francis' family as a father. (Adapted from Celano, First Life of St. Francis, 73)

LIVING AS FRANCIS DID

Francis rose to the occasion and did not cause grief for Cardinal Hugolino. The Poor Man of Assisi could not restrain God's Spirit that prompted his words.

GROWING WITH FRANCIS

Like Francis, walk the talk.

NOVEMBER 16

Ponder Humility

Francis' highest intention, his chief desire, his uppermost purpose was to observe the holy Gospel in all things and through all things and, with perfect vigilance, with all zeal, with all the longing of his mind and all the fervor of his heart, "to follow the teaching and the footsteps of our Lord Jesus Christ" [from the Rule of 1221]. He would recall Christ's words through persistent meditation and bring to mind his deeds through the most penetrating consideration. The humility of the incarnation and the charity of the passion occupied his memory particularly, to the extent that he wanted to think of hardly anything else. (Celano, First Life of St. Francis, 84)

LIVING AS FRANCIS DID

Francis followed Mary's example by pondering words of Scripture and events of daily life, trying to see how the Bible could illuminate what might seem to be jumbled events. From Jesus's Sermon on the Mount (Matthew 5–8), Francis learned which words and actions could fit through heaven's gate. An inflated sense of self and actions flowing from it would need to go on a diet, so to speak, in order to fit through that gate. Many of Francis's contemporaries saw the Incarnation as necessary for our redemption, but they were not deeply touched by the humility of the Incarnation. Francis's strong conviction changed that for many people.

GROWING WITH FRANCIS

How will the humility of the Incarnation influence your decisions today?

NOVEMBER 17

Holy Newness

For in this last time [1 Peter 1:5] this new evangelist [Francis], like one of the rivers that flowed out of paradise, diffused the waters of the Gospel over the whole world by his tender watering, and preached by his deeds the way of the Son of God and the doctrine of truth. Accordingly, in him and through him there arose throughout the world an unlooked for happiness and a holy newness, and a shoot of the ancient religion suddenly brought a great renewal to those who had grown calloused and to the very old. A new spirit was born in the hearts of the elect, and a saving unction was poured out in their midst, when the servant and holy man of Christ, like one of the lights of the heavens, shone brilliantly with a new rite and with new signs. Through him the miracles of ancient times were renewed, while there was planted in the desert of this world, by a new order but in an ancient way, a fruitful vine bearing flowers of sweetness unto the odor of holy virtues by extending everywhere the branches of a sacred religion [religious community]. (Celano, First Life of St. Francis, 89)

LIVING AS FRANCIS DID

Francis indeed represented an "unlooked for happiness and a holy newness." To the extent that his followers drew their inspiration from Scripture and the sacraments, they lived out these same qualities.

GROWING WITH FRANCIS

Allow God's grace to produce an "unlooked for happiness and a holy newness" in your life.

NOVEMBER 18

Speak Jesus

Francis's body began to be burdened with various and more serious sicknesses than before. For he suffered frequent infirmities in as much as he had chastised his body and brought it into subjection [1 Corinthians 9:27] during the many years that had preceded. For during the space of eighteen years, which was now completed, his body had had little or no rest while he traveled through various very large regions so that that willing spirit [Matthew 26:41], that devoted spirit, that fervent spirit that dwelt within him might scatter everywhere the seeds of the word of God [Luke 8:11]. He filled the whole earth with the Gospel of Christ, so that often in one day "he made a circuit of" [Mark 6:6] four or five villages and even cities, "proclaiming and bringing the good news of the kingdom of God" (Luke 8:1) to every one; and edifying his hearers not less by his example than by his word, he made a tongue out of his whole body. (Celano, First Life of St. Francis, 97)

LIVING AS FRANCIS DID

Francis "made a tongue out of his whole body." What an image! Everything about Francis pointed not to himself but to God whom Francis came to know and love more deeply through praying Scripture. Some of his contemporaries used Scripture to illustrate how the Church differed from what Jesus preached. Francis read the same words, seeing primarily God's love and compassion.

GROWING WITH FRANCIS

Read 1 Corinthians 13, and allow the words to speak through your life.

NOVEMBER 19

God's Guidance

Finally he ordered the book of the Gospels to be brought and commanded that the Gospel according to St. John be read from that place where it begins: "Six days before the Passover, Jesus, knowing that the hour had come for him to pass from this world to the Father [John 12:1; 13:1]." The minister general [Brother Elias] had intended to read this Gospel, even before he had been commanded to do so; this passage had also appeared at the first opening of the book earlier, although the book was the whole and complete Bible in which this Gospel was contained. Francis then commanded that a hair shirt be put upon him and that he be sprinkled with ashes, for he was soon to become dust and ashes. Then, when many brothers had gathered about, whose father and leader he was, and while they were standing reverently at his side awaiting his blessed death and happy end, his most holy soul was freed from his body and received into the abyss of light, and he died in the Lord (Acts 7:60). (Celano, First Life of St. Francis, 110)

LIVING AS FRANCIS DID

Jesus at the Last Supper promised the apostles that he would send them the Paraclete (the Holy Spirit) to guide them. By having this passage read as he was dying, Francis reminded the friars that the word of God will always be available to guide them.

GROWING WITH FRANCIS

Read chapter 13 of the Gospel of John and consider its meaning in your life.

An Inheritance

The lord pope [Innocent III] wondered at the parable proposed to him and recognized without doubting that Christ had spoken in man. He recalled a certain vision he had had a few days before, which, he affirmed, under the guidance of the Holy Spirit, would be fulfilled in this man. He had seen in his sleep the Lateran basilica about to fall to ruin, when a certain religious, small and despised, propped it up by putting his own back under it lest it fall. "Surely," he said, "this is that man who, by his works and by the teaching of Christ, will give support to the Church." For this reason the lord pope readily gave in to the petition of Francis. Therefore, filled with love of God he always showed a special love toward the servant of Christ. And therefore he quickly granted what had been asked, and he promised to grant even greater things than these. Francis, therefore, by reason of the authority granted him, began to scatter the seeds of virtue, going about the "cities and villages" (Matthew 9:35) preaching fervently. (Celano, Second Life of St. Francis, 17)

LIVING AS FRANCIS DID

A poor woman in the desert married the king and gave birth to his sons. When they were grown, she sent her sons to the king to claim their inheritance. Francis and his brothers were like the sons of the king. They preached their inheritance, the word of God. (See entry for August 3.)

GROWING WITH FRANCIS

What inheritance from God awaits you?

NOVEMBER 21

Loving Lady Poverty

While he was in this valley of tears, that blessed father considered the common wealth of the sons of men as trifles, and, ambitious for higher things, he longed for poverty with all his heart. Looking upon poverty as especially dear to the Son of God, though it was spurned throughout the whole world, he sought to espouse it in perpetual charity. Therefore, after he had become a lover of her beauty, he not only left his father and mother, but even put aside all things, that he might cling to her more closely as his spouse and that they might "become one flesh" (Genesis 2:24b). Therefore he gathered her to himself with chaste embraces and not even for an hour did he allow himself not to be her husband. This, he would tell his sons, is the way to perfection, this the pledge and earnest of eternal riches. There was no one so desirous of gold as he was desirous of poverty, and no one so solicitous in guarding his treasure as he was solicitous in guarding this pearl of the Gospel. (Celano, Second Life of St. Francis, 55)

LIVING AS FRANCIS DID

In Celano's First Life of St. Francis, Lady Poverty is a noble woman, loved and served from afar in the tradition of courtly love. In the Second Life, Lady Poverty is Francis's spouse. Everything that Francis knew about her came to him through the Scriptures.

GROWING WITH FRANCIS

Is your life becoming increasingly more God-centered? What part is Scripture playing in the process?

NOVEMBER 22

Scripture Educates

Although this blessed man had been educated in none of the branches of learning, still, grasping the wisdom that is of God from above and enlightened by the rays of eternal light, he had a deep understanding of the Scriptures. For his genius, free from all stain, penetrated the hidden things of mysteries, and where the knowledge of the masters is something external, the affection of one who loves enters within the thing itself. At times he would read the sacred books and what he put into his mind once he wrote indelibly in his heart. (Celano, Second Life of St. Francis, 102)

LIVING AS FRANCIS DID

Francis could not read Hebrew or Greek, the original languages of the Bible. He did not engage in university studies of the Bible. Even so, he had an understanding of the Scriptures that sometimes caused those more learned than he to consult him about the meaning of certain passages. He learned the Bible through personal prayer and through the Church's liturgy (the Eucharist and the Liturgy of the Hours). In several of his Admonitions, Francis warned the friars not to treat Scripture as an object to be mastered and then manipulated; it is a guide to life.

GROWING WITH FRANCIS

Love naturally leads to greater knowledge; knowledge by itself may lead to greater knowledge but not to greater love. Read a favorite Scripture passage, and allow it to lead you into a deeper love of God.

NOVEMBER 23

Yes, But

His memory substituted for books, for he did not hear a thing once in vain, for his love meditated on it with constant devotion. This he would say was a fruitful way of learning and reading, not by wandering about through thousands of treatises. Him he considered a true philosopher who put nothing before his desire for eternal life. But he often said that that man would easily move from knowledge of himself to a knowledge of God who would set himself to study the Scriptures humbly, not presumptuously. He often explained doubtful questions word for word, and though he was unskilled in words, he set forth the sense and meaning admirably. (Celano, Second Life of St. Francis, 102)

LIVING AS FRANCIS DID

Knowledge of anything can reinforce a deeper love for it, but knowledge alone cannot create a deeper love. A person could become a world expert in some field that he or she finds truly boring and incapable of enriching that person's life. Such was not the knowledge Francis of Assisi acquired about the Bible. He read it with great humility, knowing that was the only way to receive God's self-revelation that Scripture contains.

GROWING WITH FRANCIS

Are you growing in greater love for God and others as a result of hearing the Scriptures and praying over them? Do you allow the Scriptures to challenge your values, your choices?

Identify one Scripture verse about which you are tempted to say "Yes, but…." Pray over that verse today, confronting the "but" in your response.

NOVEMBER 24

Observe with Compassion

While Francis was staying at Siena, it happened that a certain friar of the Order of Preachers [the Dominicans] came there; he was a spiritual man and a doctor of Sacred Theology. Since he had come to visit the blessed Francis, that learned man and the saint enjoyed a long and pleasant conversation about the words of God. The aforesaid master [of theology] questioned Francis about that saying of Ezekiel: "If I [God] say to the wicked, "You shall surely die," and you give them no warning…their blood I will require at your hand" [3:18]. For he [the Dominican] said: "Good Father, I know many who, to the best of my knowledge, are in the state of mortal sin, but I do not always proclaim their wickedness. Will the souls of such men be required at my hand?" (Celano, Second Life of St. Francis, 103)

LIVING AS FRANCIS DID

Francis's holy life prompted a learned Dominican theologian to seek his help in interpreting a passage from Ezekiel. Francis did not "hang out his shingle," so to speak, as an interpreter of Scripture. People who observed his holy life, however, rightly believed that he could help them unlock the power and divine self-revelation that a passage contains. This particular one from Ezekiel could lead a person to become scrupulous.

GROWING WITH FRANCIS

Prayer and a generous love can help us see things that might otherwise go unnoticed. Make sure your eyes are open.

NOVEMBER 25

Speak, Lord

The blessed Francis said that he was unlettered and therefore it would be more fitting for him to be taught by that master than for him to interpret the meaning of Scripture. And the humble master said: "Brother, though I have heard these words interpreted by learned men, I would be glad to hear your understanding of the passage." The blessed Francis said to him: "If the passage is to be understood in a general meaning, I would take it that the servant of God should be so aflame in his life and his holiness that he would reprove all wicked men by the light of his example and by the words of his conversation. So, I say, the splendor of his life and the renown of his fame will proclaim to all their wickedness." That man, therefore, went away much edified, and he said to the companions of the blessed Francis: "My brothers, the theology of this man, based upon purity of life and contemplation, is a soaring eagle; but our learning crawls on its belly on the ground." (Celano, Second Life of St. Francis, 103)

LIVING AS FRANCIS DID

The Dominican's question was whether as a preacher he must reprove sinners at every opportunity. Francis's response was that the preacher's holy and integrated life is a reminder that the sinner has chosen a dead end path. A preacher's words of reproof work only if supported by a holy life.

GROWING WITH FRANCIS

Listen to God speaking through someone else's life today.

NOVEMBER 26

Open to Love

When Francis was ill and filled throughout with pains, his companion once said: "Father, you have always sought refuge in the Scriptures, and they have always given you remedies for your pains. I pray you to have something read to you now from the prophets: perhaps your spirit will rejoice in the Lord." The saint said to him: "It is good to read the testimonies of Scripture: it is good to seek the Lord our God in them. As for me, however, I have already made so much of Scripture my own that I have more than enough to meditate on and revolve in my mind. I need no more, son; I know Christ, the poor crucified one." (Celano, Second Life of St. Francis, 105)

LIVING AS FRANCIS DID

Francis was not displaying arrogance here. He had prayed so intently over biblical texts that they had become part of him. He remembered the passages and breakthroughs they represented for him. He could almost certainly recall how praying over and acting on those passages had changed his life. Francis knew the poor and crucified Christ from the Scriptures, from private and communal prayer, and from meeting that Christ in the women and men whom Francis served by his preaching and by the corporal and spiritual works of mercy.

GROWING WITH FRANCIS

Pray over a Scripture text that you find problematic, opening yourself to a new revelation of God's love.

NOVEMBER 27

Greater Freedom

Francis wanted such men to be ministers of the word of God [Acts 6:4] who give themselves to the study of spiritual things and are not hindered by other duties. For these, he used to say, have been chosen by a certain great king to deliver to the people the edicts that proceed from his mouth. But he said: "The preacher must first draw from secret prayers what he will later pour out in holy sermons; he must first grow hot within before he speaks words that are in themselves cold." He said that this is an office to be revered and that those who administer it should be reverenced by all. "These," he said, "are the life of the body; they are the attackers of the devils; they are the light of the world" [Matthew 5:14]. (Celano, Second Life of St. Francis, 163)

LIVING AS FRANCIS DID

Francis had a great respect for preachers—not because they were always saints but because their ministry required integrity. They were leading people into the freedom that God always wanted them to have. To some extent, every preacher reveals God and yet obscures God by a life not yet totally converted to the Lord's ways. Francis chose to emphasize the good done and pray that the preacher would yet recognize any blind spots still present.

GROWING WITH FRANCIS

Be ready for the possibility that the next homily you hear will lead you into greater freedom regarding God's ways.

NOVEMBER 28

The Power of Silence

Repeatedly asked by his vicar [Brother Elias] to preach the word of God to his daughters when he stopped off for a short time at St. Damian's, Francis was finally overcome by his insistence and consented. But when the nuns had come together, according to their custom, to hear the word of God, though no less also to see their father, Francis raised his eyes to heaven, where his heart always was, and began to pray to Christ. He then commanded ashes to be brought to him and he made a circle with them around himself on the pavement and sprinkled the rest of them on his head. (Celano, Second Life of St. Francis, 207)

LIVING AS FRANCIS DID

Like the prophets Jeremiah and Ezekiel especially, Francis understood the power of silence and gesture. Neither was used to call attention to himself but only to convey the message entrusted to him by God. Francis did not have an opportunity for formal study of the Scriptures, but he attentively participated at Mass and was very aware of the Gospel readings. The Liturgy of the Hours brought him into constant contact with the Psalms, with their prayers arising from a wide range of human emotions: praise, thanksgiving, awe, and petition.

GROWING WITH FRANCIS

Today pray the psalm whose number matches your age. What can it teach you about God and about yourself?

Have Mercy!

But when they waited for him to begin and the blessed father remained standing in the circle in silence, no small astonishment arose in their hearts. The saint then suddenly rose and to the amazement of the nuns recited the "Have mercy on me, O God" (Psalm 51), in place of a sermon. When he had finished, he quickly left. The servants of God were so filled with contrition because of the power of this symbolic sermon that their tears flowed in abundance and they could scarcely restrain their hands from inflicting punishment on themselves. (Celano, Second Life of St. Francis, 207)

LIVING AS FRANCIS DID

Psalm 51 is associated with King David, perhaps composed after the death of the son born of his adultery with Bathsheba, wife of Uriah the Hittite. The child was clearly innocent; David was not. Repentance clears away the big and small lies with which people sometimes surround themselves. The most dangerous lies that people tell are not to other people but to themselves.

The incident recorded here tells us that Francis himself was ready to repent and urge St. Clare and her sisters to do the same. Repentance leads us more deeply into the truth about God, ourselves, and others. Francis's contemporaries did not resent his encouragement that they repent because they knew that he never considered his own repentance totally complete.

GROWING WITH FRANCIS

Pray and ponder Psalm 51 today.

NOVEMBER 30

Conversion Always

Francis glowed most ardently for the common profession and the rule, and he blessed with a very special blessing those who would be zealous about it. For he called the rule the "book of life" [Revelation 3:5], the "hope of salvation" [1 Thessalonians 5:8], the marrow of the Gospel, the way of perfection, the key to paradise, the agreement of an "everlasting covenant" (Genesis 17:13). He wanted it to be had by all, to be known by all, and he wanted it to speak everywhere to the interior man unto his comfort in weariness and unto a remembrance of the vows he had made. He taught them to keep it ever before their eyes as a reminder of the life they were to live, and, what is more, that they should die with it. (Celano, Second Life of St. Francis, 208)

LIVING AS FRANCIS DID

Who can say that he or she has perfectly observed the Gospel? Who of us has no need for further conversion? Rules are only useful when obeyed. Francis knew that bones have marrow, but he could scarcely have guessed how important marrow is to the health of bones or a person's blood. When marrow does not function properly, a transplant may be needed. When marrow works as it should, the whole body is healthy.

GROWING WITH FRANCIS

How has Scripture helped in your ongoing conversion? Continue this practice.

Joy

Joy is much deeper than happiness, which can be mostly a reflection of circumstances and decisions on the part of other people. Think, for example, about the joy of being on the receiving end of a surprise party. We treasure the thoughtfulness, the ingenuity, the friendship, and the generosity needed by many people in order to make such a party a success.

Francis of Assisi was not always a happy person (no one can be happy about his or her sins, for example), but Francis was always deeply joyful. These two terms reflect different horizons in a person's life. A miser can be happy—but only momentarily. Sooner or later, whatever money, property, or sound investments have been acquired will start to fade. The black hole of "I don't have enough" will become a sinkhole of despair.

The same is true for wealth that is not strictly monetary. Alexander the Great is reported to have wept that there were no more worlds to conquer. That overlooks the fact that he had not completely conquered his internal world of wants and desires. It's very easy to think that "if only" we had this physical object, more success or recognition from others, then we could be happy. People whose lives are dominated by "if only" thinking will, in fact, never be truly happy because the ante for their happiness is always going up.

Joy, on the other hand, is not so fragile because it has much deeper roots. We see this especially in the "perfect joy" story recounted in the entries for December 29 and 30. Francis was in touch with joy's deepest roots, sharing in the life of grace and freedom that God wants for each person.

Francis knew that people can pursue happiness "in all the wrong places," as a song says. People can mistakenly see sin as a shortcut to happiness rather than as the dead end that sin always represents. Someone can presume that other people have the ability to make him or her completely happy.

In a sense, Francis's joy was the culmination of all the virtues that are the themes for this book's chapters. Poverty could have made Francis bitter; it did not. Prayer could have made him self-righteous; it did not. He might have acted as though he alone understood Jesus; Francis shunned that thought. He did not so much create peace as accept it from God.

Francis could have become bitter as he started to go blind, as travel became much more difficult for him, or as disputes arose among the friars. Clearly, not all of them were saints! And yet Francis refused to become bitter. Toward the end of his life, Francis told the friars, "I have done what was mine to do. May the Lord teach you yours" (Celano, First Life of St. Francis, 214). Only a man who had a very deep sense of joy could have said that.

May Francis lead us to our deepest joy!

DECEMBER 1

Risk with Faith

For before he gained access to the sultan, though he was captured by the sultan's soldiers, was insulted and beaten, still he was not frightened; he did not fear the threats of torture and, when death was threatened, he did not grow pale. But though he was treated shamefully by many who were quite hostile and hateful toward him, he was nevertheless received very honorably by the sultan. The sultan honored him as much as he was able, and having given him many gifts, he tried to bend Francis' mind toward the riches of the world. But when he saw that Francis most vigorously despised all these things as so much dung, he was filled with the greatest admiration, and he looked upon him [Francis] as a man different from all others. He was deeply moved by his words and he listened to him very willingly. (Celano, First Life of St. Francis, 57)

LIVING AS FRANCIS DID

Francis had a deeply rooted joy that enabled him to take great risks without fear. This incident took place near Damietta, Egypt. Francis had accompanied the Fifth Crusade and set out to meet Sultan Malik al-Kamil, hoping to preach the Gospel to him. Francis survived this meeting because of his obvious holiness. This encounter is the subject of one of Giotto's frescoes in the Upper Basilica of St. Francis in Assisi.

GROWING WITH FRANCIS

Allow your faith to move you at least slightly out of your comfort zone today.

DECEMBER 2

Portrait of Francis

He was a most eloquent man, a man of cheerful countenance, of kindly aspect; he was immune to cowardice, free of insolence. He was of medium height, closer to shortness; his head was moderate in size and round, his face a bit long and prominent, his forehead smooth and low; his eyes were of moderate size, black and sound [Matthew 6:22]; his hair was black, his eyebrows straight, his nose symmetrical, thin and straight; his ears were upright, but small; his temples smooth. His speech was peaceable [Proverbs 15:4], fiery and sharp; his voice was strong, sweet, clear, and sonorous. His teeth were set close together, even, and white; his lips were small and thin; his beard black, but not bushy. His neck was slender, his shoulders straight, his arms short, his hands slender, his fingers long, his nails extended; his legs were thin, his feet small. His skin was delicate, his flesh very spare. He wore rough garments, he slept but very briefly, he gave most generously. (Celano, First Life of St. Francis, 83)

Living as Francis Did

This is the earliest and most extensive physical description of St. Francis, a word portrait. His peaceable speech, humility and mildness flowed from his joy over being loved by God and his desire that all people might realize how much they are loved by God. We can most closely resemble Francis by living the virtues that characterized his life.

Growing with Francis

Make sure your speech is peaceable today.

DECEMBER 3

Risk Rejection

Accordingly, while he was sleeping one night, someone addressed him a second time in a vision and questioned him solicitously as to whether he intended to go. When he had told his purpose to him who was asking and said that he was going to Apulia to fight, he was asked earnestly who could do better for him, the servant or the Lord. And Francis said: "The Lord." The other answered: "Why then are you seeking the servant in place of the Lord?" And Francis said: "Lord, what do you want me to do?" And the Lord said to him: "Go back to the place of your birth for through me your vision will have a spiritual fulfillment." He went back without delay, for he had already become a model of obedience and, giving up his own will, he became a Paul in place of a Saul. Saul is thrown to the ground and heavy blows beget sweet words. Francis, however, changes his carnal weapons into spiritual ones and in place of military glory he receives the knighthood of God. (Celano, Second Life of St. Francis, 6)

LIVING AS FRANCIS DID

This dream came to Francis in Spoleto. On his way to war, Francis hoped to become a knight. Celano tells the story almost nonchalantly. Going back to Assisi to await God's direction risked family rejection and public humiliation.

GROWING WITH FRANCIS

Remember that what God asks can be very difficult.

DECEMBER 4

In-Between Time

He was then filled with such divine sweetness, as he himself said, that he became speechless and was totally unable to move from the place. Then a certain spiritual affection took hold of him and carried him away to things invisible, by virtue of which he judged all earthly things to be of no importance but entirely worthless. Stupendous indeed is the condescension of Christ, which gives the greatest gifts to those who are doing the least and in a flood of many waters [Psalm 32:6] preserves and advances the things that are his. For Christ fed the multitudes with bread and fishes, neither did he repel sinners from his banquet. When they sought him to make him king, he took to flight and went up to the mountain to pray [Matthew 14:23]. These were the mysteries of God Francis was learning; and ignorant as he was, he was being led unto perfect knowledge. (Celano, Second Life of St. Francis, 7)

LIVING AS FRANCIS DID

Conversions tend to appear much easier to onlookers and after the fact than to the person being converted. A deep joy rooted in God enabled Francis to live in the in-between time of his hopes for knightly glory and the waiting for God to reveal more fully what Francis should do. You can easily imagine that that Francis's in-between time led to much gossiping in the small town of Assisi about "poor Pietro Bernardone's son."

GROWING WITH FRANCIS

Be gentle with someone who seems to be living in an in-between time.

DECEMBER 5

Act Charitably

One night one of the sheep cried out while the rest were sleeping: "I am dying, brothers, I am dying of hunger." Immediately the good shepherd got up and hastened to give the ailing sheep the proper remedy. He commanded the table to be set, though it was filled with poor things, and…where wine was lacking water took its place.

First he [Francis] himself began to eat, and then he invited the rest of the brothers to share this duty of charity, lest that brother should waste away from shame. When they had eaten the food with fear of the Lord, the father wove a long parable for his sons about the virtue of discretion, lest something should be lacking in the offices of charity. He commanded them always to give to the Lord a sacrifice seasoned with salt, and carefully admonished each one to consider his own strength in the service of God. He said that to deprive the body indiscreetly of what it needs was a sin just the same as it is a sin to give it superfluous things at the prompting of gluttony. And he added: "Know, dearest brothers, that what I have done in eating, I have done by dispensation, not by desire, because fraternal charity commanded it. Let this charity be an example to you." (Celano, Second Life of St. Francis, 22)

LIVING AS FRANCIS DID

For Francis, the needs of others superseded following rules.

GROWING WITH FRANCIS

Let charity direct you.

Choices

St. Francis maintained that the safest remedy against the thousand snares and wiles of the enemy is spiritual joy. For he would say: "Then the devil rejoices most when he can snatch away spiritual joy from a servant of God. He carries dust so that he can throw it into even the tiniest chinks of conscience and soil the candor of mind and purity of life. But when spiritual joy fills hearts," he said, "the serpent throws off his deadly poison in vain. The devils cannot harm the servant of Christ when they see he is filled with holy joy. When, however, the soul is wretched, desolate, and filled with sorrow, it is easily overwhelmed by its sorrow or else it turns to vain enjoyments." (Celano, Second Life of St. Francis, 125)

LIVING AS FRANCIS DID

Satan works in an atmosphere of discouragement, prodding us to think that what God asks of us is not humanly possible, that previous failures make it impossible to choose a different path, that others enjoy life because of selfish choices. Satan is the father of lies. Nowhere is this more evident than in which choices will bring us lasting joy or lasting sorrow. Holy joy doesn't come from denying reality but from looking deeply into it, connecting the dots, so to speak, to see where Satan's promises lead.

GROWING WITH FRANCIS

Connect the dots in your life more carefully. Which decisions led to genuine joy? Which choices turned out to be dead ends?

DECEMBER 7

Trust Prayer

The saint, therefore, made it a point to keep himself in joy of heart and to preserve the unction of the Spirit and the oil of gladness [Psalm 45:7]. He avoided with the greatest care the miserable illness of dejection, so that if he felt it creeping over his mind even a little, he would have recourse very quickly to prayer. For he would say: "If the servant of God, as may happen, is disturbed in any way, he should rise immediately to pray and he should remain in the presence of the heavenly Father until he restores unto him the joy of salvation [Psalm 51:14]. For if he remains stupefied in sadness [Habakkuk 2:3], the Babylonian stuff will increase, so that, unless it be at length driven out by tears, it will generate an abiding rust in the heart. (Celano, Second Life of St. Francis, 125)

LIVING AS FRANCIS DID

What God asks of us may be difficult (think of Francis kissing the leper), but it can be carried out with the deep joy of knowing that we are cooperating with God's grace. Prayer helped to keep Francis rooted in the joy of living more deeply and more consistently according to God's values. Although our inclination to pray can be governed by our moods, it is precisely in times of temptation and discouragement that we most need to pray.

GROWING WITH FRANCIS

Be ready to pray today, especially if things start to go wrong.

DECEMBER 8

Point to God

Francis once saw a certain companion of his with a peevish and sad face, and not taking this lightly, he said to him: "It is not becoming for a servant of God to show himself sad or upset before men, but always he should show himself honorable. Examine your offenses in your room and weep and groan before your God. When you return to your brothers, put off your sorrow and conform yourself to the rest." And after a few more things he said: "They who are jealous of the salvation of men envy me greatly; they are always trying to disturb in my companions what they cannot disturb in me." So much, however, did he love a man who was full of spiritual joy that he had these words written down as an admonition to all at a certain general chapter: "Let the brothers beware lest they show themselves outwardly gloomy and sad hypocrites; but let them show themselves joyful in the Lord, cheerful and suitably gracious." (Celano, Second Life of St. Francis, 128)

LIVING AS FRANCIS DID

Our ideas about what constitutes holiness can get twisted; people whom we naturally avoid are not necessarily holy or unholy. Yet a frequently sad Franciscan does not point people to God. We should be sad over our sins, but once we confess them and receive absolution, our lives should point to a loving and generous God.

GROWING WITH FRANCIS

Make choices that encourage others to believe in a generous God.

DECEMBER 9

Glory to God

Francis would often say to his brothers: "No one should flatter himself with evil praise over what a sinner can do. "A sinner," he said, "can fast, pray, weep, mortify his flesh. This, however, he cannot do, namely, be faithful to his Lord. Therefore in this should we glory, that we give glory to God, that we serve him faithfully, that we ascribe to him whatever he has given us. The greatest enemy of man is his flesh; it does not know how to recall anything to grieve over it; it does not know how to foresee things to fear them; its only aim is to misuse the present time. But what is worse," he said, "it claims as its own, it transfers to its own glory what was not given to it but to the soul. It seeks for praise for its virtues and the external favor of men for its watchings and prayers. It leaves nothing to the soul, but seeks a reward even for its tears." (Celano, Second Life of St. Francis, 134)

Living as Francis Did

Both Francis and the Gospel of John use the term "flesh" to sum up everything opposed to God while presenting itself as more real than what God wants. Francis was joyful because he saw God constantly at work in the world, inviting people to live in the freedom God wants them to have.

Growing with Francis

Live wholeheartedly in God's love and freedom, giving glory on high.

Preserve Unity

It was always Francis's anxious wish and careful watchfulness to preserve among his sons the bond of unity, so that those whom the same spirit drew together and the same father brought forth might be nurtured peacefully in the bosom of one mother. He wanted the greater to be joined to the lesser, the wise to be united with the simple by brotherly affection, the distant to be bound to the distant by the binding force of love. (Celano, Second Life of St. Francis, 191)

LIVING AS FRANCIS DID

People have a hard time preserving unity because every difference can be perceived as a threat, as a reproach for my choices that are different from others. Centrifugal force (movement outward, separation) often seems much more natural than centripetal force (movement inward, unity). "Sin divides; love unites," St. Augustine of Hippo once wrote. Francis of Assisi knew this reality even if he knew very little or nothing about St. Augustine. It is always easier to sow discord within a group than to build unity. We can question another person's motives when such questioning arises from jealousy or some other motive we may wish to hide. Human motivation can be incredibly complex. A divisive person within a group may succeed in claiming simply to be more realistic than other members of the group. Such actions will eventually reveal what that person was after.

GROWING WITH FRANCIS

Work to promote more understanding at home and in your local community.

DECEMBER 11

Silent Miracle

However, a new miracle turned their laments [over the death of St. Francis] to joy and their weeping to jubilation. They saw the body of their blessed father adorned with the stigmata of Christ, in the middle, namely, of his hands and feet; not indeed the holes made by nails, but the nails themselves formed out of his flesh, indeed imbedded in that same flesh, and retaining the blackness of iron; and his right side was red with blood. His flesh, naturally dark before, but now gleaming with a dazzling whiteness, gave promise of the rewards of the future life. His members, finally, had become pliable and soft, not rigid as they generally are in the dead; and they were changed into the likeness of the members of a little child. (Celano, Second Life of St. Francis, 217)

LIVING AS FRANCIS DID

Francis kept his stigmata a secret as much as he could because of the danger that it would be misinterpreted, especially that some of his followers might think they were entitled to bask in the glow of this unusual gift to Francis. If the stigmata showed the closeness of Francis to Jesus Christ, it also signaled why self-emptying to rid oneself of selfishness is so important.

GROWING WITH FRANCIS

Saints encourage us to make our own good choices, not to live in a parasitic way off their choices. Consider what small and silent miracles have been brought about by your own choices.

DECEMBER 12

Joy Follows Truth

He withdrew from the busy life of his trade and begged God in his goodness to show him what he should do. He prayed constantly until he was consumed with a passionate longing for God and was ready to give up the whole world in his desire for his heavenly home and think nothing of it. He realized that he had discovered the treasure hidden in the field, and like the wise trader in the Gospel [Matthew 13:44–46], he could think of nothing but how he might sell all that he had and buy the pearl he had found. He still did not know how to go about it, but at the same time he was forced to conclude that a spiritual venture could only begin by rejecting the world and that victory over himself would mark the beginning of his service of Christ. (Bonaventure, Major Life of St. Francis, I, 4)

LIVING AS FRANCIS DID

Francis's victory over himself might seem an unlikely foundation for a life of joy, but that it was. Francis saw all sin as rooted in an appropriation of what belongs to God alone. Only a spirit of expropriation, recognizing everything as a gift from God, enables a person to live in the deepest truth about his or her life. Joy naturally follows when a person lives in such a truth.

GROWING WITH FRANCIS

What truth have you discovered recently that brings you joy?

DECEMBER 13

Prepare the Way

Then as he was walking through the forest joyfully singing in French and praising God, he was suddenly set upon by robbers. They threatened him and asked him who he was but he replied intrepidly with the prophetic words, "I am the herald of the great King." Then they beat him and threw him into a ditch full of snow, telling him, "Lie there, rustic herald of God." With that they made off and Francis jumped from the ditch, full of joy, and made the woods re-echo with his praise to the Creator of all. (Bonaventure, Major Life of St. Francis, II, 5)

LIVING AS FRANCIS DID

God's love was so deeply rooted in Francis that he was not deeply shaken by an incident such as this one. He wanted them to know what a great inheritance they were ignoring and patiently tried to get that message across to all people. A herald prepares people for the arrival of a more important person. In that sense, John the Baptist was a herald for Jesus. If people want to look down on the herald's role as demeaning, they have already set themselves on a dead-end path because they will almost certainly claim what does not belong to them.

GROWING WITH FRANCIS

Many people become more irritable in December because they try to do too much. Consider your preparations for the Christmas season as an act of joy, and proceed accordingly.

DECEMBER 14

Build Up Peace

By divine inspiration he now began to strive after Gospel perfection, inviting others also to lead a life of penance. His words were full of the power of the Holy Spirit, never empty or ridiculous, and they went straight to the heart, so that his hearers were amazed. In all his sermons he began by wishing his hearers peace, saying to them, "God give you peace," a form of greeting which he had learned by a revelation, as he afterwards asserted. He was moved by the spirit of the prophets and he proclaimed peace and salvation. By his salutary warnings he united in the bond of true peace great numbers of people who had been at enmity with Christ and far from salvation. (Bonaventure, Major Life of St. Francis, III, 2)

LIVING AS FRANCIS DID

Filled with the Holy Spirit, Francis was constantly joyful. Because of this, his words touched people's hearts. Peace cannot be built up grimly. Never an easy task, it is always a joyful one, one that frees people to live as God intended. Living peacefully requires that we recognize outright lies and seductive half-truths that we encounter. What we watch on TV and other forms of entertainment, or how we use social media can build up or tear down peace.

GROWING WITH FRANCIS

Take an honest look at how you use various means of social communication and for what purpose. Does your use reflect deep, God-given joy?

DECEMBER 15

Invitation to Prayer

One day when he was in a lonely place by himself, weeping for his misspent years in the bitterness of his heart, the joy of the Holy Spirit was infused into him and he was assured that all his sins had been forgiven. He was rapt in ecstasy and completely absorbed in a wonderful light, so that the depths of his soul were enlightened and he saw what the future held in store for himself and his sons. Then he returned to the friars once again and told them, "Have courage, my dearly beloved, and rejoice in God. There is no need to be upset because there are only a few of us, nor any need to be afraid because we have no experience. God has shown me beyond all shadow of doubt that he will make us grow into a great multitude and that the Order will spread far and wide, by the favor of his blessing." (Bonaventure, Major Life of St. Francis, III, 6)

LIVING AS FRANCIS DID

Francis knew great joy from moments such as this, but also sorrow because some friars looked for a shortcut to Gospel living, a path that didn't require victory over self. Francis had moments of self-doubt. He used these as a springboard for prayer rather than as the final word about any situation. Thus he maintained the joy needed to complete the work that God had begun in him.

GROWING WITH FRANCIS

View self-doubt as an invitation to more fervent prayer.

DECEMBER 16

Choose Happiness

Although his spirit was one of poverty and lowliness, free from all pretense and devoid of life-giving powers, Francis had already attracted seven followers and he was anxious to invite the whole world to repent and give it new life in Christ. So he told his companions, "Go and bring to all men a message of peace and penance, that their sins may be forgiven. Be patient in trials, watchful in prayer, and never cease working. Be considerate in your speech, well-ordered in your actions, and grateful to your benefactors. Remember that for all this an eternal kingdom is being made ready for you." The friars humbly cast themselves on the ground before him and welcomed the command of obedience with true spiritual joy. (Bonaventure, Major Life of St. Francis, III, 7)

LIVING AS FRANCIS DID

These first friars left in pairs on their missionary experience not knowing how they would be received but assured that their humble preaching and virtuous lives would open listeners to what God wanted for them. A message of peace and penance, preached and lived with joy, would make people more joyful than any alternative to Christ's ways they might explore. Joy would keep conversion going deeper and wider in the lives of those who heard and observed the friars.

GROWING WITH FRANCIS

"People are about as happy as they decide to be," someone once said. How happy have you decided to be today?

DECEMBER 17

Less Is More

Poverty, which was all they had to meet their expenses, made them ready to undertake any task, while giving them strength for any kind of toil and leaving them free to travel without difficulty. They possessed nothing that belonged to this world; they loved nothing, and so they feared to lose nothing. They were free from care, with no anxiety to disturb them or worry to distract them. Their hearts were at peace as they lived from day to day, looking forward to the morrow without a thought as to where they would find shelter for the night. In those parts of the world where they were unknown and despised, they were often insulted, but they were so meek in their devotion to Christ's Gospel that they preferred to remain where they had to endure physical persecution, rather than return where their holiness was recognized and they might become proud of the honor shown them. Their very poverty seemed to them overflowing abundance as, in the words of the prophet, they "made much of the little they had" (Sirach 29:30). (Bonaventure, Major Life of St. Francis, IV, 7)

LIVING AS FRANCIS DID

Some people find it hard to believe that the life described here could be truly happy. By keeping their egos from becoming overinflated and less grasping, these friars were more available for God's work. They were poor in possessions but rich in God's love and grace.

GROWING WITH FRANCIS

Is less sometimes more? Act today as if it were.

DECEMBER 18

Prepare a Place for Him

In that place there was a certain man by the name of John, of good reputation and an even better life, whom blessed Francis loved with a special
love, for in the place where he lived he held a noble and honorable position
in as much as he had trampled upon the nobility of his birth and pursued
nobility of soul. Blessed Francis sent for this man, as he often did, about
fifteen days before the birth of the Lord, and he said to him: "If you want
us to celebrate the present feast of our Lord at Greccio, go with haste
and diligently prepare what I tell you. For I wish to do something that
will recall to memory the little Child who was born in Bethlehem and set
before our bodily eyes in some way the inconveniences of his infant needs,
how he lay in a manger, how, with an ox and an ass standing by, he lay upon
the hay where he had been placed." When the good and faithful man heard
these things, he ran with haste and prepared in that place all the things the
saint had told him. (Celano, First Life of St. Francis, 84)

Living as Francis Did

See God's extraordinary love in the Christmas crib when you come upon
one this month.

Growing with Francis

Slow down today and praise God's rich blessings.

DECEMBER 19

Amid the Rush

But the day of joy drew near, the time of great rejoicing came. The brothers were called from their various places. Men and women of that neighborhood prepared with glad hearts, according to their means, candles and torches to light up that night that has lighted up all the days and years with its gleaming star. At length the saint of God came, and finding all things prepared, he saw it and was glad [John 8:56]. The manger was prepared, the hay had been brought, the ox and ass were led in. There simplicity was honored, poverty was exalted, humility was commended, and Greccio was made, as it were, a new Bethlehem. The night was lighted up like the day, and it delighted men and beasts. The people came and were filled with new joy over the new mystery. The woods rang with the voices of the crowd and the rocks made answer to their jubilation. (Celano, First Life of St. Francis, 85)

LIVING AS FRANCIS DID

Francis combined love for Christ's crib, Christ's cross, and the Eucharist in a way that attracted even people whose faith was lukewarm. Christmas is celebrated year-round at Greccio. The crib that Francis made there emphasized the great love and humility of the Son of God in becoming one of us so that we might share divine life.

GROWING WITH FRANCIS

Amid the rush to prepare for Christmas, take time to thank God for the tremendous gift of Jesus's birth in Bethlehem.

DECEMBER 20

Jesus, the Reason

The brothers sang, paying their debt of praise to the Lord, and the whole night resounded with their rejoicing. The saint of God stood before the manger, uttering sighs, overcome with love, and filled with a wonderful happiness. The solemnities of the Mass were celebrated over the manger and the priest experienced a new consolation.

The saint of God was clothed with the vestments of the deacon, for he was a deacon, and he sang the holy Gospel in a sonorous voice. And his voice was a strong voice, a sweet voice, a clear voice, a sonorous voice, inviting all to the highest rewards. Then he preached to the people standing about, and he spoke charming words concerning the nativity of the poor King and the little town of Bethlehem. Frequently too, when he wished to call Christ Jesus, he would call him simply "the Child of Bethlehem," aglow with overflowing love for him; and speaking the word "Bethlehem," his voice was more like the bleating of a sheep. His mouth was filled more with sweet affection than with words. Besides, when he spoke the name "Child of Bethlehem" or "Jesus," his tongue licked his lips, as it were, relishing and savoring with pleased palate the sweetness of the words. (Celano, First Life of St. Francis, 85–86)

LIVING AS FRANCIS DID

Francis preached with great devotion about a Gospel that he lived 24 hours a day, 365 days a year.

GROWING WITH FRANCIS

Remember, Jesus is the reason for the season.

DECEMBER 21

Everything Changed

The gifts of the Almighty were multiplied there, and a wonderful vision was seen by a certain virtuous man. For he saw a little child lying in the manger lifeless, and he saw the holy man of God go up to it and rouse the child as from a deep sleep. This vision was not unfitting, for the Child Jesus had been forgotten in the hearts of many; but, by the working of his grace, he was brought to life again through his servant St. Francis and stamped upon their fervent memory. At length the solemn night celebration was brought to a close, and each one returned to his home with holy joy. (Celano, First Life of St. Francis, 86)

Living as Francis Did

The custom of setting up a Christmas crib in one's home—not simply outside a church—reinforces the personal challenge represented by the Incarnation. The Incarnation changes everything in human history. We become different people because of it. In Francis's day, many thought first of Jesus dying on the cross and only later about his birth in Bethlehem. Popularizing the crib reminded people of the great love that led to Jesus's becoming one of us without compromising his divine nature. After that celebration in Greccio, participants could well have said, "This changes everything!"

Growing with Francis

We could admire Jesus's birth as an historical moment that becomes more distant with each passing year, or with Francis's help, we can see it as an ongoing event and act accordingly.

Celebrate!

The birthday of the Child Jesus Francis observed with inexpressible eagerness over all other feasts, saying that it was the feast of feasts, on which God, having become a tiny infant, clung to human breasts. Pictures of those infant members he kissed with thoughts filled with yearning, and his compassion for the Child flooded his heart and made him stammer words of sweetness after the manner of infants. His name was like honey and the honeycomb in Francis's mouth. When the question arose about eating meat that day, since that Christmas day was a Friday, he replied, saying to Brother Morico: "You sin, Brother, calling the day on which the Child was born to us [allusion to the opening verse of Christmas Mass] a day of fast. It is my wish," he said, "that even the walls should eat meat on such a day, and if they cannot, they should be smeared with meat on the outside." (Celano, Second Life of St. Francis, 199)

Living as Francis Did

Francis was ready to splurge in celebrating the anniversary of Christ's birth, the focal point of human history. In a year when Christmas fell on a Friday, Francis considered it perfectly obvious that the rule about abstaining from meat on Fridays did not apply that year. Francis frequently reminded his listeners that Mary and Joseph gladly shared the poverty into which Jesus was born.

Growing with Francis

Remember the needs of food banks, soup kitchens, and homeless shelters in this season.

Take Time

Three years before he died, St. Francis decided to celebrate the memory of the birth of the Child Jesus at Greccio, with the greatest possible solemnity. He asked and obtained the permission of the pope for the ceremony, so that he could not be accused of being an innovator, and then he had a crib prepared, with hay and an ox and an ass. The friars were all invited and the people came in crowds. The forest re-echoed with their voices and the night was lit up with a multitude of bright lights, while the beautiful music of God's praises added to the solemnity. The saint stood before the crib and his heart overflowed with tender compassion; he was bathed in tears but overcome with joy. The Mass was sung there and Francis, who was a deacon, sang the Gospel. Then he preached to the people about the birth of the poor King, whom he called the Babe of Bethlehem in his tender love. (Bonaventure, Major Life of St. Francis, X, 7)

Living as Francis Did

St. Bonaventure was born a couple years before Francis died. When Bonaventure wrote his Life of Francis forty years later, he felt the need to add that Francis had the pope's permission for the Christmas crib at Greccio. The Poor Man of Assisi worked with the Church as he found it— not as he imagined it could be.

Growing with Francis

Today take time to enjoy music that reflects the deepest meaning of Christmas.

DECEMBER 24

Share the Story

A knight called John from Greccio, a pious and truthful man who had abandoned his profession in the world for love of Christ and was a great friend of St. Francis, claimed that he saw a beautiful child asleep in the crib, and that St. Francis took it in his arms and seemed to wake it up.

The integrity of this witness and the miracles which afterwards took place, as well as the truth indicated by the vision itself, all go to prove its reality. The example which Francis put before the world was calculated to rouse the hearts of those who are weak in the faith, and the hay from the crib, which was kept by the people, afterwards cured sick animals and drove off various pestilences. Thus God wished to give glory to his servant Francis and prove the efficacy of his prayer by clear signs. (Bonaventure, Major Life of St. Francis, X, 7)

LIVING AS FRANCIS DID

The celebration that Francis arranged at Greccio was so inspiring that people had their faith enkindled. If they truly took this experience to heart, there was no danger that this would become a one-time event destined to become a dim memory as the years rolled on. A deeper personal relationship with Jesus was the fruit of this celebration—a deeper relationship for Francis and for others who participated.

GROWING WITH FRANCIS

This week, share this Greccio story with someone who has never heard of it.

DECEMBER 25

God the Source

Hurrying to leave this world in as much as it is the place of exile of our pilgrimage, this blessed traveler was yet helped not a little by the things that are in the world. With respect to the world-rulers of this darkness [Ephesians 6:12a], he used it as a field of battle; with respect to God, he used it as a very bright image of his goodness [Wisdom 7:26b]. In every work of the artist he praised the Artist; whatever he found in the things made he referred to the Maker. He rejoiced in all the works of the hands of the Lord and saw behind things pleasant to behold their life-giving reason and cause. In beautiful things he saw Beauty itself; all things were to him good. "He who made us is the best," they cried out to him. Through his footprints impressed upon things he followed the Beloved everywhere; he made for himself from all things a ladder by which to come even to his throne [Job 23:3]. (Celano, Second Life of St. Francis, 165)

LIVING AS FRANCIS DID

Whatever is good, true, or beautiful comes from a single source: God. The generosity and faithful love that God showed in creation can become a constant reminder of our need to live out a generous and faithful love. Our ability to do that grows as we grow.

GROWING WITH FRANCIS

Create a moment today to thank God for Jesus's Incarnation and be ready for that to change your life.

Justice and Peace

On this day [Christmas] Francis wanted the poor and the hungry to be filled by the rich, and more than the usual amount of grain and hay given to the oxen and asses. "If I could speak to the emperor," he said, "I would ask that a general law be made that all who can should scatter corn and grain along the roads so that the birds might have an abundance of food on the day of such great solemnity, especially our sisters the larks." (Celano, Second Life of St. Francis, 200)

LIVING AS FRANCIS DID

We need to show compassion for those in need during this season and year-round. We miss the point of the Incarnation if we feel that feeding the hungry and sheltering the homeless are activities for this season only. Educational theorist John Dewey said, "All education is about making connections." We can never exhaust the connections that the Incarnation invites. Francis recognized this by linking this feast to extra generosity for humans in need, for oxen, asses, and even the lowly larks. The Incarnation of Jesus is a testament to God's universal love and compassion. It becomes a constant reminder of a biblical saying that Pope Paul VI made popular: "Peace is a work of justice."

GROWING WITH FRANCIS

Be as committed to justice for everyone as you are to peace for everyone.

Imitate Integrity

[At the canonization of St. Francis], Pope Gregory preached to all the people, and with a sweetly flowing and sonorous voice he spoke the praises of God. He also praised the holy father Francis in a noble eulogy, and recalling and speaking of the purity of his life, he was bathed in tears. His sermon had this text: He shone in his days as the morning star in the midst of a cloud, and as the moon at the full. And as the sun when it shineth, so did he shine in the temple of God [Sirach 50:6–7]. When the faithful saying and worthy of all acceptation [1 Timothy 1:15] was completed, one of the lord pope's subdeacons, Octavian by name, read the miracles of the saint before all in a very loud voice, and the lord Raynerius, a cardinal deacon, a man of penetrating intellect and renowned for his piety and life, spoke about them with holy words and with an abundance of tears. The Shepherd of the Church was carried away with joy, and sighing from the very depths of his being and sobbing, he shed torrents of tears. (Celano, First Life of St. Francis, 125)

LIVING AS FRANCIS DID

Francis brought great joy to his contemporaries by the integrity of his life. Pope Gregory IX, formerly Cardinal Hugolino and a great friend of Francis, felt privileged to declare officially what people had long recognized: Francis of Assisi was a saint.

GROWING WITH FRANCIS

Honor Francis by imitating the integrity of his life.

DECEMBER 28

Perfect Joy

St. Francis called to Brother Leo, who was walking a bit ahead of him and he said: "Brother Leo, even if the Friars Minor in every country give a great example of holiness and integrity and good edification, nevertheless write down and note carefully that perfect joy is not in that."

And when he had walked on a bit, St. Francis called him again, saying: "Brother Leo, even if a Friar Minor gives sight to the blind, heals the paralyzed, drives out devils, gives hearing back to the dear, makes the lame walk, and restores speech to the dumb, and what is still more, bring back to life a man who has been dead four days, write that perfect joy is not in that." And going on a bit, St. Francis cried out again in a strong voice: "Brother Leo, if a Friar Minor knew all languages and all sciences and Scripture, if he also knew how to prophesy and to reveal not only the future but also the secrets of the consciences minds of other, write down and note carefully that perfect joy is not in that." (Little Flowers of Saint Francis, 8)

LIVING AS FRANCIS DID

Francis wanted his followers to understand that seeking perfection in a human way would not achieve perfect joy.

GROWING WITH FRANCIS

Remember to thank God daily for all the successes you experience in life because they are God's gifts to you.

DECEMBER 29

Illusions of True Joy

One day at St. Mary, St. Francis called Brother Leo and said: "Brother Leo, write this down."

He answered: "I'm ready."

"Write what true joy is," he said. "A messenger comes and says that all the masters of theology in Paris have joined the Order—write: that is not true joy. Or all the prelates beyond the mountains—archbishops and bishops, or the King of France and the King of England—write: that is not true joy. Or that my friars have gone to the unbelievers and have converted all of them to the faith; or that I have so much grace from God that I heal the sick and I perform many miracles. I tell you that true joy is not in all those things." (The Perfect Joy)

LIVING AS FRANCIS DID

Francis used examples from life of the times in which he lived—kings and prelates, even bishops and archbishops—to depict the illusions of what some might imagine could produce joy, so that the sublime truths of faith and true joy might be revealed.

GROWING WITH FRANCIS

Be on guard against belief that power and prestige might be the path to joy.

Humble Joy

"But what is true joy?" [asked Brother Leo].

"I [Francis] am returning from Perugia and I am coming here at night, in the dark. It is winter time and wet and muddy and so cold that icicles form at the edges of my habit and keep striking my legs, and blood flows from such wounds. And I come to the gate, all covered with mud and cold and ice, and after I have knocked and called for a long time, a friar comes and asks: 'Who are you?' I answer: 'Brother Francis,' And he says: 'Go away. This is not a decent time to be going about. You can't come in.'

"And when I insist again, he replies: 'Go away. You are a simple and uneducated fellow....

"But I still stand at the gate and say: 'For the love of God, let me come in tonight.' And he answers: 'I won't! Go the Crosiers' Place and ask there.'

"I tell you that if I kept patience and was not upset—that is true joy and true virtue and the salvation of the soul." (The Perfect Joy)

Living as Francis Did

Francis related an exaggerated, imaginary incident to enable Brother Leo to understand that true joy and true virtue are spawned by patience and humble acceptance.

Growing with Francis

Strive to exchange pride and ego for pure joy and true virtue.

DECEMBER 31

Follow Joy with All Your Heart

And may whoever observes all this be filled in heaven with the blessing of the most high Father, and on earth with that of his beloved Son, together with the Holy Spirit, the Comforter, and all the powers of heaven and all the saints. And I, Brother Francis, your poor worthless servant, add my share internally and externally to that most holy blessing. Amen. (Testament)

LIVING AS FRANCIS DID

The truthful, humble, and generous type of life that Francis encourages us to lead is already a blessing in itself. Some days it may feel more like the "perfect joy" story recounted in the entries for December 28–30. Francis had no monopoly on dealing patiently with rude people, with people who misjudged his motives, with people who should have been grateful but were not.

Francis took what his contemporaries would have considered great risks: embracing a leper, asking approval from Pope Innocent III for a new way of living the Gospel, or going unarmed into Sultan Malik al-Kamil's camp. He took those risks not for publicity or adulation but because he believed with all his heart that God was leading him.

GROWING WITH FRANCIS

This day and throughout the coming year, take whatever risks you believe God is calling you to take. Live in perfect joy, as Francis did.

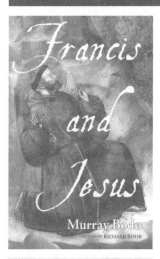
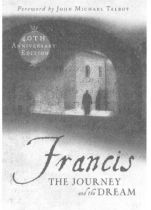

ABOUT THE AUTHOR

Pat McCloskey, O.F.M., is the Franciscan editor of *St. Anthony Messenger* magazine and the author of *Ask a Franciscan: Answers to Catholic Questions.* He has edited and contributed to *Saint of the Day* as well as *Come and See: An RCIA Sourcebook.*